The Teradata Database

Introduction and SQL

Brian Marshall

Published By

Education in Parallel
Yucca Valley, California

ISBN 0-9665493-3-3
Library of Congress Catalog Number: TX-4648933

Printed in the United States of America

Published by
Education in Parallel
Yucca Valley, California 92284
E-Mail: brianmary@yahoo.com

To my wife Mary,
without whose help, unfailing support and encouragement,
this book would have never been written.

ACKNOWLEDGEMENTS

My association with the Teradata Corporation and NCR now stretches back for more than a decade. During that time, I have always had the strong and enthusiastic support of the brightest bunch of people it has ever been my privilege to know.

In particular, I would like to thank Mark Jahnke, who provided many hours of painstaking research on how companies use the Teradata Database", Todd Walters without whom much of Teradata Version 2 Release 2 would still be a mystery to me, and Alan Chow, who continues to field the strongest team in the business.

Foreword

Some time ago, when attempting to eliminate the uninterested from the mailing list, we received an impassioned call from the resident programmer of a small college deep in Kentucky, who implored up to please keep him on the list. He would never buy any education from us, but he was the sole user of a Model 1 DBC/1012 which had been donated by the Teradata Corporation several years before. He dearly loved the system, but his college was under-funded, and had no budget for upgrade or education in the Teradata product. As a result, our education catalog was his only link to what was happening to Teradata in the great world outside. Naturally, with devotion such as that, we kept him on the list.

Nevertheless we began to wonder how many others there were like him. Teradata had always been generous in donating the older machines returned for upgrade to deserving causes, and there is now a flourishing secondary market in Teradata hardware. Formal classroom education is costly both in fees and time away from the job, and despite the old adage, "If you think education is expensive, try ignorance," it tends to be limited to none but the chosen few. In addition, while Teradata has had a large effect on the lives of almost all people in the developed world, outside of the initiated priesthood, few have even heard about it. Yet it is a story which deserves to be told and now, at last, it has.

It is a story of stubborn persistence, despite the concentrated efforts of the established main-frame elite to crush the troublesome newcomer. It is a story of the dogged application of quiet reason over obsolete beliefs and, best of all, it has a happy ending.

Teradata makes super stores possible. It helps telephone companies like AT&T to deliver the finest communications in the world. It provided the logistics which helped huge armies to secretly re-position during the

Gulf War. It plays a part in NASA's conquest of space. It identifies tax dodgers in the USA, inside traders in Chicago, welfare cheats in Australia and spies in Europe. Most of all, its consistent standards of excellence have forced the computer giants of yesteryear into a grudging attempt to emulate it.

In this book, I have attempted not only to describe what the Teradata Database does and how it does it, but also the reason why it does it. What we could not do was to identify all the brilliant people who made it possible. But their legacy is a superb product, which just gets better, year after year.

Table of Contents

Chapter 1

Stealth Marketing 1

History 3

Chapter 2

The Relational Database 7

The Relational Data Model 8
- Components of The Relational Database 9
- Tables - The Building Blocks 9
- Primary Keys and Foreign Keys 11
- Attributes 14
- Domains 14
- The Physical Database 16
- Differences between Keys and Indexes 17

The Teradata Database 17
- Physical Tables 18
- Views 18
- Macros 19
- Access Rights 20

Chapter 3
Accessing The Teradata Database 21

Data Types supported by The Teradata Database 23
Sending The SQL to Teradata 25
Teradata Structured Query language (SQL) 25
- Data Definition Language (DDL) 25
- Data manipulation language (DML) 30
  - The Select Statement 31
  - The Insert, Update and Delete 34
- Data Control language (DCL) 34
- Teradata Enhancements 34

Sequential Processing VS Parallelism 35

Chapter 4 -
Evolution of The Teradata Database 37

The Concept 38
The DBC/1012 - Access from a Main Frame 39
- The Interface Processor (IFP) 41
- The Ynet 42
- The Access Module Processor (AMP) 44

The DBC/1012 - Access from a local Area Network 46
- The Communications processor (COP) 47

Linear performance Characteristics 48
The Agreement with NCR 49
The NCR 3600 50
Teradata Goes Open 52
The NCR 3550 53
The WorldMark 5100 54
The Bynet 56

Chapter 5
Parallelism 57

Full Table Scan 57
The hashing Algorithm 58
Search by Index 59
Primary Index 61
    Using The Primary Index to Locate a Row 62
    Hash Collisions and Duplicates 64
    The Data Dictionary DD/D 66
    Locating a row using The Primary Index 67

Chapter 6
Choosing a Primary Index 73

Keys VS Indexes 73
Distribution of The Rows 74
Primary Index Access 77

Chapter 7
Secondary Indexes and Full Table Scans 85

The Unique Secondary Index(USI) 88
The Non-Unique Secondary Index (NUSI) 89
The Full Table Scan (FTS) 91

Chapter 8
Sending The SQL to Teradata 95

Programming Interfaces 97
    Call level Interface 97

Chapter 8

Sending The SQL to Teradata 95

Programming Interfaces 97
Call level Interface 97
The Teradata Pre-Processor 97
The Teradata ODBC Driver 98
The Application Utilities 99
Basic Teradata SQL (BTEQ) 101
BulkLoad 105
FastLoad 108
MultiLoad 110
FastExport 113
Continuing utility Development 116

Chapter 9

Data Protection and Recovery 119

Protection from Unauthorized Users 119
Teradata Logon 120
Access Rights 120
Locks and Priorities 121
Automatic Locks 123
Priorities 125
Transaction Boundaries 126
Deadlocks 128
Protection Against Transaction Failure 129
The Transient Journal 129
The Before Image Journal 129
Protection From Hardware Failure 130
FALLBACK Protection 130
Disk Arrays 133
RAID 1 134

Chapter 10

Who's Using Teradata? 143

The Biggest databases 143
The Largest Tables 144
The Largest Number of Users 145
Retail 146
Consumer Goods/retail Supply 147
The Cargo Transportation Industry 148
The Passenger Transportation Industry 149
The TeleCommunications Industry 150
The Health Care Insurance Industry 152
The Banking and Financial Industry 153
The Public Sector 155
Other Industries 156

The Teradata Database - SQL

Table of Contents

Chapter 1
Teradata SQL 159

Chapter 2
The Database 165

The "Classics" Database 166
SQL Naming Convention 170
Keys 170
  Primary Keys 170
  Foreign Keys 171
Referential Integrity 172
Indexes 172
  Primary Indexes 173
  Secondary Indexes 173
  Unique Secondary Index (USI) 174
  Non Unique Secondary Index (USI) 174
Domains 175
  Synonyms 177
  Homonyms 178
  Identifying Columns in the Same Domain 178

Chapter 3

BTEQ 181

Accessing BTEQ 181
    Access via a Main Frame 182
Access via a Local Area network (LAN) 183
Access via NCR 3600 or Worldmark 5100 UNIX 183
ANSI or Teradata Mode 183
Initialization and Logon (Interactive mode) 184
BTEQ in Batch mode 185
BTEQ Output 186
BTEQ Error reporting 188
Setting Up the "Classics" Database 189

Chapter 4

Getting Started 191

Sets 191
SQL Functions 192
Data Definition Language (DDL) 182
Data Manipulation Language (DML) 182
Data Control Language (DCL) 182
Relation Query Functions 193
SELECT 193
    Selecting ALL the Data 195
    WHERE 197
    Items in a List 197
    ORDER BY 198
    DISTINCT 199
Hands On Exercises 201

Chapter 5

Help, Show and Explain 203

The ANSI Flagger Program 204
HELP 205
FOLDLINE and SIDETITLES 207
SHOW 209
SHOW CONTROL 211
EXPLAIN 213
Hands On Exercises 216

Chapter 6

Logical Expressions 217

Logical Operators - AND, OR, NOT 217
- AND 219
- OR 219
- Multiple AND/OR 220
- NOT 222

Range Test Operators -BETWEEN AND 223
The UPPER Function 225
Partial string Operator - LIKE 226
- LIKE with ANY, ALL or SOME 227
- The ESCAPE Feature of LIKE 228

The SET Operators IN/NOT IN 229
Hands On Exercises 231

Chapter 7
Computations and Conversions 233

Arithmetic Operators 235
Computed Values 236
Arithmetic Data Conversions 237
DATE, TIME and USER 237
- MODULO Operator 238
- Dates 239
- The EXTRACT Statement 241
- ADD_MONTHS 241

Data Type Conversions 242
- The CAST Function 243

Data Type Comparisons 244
Hands On Exercises 245

Chapter 8
Titles, Formats and Names 247

The TITLE Function 247
The NAMED Function 248
The FORMAT Function 249
Hands On Exercise 254

Chapter 9
Aggregates and Totals 255

GROUP BY 258
- Mixed Aggregates and Non-Aggregates 259
- GROUP BY, WHERE and ORDER BY 260
- GROUP BY on Multiple Columns 261
- GROUP BY and HAVING 261

Using WITH … BY for Subtotals 262
Multiple Subtotals 263
Multiple Subtotal Levels 264
Using WITH for Grand Totals 266
WITH … BY and WITH 266
Hands On Exercises 269

Chapter 10
NULL 271

Arithmetic and Comparison Operations on NULL 272
NULL in the SELECT 273
CASE 274
The Valued CASE Expression 275
The Searched CASE Expression 275
NULLIF 277
COALESCE 278
NULLIFZERO and ZEROIFNULL 280
NULLIFZERO for Division 281
Hands On Exercises 283

Chapter 11
String Functions 285

Concatenation 285
TRIM 286
CHARACTERS 288
SUBSTR and SUBSTRING 289
SUBSTR or SUBSTRING on Numerics 290
INDEX 292
Hands On Exercise 293

Chapter 12
Subqueries and Joins 295

Subqueries 295
Defining and Using ALIAS Names 298
Correlated Subqueries 299
The EXISTS Function 300
JOINS 301
- DOMAINS 301
- Self Joins 305
- Cartesian Product Joins 306

Subquery VS Join 307
- The EXPLAIN 311

Hands On Exercises 311

Chapter 13
Outer Joins, Set Operators
and Derived Tables 313

Types of Join 314
SET Operators 317
Set Operators - Rules for Usage 317
- The UNION Operator 318
- MINUS 319
- INTERSECT 320

Derived Tables 321
Hands On Exercises 322

Chapter 14

Insert, Update and Delete 323

INSERT 323
    The Positional Form 324
    The Non-Positional Form 325
The UPDATE 326
    UPDATE in a Subquery 327
    UPDATE in a Join 328
The DELETE 328
Hands On Exercises 330

Chapter 15

Macros 331

CREATE MACRO 333
REPLACE MACRO 333
EXECUTE macroname 334
DROP MACRO 334
Parameterized Macros 335
Transaction Integrity 336
Syntax Options 337
Data, Transaction and Referential Integrity 338
Hands On Exercises 341

Chapter 16

Databases Tables and Views 343

Users and Databases 345
Tables 347
    CREATE USER/DATABASE Parameters 349
    Referential Integrity 352
    Primary Keys and Primary Indexes 352
    Foreign Keys 354
    CONSTRAINT 354
COMMENTS 355
ALTER Table 356
Secondary Indexes 356
Views 357
    Creating/Replacing Views 358
Hands On Exercises 362

Chapter 17

Ownership and Access Rights 365

Hierarchical Terms 366
Access Rights 368
    GRANT 368
    Access Rights Mechanisms 370
MONITOR Privileges 373
The REVOKE Statement 375
    What REVOKE does and does not do 376
Transfer of Ownership and Access Rights 377
Hands On Exercises 379

Chapter 18 -
Report Writing 381

BTEQ .EXPORT Command 382
BTEQ Format Control Commands 383

Solutions to Hands On Exercises 391

"Classics" Database Create Script 431

Index 447

Glossary 455

List of Acronyms 463

The Teradata Database

Introduction

Brian Marshall

1 Stealth Marketing

If you go to the summit of a high mountain, you can hear a subtle whisper. It is not the sound of the background radiation left over from the "Big Bang". It is the quiet tapping of billions of fingers on hundreds of millions of keyboards, the almost sub-audible squeak of legion upon legion of mice scampering over mile upon mile of mouse pads, the incessant hum of hard-drives and the quiet chatter of the Internet. You are listening to the Information Revolution and, whether or not you approve, if you own a personal computer, a television set or even a quartz crystal wrist-watch you are, however innocently, already marked as a co-conspirator.

Future historians might well trace the beginning of this revolution to some point in the long distant past, but the effects only began to make themselves felt by the population at large with the introduction of the inexpensive micro computer in the 1970's. Until then most people were able to comfortably ignore the fact that the government used sophisticated counting machines to evaluate the national census, or that banks used similar machines to keep track of checks and deposits. These were relatively primitive applications after all. It was the invention of the silicon chip which set the world on an ever-accelerating course in search of information. Information about anything. Information about everything. Knowledge is power and information is the sustenance of knowledge.

You might well argue, "Yes, but I have no interest in this information revolution. It has nothing to do with me", but whether you are a mover or the moved, the predator or the prey, the very substance of your life has already irrevocably changed in the last few years and will continue to change in the future at an ever-increasing pace, in ways you can scarcely imagine.

The amount of information which exists about you right now in thousands of computer files and databases throughout the world is truly frightening. You have already been identified, catalogued, analyzed and manipulated in a thousand ways of which you are barely aware. While up to now you might have been successful in preserving some vestige of anonymity by avoiding the use of tell-tale credit card records, all this is about to change. The technology is already in place, and your disposable, and even non-disposable income has been carefully identified as the target.

Using this new technology to analyze the contents of shopping baskets at check-out, a major Canadian retailer discovered that when customers buy auto polish, they often buy Q-Tips for cleaning the air-conditioning vents. Consequently they positioned the Q-Tips in the auto polish section, and sales of Q-Tips sky-rocketed. Another discovered that when husbands are sent out of an evening to buy disposable diapers, they invariably return with beer as well. By relocating the beer next to the disposable diapers, and the disposable diapers next to the beer, sales of both items have improved in logarithmic fashion. The Internal Revenue Service has announced it will no longer conduct random audits. It too is using this new information technology to identify "non-compliant" taxpayers with a pin-point accuracy never before possible.

The technology is already available for retailers to photograph you on arrival. They will recognize you in the database, and follow your progress throughout the store. They can carefully note the displays which attract your attention, and record whether or not you are motivated to buy. Physicians will shortly be able to rely on computers to locate, identify and diagnose abnormalities on X-Ray and Magnetic Resonance Imaging (MRI) scans. By the year 2000, 2 trillion bytes of information per day will be received from near-Earth satellites alone. All of this will need to be recorded and analyzed, and this is only the beginning.

The purpose of this book then, is to identify the major product which, more than any other, has already changed the world in thousands of ways, and is committed to spear-heading the information revolution for the foreseeable future - the Teradata Database.

History

During the late 1970's, Transaction Technology Incorporated (later unofficially renamed the "Teradata Training Institute"), was charged with developing a solution to the mushrooming data needs of CitiBank. CitiBank was rapidly becoming the largest organization of its kind in the world, and they needed answers in a hurry. They turned to Dr. Jack Shemer for advice.

Dr. Shemer worked closely with another brilliant young engineer, Dr. Phil Neches, and together they devised a solution which took full advantage of the newly emerging micro-computer technology to provide a combined hardware and software solution to Citibank's problem.

While the theory was sound, the solution would take time to develop and Citibank had more immediate needs. Nevertheless they did agree to become one of the earliest stockholders in a new company headed by Dr. Shemer who, showing a degree of confidence bordering on braggadocio, named the new organization "Teradata" after the terabyte, one trillion (1,000,000,000,000) bytes. Despite the fact that a computer system which could handle trillion-byte databases was as far ahead of the technology of the day as the Sopwith Camel was from the Boeing 747, Dr. Shemer managed to raise more than $50 million of venture capital, and hired six more people. The stage was thus set for the great adventure to begin in the garage of Dr. Shemer's home in Brentwood, California in 1978.

If you want to know what people will buy, it is a good idea to ask them, and with that in mind the new company identified fourteen Fortune 100 companies to find out what they were looking for in the computer of the future.

They wanted:

A machine to handle large Relational Databases

High Performance

A single data store for multiple "host" computers

Network connectivity

Manageable growth

Fault tolerance

Data Integrity

Structured Query Language (SQL).

Initial development took rather longer than expected, but by the summer of 1985 the first large full-scale massively parallel relational database production machines (DBC/1012) were built and, with great ceremony, shipped to AT&T and K-Mart.

By now the Teradata Corporation had grown to more than 120 employees, and already identified as a serious competitor by the giant IBM, now began to emerge as the major supplier of machines capable of sustaining highly efficient complex queries against large relational tables. The Data Warehouse needed by the Information Revolution was now in place, and Teradata's destiny was assured.

By 1991, the Teradata Corporation, now headquartered in El Segundo, California had become a world-wide operation with more than 1000 employees. Its customer base, though numbering fewer than 200 companies, was extremely high profile and drawn almost exclusively from Fortune 500 companies and governmental agencies world-wide.

Nevertheless since Teradata relied almost exclusively on word-of-mouth advertising, humorously referred to within the company as "stealth marketing", it remained almost unknown to the general public.

Teradata management had decided that large computer systems costing millions of dollars were unlikely to be sold through media advertising. They believed instead that money saved on advertising could be more effectively invested in a high degree of customer service, and adopted the maxim that the visible success of one customer would effectively the motivate the next.

Recognizing that Teradata was not in the computer-parts manufacturing business, and could never produce computer chips as well as INTEL, or disks as good as CDC, Fujitsu or Hitachi, the DBC/1012 was built largely of parts readily available in any computer store. The only item specifically patented was the Ynet, the intelligent interconnect which permitted the multiple processors to function as a single, well-coordinated unit. Consequently, as Intel replaced the 8086 chip with the 286, the 386 and the 486, and larger, faster and more reliable disk drives were introduced by various vendors, Teradata was able to quickly introduce new generations of the DBC/1012, each of which was faster and better than the one before. By 1990 the Teradata Corporation had been identified as the database vendor of choice for more than 70% of the world's very large relational database market.

Nevertheless much continued to be learned, and lacking the necessary resources to use the accumulated knowledge to build a completely re-designed machine for the late 1990's and beyond, Teradata eagerly sought a new cash-rich partner with the networking experience it believed it needed. In 1988 Teradata and NCR entered into an agreement to pool resources to develop this new machine independently of the DBC/1012. In the meantime, using the Teradata Ynet, NCR would compete directly with Teradata with a UNIX-based machine called the 3600.

In the meantime, Teradata's patron and largest single customer, AT&T had decided to acquire NCR. In view of the 3-way relationship between AT&T, NCR and Teradata, it also purchased Teradata and merged it with NCR. Despite an interim name change to "AT&T Global Information Solutions" (AT&T GIS), NCR was spun off from AT&T in December, 1996.

Under NCR, the proprietary architecture of the DBC/1012 gradually evolved into a virtual architecture software product renamed the "Teradata Database" running mainly, but not exclusively, on the highly-acclaimed, massively parallel, high-performance, UNIX-based super-computer known as the WorldMark 5100. It is the WorldMark 5100 therefore which promises to become the standard database workhorse of the 21st century, and the only one at present capable of handling the huge amounts of information needed to satisfy the rapacious appetite of the ever-expanding Internet.

2 The Relational Database

The concept of the Relational Database is not new. While the SET MATHEMATICS and the rules on which it is based were defined in the 20th century, the concept of storing information in tabular form is at least as old as 5,000 BC. After all, what more sensible method is there of conveying large amounts of information than as a simple two-dimensional table?

You might therefore wonder why computer technology has waited so long to take advantage of this clearly superior method of storing information. You might indeed ask why it has until recently doggedly relied on complex file systems which require prodigious amounts of explanation before they can be understood by the uninitiated. While it is tempting to blame the technical priesthood for jealously guarding their secrets, the real reason has more to do with the enormous expenditure of computer resources needed to support this kind of data representation.

Computer implementation of the relational data tables was destined to wait until the commercial introduction of the inexpensive silicon computer chip in the late 1970s. While the main-frame environment had previously supported such stop-gap devices as hierarchical databases and indexed files, implementation of truly relational tables required resources inexpensive enough to squander.

Prior to that time only as much data as absolutely necessary was collected as fuel for mission-critical applications. As a result, important business decisions were frequently based, not on real-time opportunities in the market place, but on the limited amount of information available.

As companies grew in stature, wise decisions became more profitable and bad decisions more costly, it was clearly time for a change. What was needed, was a method of maintaining a model of the business itself where decisions could be tested, and results evaluated, without incurring a high degree of risk - a source of all the relevant information needed to make important business decisions. A model was needed in fact, which could answer any and all reasonable questions about the business likely to be asked by management and deliver answers in clear, concise and unambiguous fashion. What was needed was the relational data model.

The Relational Data Model

Models are widely used in all walks of life to simulate the world around us. This allows us to play the "What if ?" game without unnecessary risk of costly failure.

Aircraft manufacturers, for example, make decisions about the optimum shape of new aircraft by building scale models of all the promising designs, and testing them in a wind tunnel.

City Planners might work with a scale model of the down town area, showing all the streets, buildings, traffic lights, subway entrances, fire hydrants etc. faithfully modeled in wood, cardboard or plastic. With such a model available, the effects of all planned changes can be observed within the safety of the laboratory environment, without submitting the already overburdened citizenry to the actual indignities of some of the wilder schemes being considered.

There is a price to be paid however for this luxury. For such a model to remain useful, it must be subject to regular update activity as the enterprise being modeled changes, to ensure it remains an accurate and faithful representation. Should this regular maintenance fail for any reason, the model quickly loses its utility and can no longer be used for its primary function.

The building blocks of the relational model are not wood, or plastic or cardboard, but a series of two-dimensional tables. These tables relate to each other by means of a key structure in such a way that if the model is properly constructed, there should be no reasonable question which could be asked about the enterprise itself which cannot be answered by the model.

Components of the Relational Database

The mathematical term used for a 2-dimensional table which conforms the specific rules outlined by Dr. Codd is a "relation", and lends its name to the relational database. A "relational" database is therefore simply a collection of "relations". While we will retain the term "relational database" to differentiate from a collection of tables which do not obey the relational rules, the more common term used for the relations themselves is simply "tables".

TABLES The building blocks

A relational database consists of a model of a business (or other) enterprise as a series of 2-dimensional tables composed of horizontal rows and vertical columns. Each table represents a person, place, thing or idea of importance to the User. Each row in a table represents a specific instance of the person, place, thing or idea, while each column represents a specific item of information about that individual instance.

Let us consider the Employee table *(Fig.2-1)* as a typical example of an Entity (Funk and Wagnall's defines "Entity" as "Thing").

EMPLOYEE

DESCRIPTION: A salaried person employed by the company

EMPLOYEE NUMBER	LAST NAME	FIRST NAME	BIRTH DATE	MANAGER EMPLOYEE NUMBER	SALARY AMOUNT	DEPARTMENT NUMBER	HIRE DATE
PK				FK		FK	
1856	Davis	Paul	04/10/60		43000.00	1	06/10/88
3111	Benson	Thomas	10/17/69	1856	35000.00	35	04/30/91
4312	Lopez	Raoul	06/15/71	3111	28000.00	22	01/10/93
1925	Lee	Robert	07/31/72	2013	39000.00	17	11/30/89
2013	Waters	Jackson	12/10/66	1856	40000.00	17	10/22/90

Figure 2-1

This entity has a number of interesting qualities:

1. A short singular name describing the entity represented.

2. A brief definition.

3. A descriptive heading for each column.

4. Each horizontal row describes one and only one employee.

5. Each column contains a single 'atomic' item of information.

6. Each horizontal row could be repositioned in the table without changing the meaning.

7. Each vertical column could be repositioned in the table without changing the meaning.

8. The information presented in the table is clear, precise and unambiguous.

This table could successfully answer a large number of questions.

For Example:

1. How many employees are there ?
2. What is the total payroll ?
3. Who was the most recently hired ?
4. How much does Davis earn ?

The number of such questions which can be successfully answered by this table is limited only by the imagination and interest of the user.

Each and every table in a relational database must have a column or combination of columns which uniquely identify each instance of the entity in a table. This column or combination of columns is known as a "Primary Key", and is generally identified by the letters "PK".

Primary Keys and Foreign Keys

The column or combination of columns designated as the Primary Key, the Employee Number in the Employee table for example, must have three essential properties:

1. It must be unique within the table. (Otherwise we could not tell the difference between two employees with the same name.)

2. It must have a value. (Otherwise the employee might be overlooked by the Payroll department)

3. The value should seldom change.

This last condition is not intuitively obvious, but it is nevertheless important.

> Assume that in this company we have decided on a scheme which permits us to tell an employee's rank by his/her employee number. Thus Waters joins the organization and is allocated the employee number of 2013. Through hard work and application, Waters is eventually promoted to management and is given a new employee number of 6009. If later we need information about the hire of employee number 2013, the record is missing.
>
> On the one hand we have an employee with a past but no present, and on the other we have an employee with a present but no past.

In addition to columns marked "PK" there are, in our model, other columns marked "FK" (Foreign Key), for it is these columns which permit one table to relate to another, and form the essential foundation of the relational database. In *Fig 2-2*, we have added another table, the Department Table. This broadens the scope of our model considerably, and provides answers to many more questions:

> Which department does Benson work for ?
>
> How many employees work for Education ?
>
> Who does Waters report to ?

The answers to these questions, and many more besides, are easily found by matching similar values in either the same table, (as in the case of Manager Employee Number and Employee Number) or in different tables (Department Number in each table).

The column "Manager Employee Number" contains the employee number of the employee's manager. Managers are also employees, and so any value appearing in this column must also appear somewhere in the table as a valid Employee Number. (Remember that the Employee Number column is marked "PK"). Several employees can report to the same manager, and the company president does not have a manager (the Manager Employee Number is missing or unknown - NULL).

Similarly any value in the Department Number column of the Employee table must be a valid value in the "PK" column (Department Number) of the Department table, or it may be NULL.

EMPLOYEE

DESCRIPTION: A salaried person employed by the company

EMPLOYEE NUMBER	LAST NAME	FIRST NAME	BIRTH DATE	MANAGER EMPLOYEE NUMBER	SALARY AMOUNT	DEPARTMENT NUMBER	HIRE DATE
PK				FK		FK	
1856	Davis	Paul	04/10/60		43000.00	1	06/10/88
3111	Benson	Thomas	10/17/69	1856	35000.00	35	04/30/91
4312	Lopez	Raoul	06/15/71	3111	28000.00	22	01/10/93
1925	Lee	Robert	07/31/72	2013	39000.00	17	11/30/89
2013	Waters	Jackson	12/10/66	1856	40000.00	17	10/22/90

DEPARTMENT

DESCRIPTION: An organizational group

DEPARTMENT NUMBER	DEPARTMENT NAME
PK	
35	Education
17	MIS
22	Personnel
1	President

Fig 2-2

The rules for a column marked "FK" thus become clear. Any value in a column marked "FK":

1. Must be a valid value in the PK column of the same or another table, or it may be NULL.

2. May be duplicate

If the columns marked "FK" adhere strictly to the above rules, they may be described as observing "referential integrity".

Attributes

While technically an attribute is the name given to any column in a table, it is frequently restricted to mean any non-key column in a table. As with columns marked "PK" and "FK", attribute columns must follow certain rules to ensure they are located in the correct tables. Attribute columns must describe:

The instance identified by the Primary Key.

All components of the Primary Key

Only the Primary Key and no other columns.

Additionally the first rule forbids repeating groups of columns such as "This Month's Sales", "Last Month's Sales", "Prior Month's Sales" etc. , whatever the naming convention may be.

These requirements are known as the *3 Rules of Normalization.* There are additional rules of normalization beyond three, but generally the first three are considered sufficient in the every-day business environment. Beyond this point they tend to become mathematic abstractions. If all columns in all tables adhere to the first three rules of normalization, the tables are said to be in *3rd Normal Form.*

Domains

Each column of every table must fall within a sub-group of columns known as a Domain. For example the column Department Number appears in both the Employee table and the Department table. If the values in both columns mean the same thing - a numeric identification for a Department - they are said to be in the same domain and should be given similar names. Imagine the confusion when the Sales Department refers to a customer as an "Account", the Legal Department refers to the same customer as a "Client" and the Bookkeeping also use the term "Account" to describe the customer record in a ledger. A good understanding of domains can help to alleviate the confusion caused by homonyms - words which sound the same but mean different things, and synonyms - words which sound different, but mean the same thing.

Each domain must have a name, a data type and a description.

If two columns can be logically added, subtracted or compared, they fall within the same domain.

Using the Employee and Department tables as an example:

> Employee Number and Manager Employee Number can be logically compared to determine an employee's manager - same domain (Employee Number, numeric)
>
> To compare Last Name with First name makes little logical sense. These columns are therefore in different domains - (Last Name, First Name, both text).
>
> Birth Date and Hire Date can be logically compared to determine the age of an employee at the date of hire - same domain (Date, date).
>
> Salary Amount could be logically compared to any other value expressed in the same currency (US$ Amount, numeric).
>
> Department Number in the Employee table can be logically compared to Department Number in the Department table - same domain (Department Number, numeric).

Not only do domains define the logical rules of access to data in relational tables, they also provide a column naming convention Each column should be called by the underlying domain name, qualified as necessary to avoid ambiguity.

> Hire Date and Birth Date fall within the same domain of "Date" which should, for that reason, become the basis for the column names. Since we cannot have two columns with identical names, the domain name of "Date" must be further qualified to "*Hire* Date" and "*Birth* Date" (not "date-of-hire" or "date-of-birth") for clarity.

The relational model can therefore be defined as a collection of:

Tables (or relations)

Keys (Primary and Foreign) and

Domains.

In order to fulfill its primary purpose of being able to provide answers to any and all questions falling within its scope, the relational model must be created independent of the specific questions which might, at some future time, be asked of it. At the same time it should completely conform to the first three rules of normalization.

Only when the logical model is complete and in 3rd Normal form, should we consider how we intend to use it. Development of the logical data model is therefore completely independent of the database vendor or computer system on which it is eventually to be implemented.

The Physical Database.

If all computer systems performed all tasks equally well, and each database vendor provided a perfect product, there would be little need for further data modeling activity. We would simply create the tables using SQL (Structured Query Language), populate them with data, and begin work.

Each database vendor and every computer system has its own peculiar eccentricities however, and it is often necessary to "skew the data" or de-normalize the tables in some way to favor high-priority tasks by exploiting the particular strengths of the computer system and avoiding its weaknesses. It must be recognized however that any departure from 3rd Normal Form will eventually restrict the generalized use of the model, and may make new applications more difficult to implement. Tables finally implemented on the computer (the *physical* model) will probably differ to a greater or lesser degree from those originally designed in the *logical* model.

Differences between Keys and Indexes

While the function of a primary *key* is to simply distinguish one row in a table from all others, the Teradata Database uses a primary *index* to physically locate and find rows on the disk. Thus *keys* are used to ensure row uniqueness and maintain referential integrity, while *indexes* are used to access data. As we have seen, a primary *key* column must be unique, never null and never changed. A primary *index*, on the other hand, may be unique or non-unique, may be null, and may be (infrequently) changed.

As a general rule-of-thumb the primary index and the primary key will be based upon the same column between 40% and 60% of the time. In this event the primary index will, of course, be unique. For those tables with multiple-component primary keys, the primary index will generally be non-unique based on one component of the primary key, or more rarely on a non-key attribute. Successful implementation and performance of the Teradata Database depends almost exclusively upon the correct choice of indexes. Choosing the correct indexes requires a thorough knowledge of the applications, together with a firm understanding of the strengths and weaknesses of the system architecture.

Additional consideration must be given to who is to be permitted access to the information, how much may be revealed, and how multiple users can be effectively insulated from each other.

The Teradata Database

In the Teradata environment each valid User is provided with a UserID, a password, and permission to use zero or more bytes of disk space for storage of data in tables. Information about all objects in the Teradata Database is recorded in a system-maintained database with a User ID of "DBC", known as the "Data Dictionary/Directory" (DD/D).

EMPLOYEE

DESCRIPTION: A salaried person employed by the company

EMPLOYEE NUMBER	LAST NAME	FIRST NAME	BIRTH DATE	MANAGER EMPLOYEE NUMBER	SALARY AMOUNT	DEPARTMENT NUMBER	HIRE DATE
PK,UPI	NUPI			FK,NUPI		FK	
1856	Davis	Paul	04/10/60		43000.00	1	06/10/88
3111	Benson	Thomas	10/17/69	1856	35000.00	35	04/30/91
4312	Lopez	Raoul	06/15/71	3111	28000.00	22	01/10/93
1925	Lee	Robert	07/31/72	2013	39000.00	17	11/30/89
2013	Waters	Jackson	12/10/66	1856	40000.00	17	10/22/90

DEPARTMENT

DESCRIPTION: An organizational group

DEPARTMENT NUMBER	DEPARTMENT NAME
PK,UPI	
35	Education
17	MIS
22	Personnel
1	President

Fig 2-3

Physical Tables

Each physical table must have a column or group of columns designated as the Primary Index. Primary Indexes may be Unique (UPI) or Non Unique (NUPI). In the Teradata Database the primary *index (Fig. 2-3)* is used to physically locate the row on the disk. Unique Secondary Indexes (USI) and Non Unique Secondary Indexes (NUSI) are used for alternate access paths.

Views

Views provide a means of controlling access to the specific rows and columns a particular user needs or is authorized to see.

EMPVIEW

EMPLOYEE NUMBER	LAST NAME	FIRST NAME	HIRE DATE	DEPARTMENT NAME
1925	Lee	Robert	11/30/89	MIS
2013	Waters	Jackson	10/22/90	MIS

Fig 2-4

A view is often described as a "virtual" table. Having no data of its own, it gathers the information it needs from the appropriate table(s). From the User's perspective however, a view appears as a table tailored specifically to that User's particular needs. The EmpView *(Fig. 2-4)* permits the user access only to employees who work in MIS, and effectively insulates sensitive information such as the Birth Date and Salary Amount from the unauthorized scrutiny of this User.

Macros

In the same way that a view can be used to limit the amount and type of data which can be seen by a user, a Teradata macro is often used to limit the type and scope of a transaction a user may request. Macros contain SQL statements and generally represent mini-applications previously authorized for the use of specified users.

Access Rights

All user access to data in the Teradata Database is governed by rights or privileges recorded as rows in the AccessRights table of the Data Dictionary

All user access to data in the Teradata Database is governed by rights or privileges recorded as rows in the AccessRights table of the Data Dictionary.

Summary

A *logical* data model may be defined as a series of tables with primary key/foreign key relationships which model a business enterprise. The logical model should be in 3rd Normal Form and capable of answering any and all questions which might be asked of the business itself.

A *physical* database is implemented on a computer system as an amount of disk space and a collection of zero or more tables, views, macros and access rights. The physical model is generally de-normalized to favor mission-critical applications by exploiting the strengths of the computer system and avoiding its weaknesses.

3 Accessing the Teradata Database

A legendary story involves the CEO of Transamerica Information Group (TIG). TIG, which was formerly part of Transamerica Corporation, insures all kinds of property for businesses including cars, boats, homes, mobile homes, skyscrapers and even North Sea oil rigs. The response time for retrieving information from the main-frame had become unacceptable, so the data was off-loaded to Teradata, and all of the Vice Presidents received canned reports on the state of the business, in preparation for the regular Monday morning meeting with the CEO. Nevertheless it seemed that no matter how much time the VPs spent in studying the reports, the CEO would always show up on Monday with a great deal of detailed knowledge, and a lot of questions the VPs could not answer.

It turned out that the CEO had taught himself to submit SQL queries to Teradata from a PC at home. As a result he was no longer dependent upon the limited information fed to him by the MIS department, but now had full and direct access to all the information in the company. It was not long before each VP had a PC at home from which he or she could also query the Teradata Database.

So what was this language which was, on the one hand, simple enough for a busy CEO to teach himself in the precious few moments of spare time available to him, and at the same time sufficiently powerful to successfully drive a major corporation?

Structured Query Language (SQL) uses a very easy-to-understand, almost plain English syntax, and has become the industry standard for relational database access. Unlike prior generations of computer languages, SQL is non-procedural. It makes no attempt to instruct the computer as to how to perform a task, but confines itself to a description of the desired answer set, and permits the computer to decide how best to achieve it.

SQL is build upon a discipline of arithmetic known as "SET MATHEMATICS". It deals not with a single record at a time, but with *ALL* the records which qualify for certain defined conditions.

For Example:

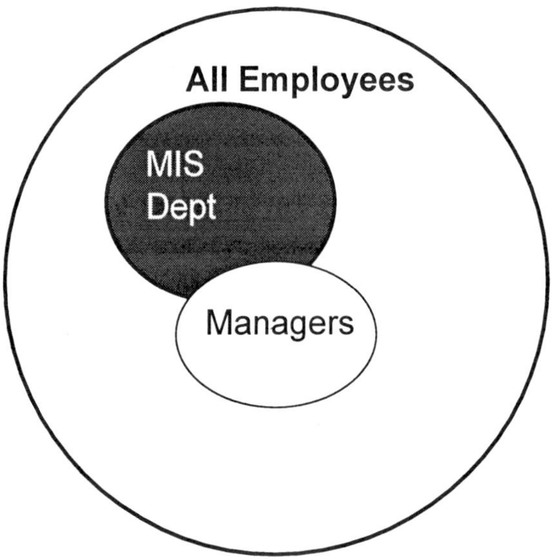

Fig 3-1

Suppose we wish to reward all the employees, except managers, working in the MIS Department with a 5 percent raise. We first consider the SET of all employees, *(Fig. 3-1)*, and within that SET, the SUBSET of just those working in MIS. There is another SET of employees who are managers. We therefore process the raise for the SET of employees who are in the "MIS Dept" SUBSET, but not in the "Managers" SUBSET.

SQL is a relatively modern language. While the broad concepts were reasonably well understood in 1978, the first definitive set of SQL standards was not agreed by the American National Standards Institute (ANSI) until 1986. Teradata therefore found itself heading, in good StarTrek fashion, "where no one had gone before". Without official standards and with a compelling and immediate need, Teradata had developed its own version of the language, called TEQUEL (Teradata SQL). Once official standards were announced, the company quickly adopted them. It had however, in the meantime developed a number of innovative and powerful enhancements particularly useful to the Teradata Database which were already widely used by its customers. As a result, Teradata decided to retain the enhancements and the name "Teradata SQL", but commit any future development to comply with ANSI standards.

The SQL language is concerned with storage and retrieval and change of data. Data, the collection of facts on which a discussion or an inference is based is, by definition, nebulous. Computers require a more precise description of the actual nature of input or output values, which includes information about the alpha/numeric representation of values and their exact lengths. Any discussion of SQL should, for that reason, begin with a discussion of data types.

Data Types Supported by the Teradata Database

In the Teradata environment, data is stored in 8 bit ASCII form, but is accepted from and returned to the user in the data representation recognized by the User's host. Nonetheless all data input or output from the database machine must be described in data types recognizable to Teradata:

NAME	BYTES	DESCRIPTION
NUMERIC		
BYTEINT	1	Values between -128 and+127
SMALLINT	2	Values between -32768 and+32767
INTEGER	4	Values -2,147,483,648 to +2,147,483,647
DATE	4	INTEGER in form "YYYMMDD"
DECIMAL (,)	2-8	Up to 18 numeric or fractional values
NUMERIC (,)	2-8	Up to 18 numeric or fractional values
FLOAT	8	IEEE floating point
FLOAT ( )	8	Floating point. Exponent -308 to +307
REAL	8	Floating point. Exponent -308 to +307
DOUBLE PRECISION	8	Floating point. Exponent -308 to +307
CHARACTER		
CHAR(n)	Up to 32000	Fixed length characters
VARCHAR(n)	Up to 32000	Variable length characters
BYTE		
BYTE(n)	Up to 32000	Fixed length bytes
VARBYTE(n)	Up to 32000	Variable length bytes
GRAPHIC		
GRAPHIC	Up to 16000	Fixed length double-bytes
VARGRAPHIC	Up to 16000	Variable length double-bytes

Also supported are double-byte character sets including Chinese Hanzi and Japanese Kanji.

Sending the SQL to Teradata

Teradata provides a number of utilities and program development tools to send the SQL requests to the Teradata Database, and process the results in reasonably user-friendly fashion. Of these the most functional and easiest to use is BTEQ (Basic Teradata SQL), which in its simplest form permits the user to sit at a terminal, type in the SQL request, hit the Enter key and see the response generated to the screen.

Teradata Structured Query Language (SQL)

The SQL language can be conveniently divided into 3 main groups of statements:

Data Definition Language (DDL)	Create, drop and alter database objects.
Data Manipulation Language (DML)	Retrieve, add, drop and change records.
Data Control Language (DCL)	Control user access to data.

Data Definition Language (DDL)

There is no known physical limit to the number of tables in a relational database. Today's large databases may typically have more than 400 tables, and this number will grow as more and more applications are consigned to this exciting medium. While computers are specially built to handle large numbers of individual items with no discomfort whatsoever, people are not. While computers have no difficulty in correctly identifying one item from many by providing each with a single numeric reference, people are easily confused. People generally prefer to assign names to other people, places or things, and when dealing with very large numbers in a set, often create sub-groups, each with its own specific name.

It is difficult to comprehend the 5 billion human inhabitants of planet Earth. It becomes easier however, if we divide them into sub-groups such as Americans, Europeans, Asians etc. So it is with objects on a computer.

While a Teradata database might be defined as a collection of tables, views and macros, its boundaries are logical rather than physical. From the computer's perspective one object is like another, and the computer sees no difficulty in comparing a value from a table in one database to a value in a table in another. From the computer's limited viewpoint, a database is:

A unique name.

A limit of disk space (PERM or PERMANENT SPACE), which can be used to store information in tables.

A maximum amount of temporary space (SPOOL) which can be utilized as work space for complex queries.

Example:

```
CREATE DATABASE MyDatabaseName
        AS PERM = 100000000, SPOOL = 200000000;
```

Each User of the Teradata Database must be identified using a unique name and a password, and is always provided with zero or more bytes of PERM. In addition, a user is expected to issue SQL requests and the system needs to be advised as to the limit of temporary work space (SPOOL) it may use to fulfill a User's requests:

Example:

```
CREATE USER MyName
        AS PERM = 0, SPOOL = 100000000,
        PASSWORD = MyPassword ;
```

Unlike most database vendors, Teradata does not require contiguous disk space to be set aside for each user or database. The values for PERMANENT SPACE are recorded only as limits. This provides three major advantages to Teradata users:

Disk space defined, but not yet used can, in the interim, be used for SPOOL or any other temporary need.

Since contiguous space is not required, reorganizations (REORGs) which plague users of other systems are never required.

User disk space requirements can be easily and dynamically modified without serious interruption of processing.

Example:

```
MODIFY USER MyName
        AS PERM = 50000000, SPOOL = 100000000
        ;
```

Data Definition Language statements are also used to create tables, and create or replace views and macros:

Example:

```
CREATE TABLE Employee
        (Employee_Number        INTEGER       NOT NULL
        , Last_Name             VARCHAR(20) NOT NULL
                                NOT CASESPECIFIC
        , First_Name            VARCHAR(15) NOT NULL
                                NOT CASESPECIFIC
        , Social_Security_Number
                                INTEGER
        ,Salary_Amount          DECIMAL(10,2) NOT NULL
        ,Hire_Date              DATE
```

```
,Birth_Date             DATE
,Department_Number  SMALLINT
,Phone_Number           INTEGER)
Unique Primary Index (Employee_Number)
;
```

SQL is free-form and not case-specific in its syntax. The "Create Table" statement provides each column of the table with:

A name, unique within the table

A data type and length for each column

Specific conditions governing when data may or may not be acceptable

Identification of the column(s) to be used as the Primary Index.

Example:

```
CREATE VIEW EmpBirthday AS
SELECT          Employee_Number
                ,Last_Name
                ,First_Name
        Birth_Date      FORMAT('MMMDD')
FROM  Employee
WHERE           Department_Number = 101
ORDER BY        Birth_Date MOD 10000
;
```

The View, EmpBirthday, is a virtual table. It has no data of its own but SELECTs or retrieves data from the Employee table. From the User's perspective however, it has all the appearance of a table which contains data specifically tailored to the User's needs. In this way the user can be permitted to view all the information he or she needs to see about any or all employees who work in department 101, but at the same time, be effectively insulated from other sensitive information in the Employee table such as "SALARY-AMOUNT", year of birth and employees from other departments.

The SQL **Macro** is a Teradata enhancement which permits multiple users from different hosts to execute a single copy of the SQL to guarantee application and transaction integrity.

Macros :

Can contain multiple SQL and utility statements

Are stored in the Teradata Database

Can contain execution-time parameters.

Guarantee transaction integrity.

Are pre-parsed and pre-checked for security and performance.

Provide an additional level of security authorization.

Example:

```
REPLACE MACRO PhoneList AS
(SELECT         Last_Name
                ,First_Name
                ,Phone_Number
FROM            Employee
WHERE           Department_Number = 101
ORDER BY        Phone_Number ;
);
```

This particular macro was created to permit the office administrator to create an employee telephone directory as and when required, by accessing information from the Employee table, but in a highly controlled way. The user of the macro is restricted to seeing employee names and phone numbers, in ascending order, for those employees working in one specific department.

Databases, Users, tables, views and macros can also be dropped from the system when they are no longer required:

```
DROP DATABASE MyName;
DROP TABLE Employee
DROP VIEW EmpBirthday;
DROP MACRO PhoneList;
```

Data Manipulation Language (DML)

The 4 DML statements, SELECT, INSERT, UPDATE and DELETE are used to:

Display or report existing records,
Add new records,
Change existing records, or
Remove records

from a table or tables.

The Select Statement

The SQL "SELECT" statement is extremely powerful, and honors all of the functions required of a relational database management system including:

SELECT	Choose some or all of the rows of a table.
PROJECT	Choose some or all of the columns of a row.
JOIN	Match rows from multiple tables based on a common domain value.
UNION	Merge the results of multiple SELECTs in a single answer set.
AGGREGATE	Divide result rows into distinct groupings, and provide inter-group and intra-group calculations.

It is the "SELECT" statement which addresses the ultimate objective of any intelligence-gathering application.

Example:

Using data from the Employee, Job and Department tables *(Fig. 3-2)*, a report is required which provides a list of employee salaries (except the President), with sub-totals for each department and a grand total for all departments.

The tables are joined by matching Department Number and Job Number in the Employee table with Department Number in the Department table and Job Number in the Job table.

The Tables:

EMPLOYEE

EMPLOYEE NUMBER	LAST NAME	FIRST NAME	BIRTH DATE	MANAGER EMPLOYEE NUMBER	SALARY AMOUNT	DEPARTMENT NUMBER	HIRE DATE	JOB NUMBER
UPI	NUSI							
3111	Benson	Thomas	10/17/69	4500	30000.00	35	04/30/91	12
1856	Davis	Paul	04/10/60		43000.00	1	06/10/88	1
4312	Lopez	Raoul	06/15/71	3111	28000.00	22	01/10/93	10
1925	Lee	Robert	07/31/72	2013	39000.00	17	11/30/89	15
2013	Waters	Jackson	12/10/66	1856	40000.00	17	10/22/90	10
4315	Chong	Kim	05/11/71	2013	24000.00	17	02/15/93	15
4411	Adams	Peter	08/31/70	2013	27000.00	17	01/30/94	15
4500	Cousins	Anne	11/11/73	1856	35000.00	35	10/31/95	10

DEPARTMENT

DEPARTMENT NUMBER	DEPARTMENT NAME
UPI	
35	Education
17	MIS
22	Personnel
1	President

JOB

JOB NUMBER	JOB TITLE
UPI	
1	President
10	Manager
12	Instructor
15	Programmer

Fig 3-2

The SQL:

```
SELECT Last_Name
       ,First_Name
       ,Department_Name     (TITLE 'Department')
       ,Job_Title           (TITLE 'Job')
       ,Salary_Amount       (TITLE 'Salary',
                            FORMAT $,$$$,$$9.99')
FROM  Employee, Department, Job
```

```
WHERE         Employee.Department_Number =
              Department.Department_Number
AND           Employee.Job_Number = Job.Job_Number
AND           Employee.Department_Number NE 1
WITH          SUM(Salary_Amount) BY Department_Name
              (TITLE ' Sub Total', FORMAT '$,$$$,$$9.99')
WITH SUM(Salary_Amount)
              (TITLE ' Grand Total',
              FORMAT '$,$$$,$$9.99')
ORDER BY      Last_Name ;
```

Note how a few easily understandable but immensely powerful instructions are required to generate a reasonably sophisticated report.

The Result:

Last Name	First Name	Department	Job	Salary Amount
Benson	Thomas	Education	Instructor	$30,000.00
Cousins	Anne	Education	Manager	$35,000.00
		Sub Total		$65,000.00
Adams	Peter	MIS	Programmer	$27,000.00
Chong	Kim	MIS	Programmer	$24,000.00
Lee	Robert	MIS	Programmer	$39,000.00
Waters	Jackson	MIS	Manager	$40,000.00
			SubTotal	$130,000.00
Lopez	Raoul	Personnel	Manager	$28,000.00
			Sub Total	$28,000.00
			Grand Total	$223,000.00

The Insert, Update and Delete

Compared to the "SELECT", the "INSERT", "UPDATE" and "DELETE" statements perform less ostentatious but nevertheless essential roles of data maintenance and management. While the "INSERT" is limited to adding a single record at a time, the "UPDATE" and "DELETE" statements provide a powerful mechanism to change or drop multiple records in a single transaction.

Data Control Language (DCL)

Data Control Language statements:

GRANT

REVOKE

GIVE

permit the System or Database Administrator to tightly control user access to data.

Teradata Enhancements

Teradata has made a significant number of enhancements to SQL not only in ways which primarily benefit Teradata Users, but also in a number of ways which significantly contribute to the overall richness of the language.

Command	Function
HELP	Permit users to see the structure of database objects.
SHOW	Returns last DDL statement against a named object.
EXPLAIN	Optimizer output in plain English
FALLBACK	Redundant copy of data for recovery purposes.
MACRO	Transaction SQL available to multiple users.
RENAME	Permits renaming of tables.
NULLIFZERO	Ignores zero values in aggregate calculations
ZEROIFNULL	Treats nulls as zeros in aggregate calculations.
WITH..BY	Calculates sub-totals for detail records
MODIFY USER/ DATABASE	Permits major changes to User/database objects including space allocation without REORG.

Sequential Processing VS Parallelism

SQL provides the world's most potent interface to the ever-expanding world of information, and provides an ultra high-level access mechanism which can be quickly learned by computer guru and novice alike. In the simplicity of its syntax it remains, in effect no more than a collection of standard input commands which describe the nature and format of the information required by the user.

ANSI standards make few stipulations about how this objective is to be achieved, nor whether this it must be completed in moments, minutes or millennia. This is left to the artistry, ingenuity and skill of the database vendor.

Imagine, for example, a major retailer with 2500 stores, each of which carries up to 5000 distinct products. To keep a record of each store's daily sales of each product item might require a table of 2500 X 5000 X 365 (over 4 billion rows) for a single year. To calculate the total sales of each item for each store would require a full table scan of up to 4 billion rows - a Herculean task for even the most powerful single CPU in existence.

This kind of workload is however routinely undertaken by users of the Teradata Database, and becomes possible by dividing workload amongst multiple state-of-the-art micro CPUs working in parallel. With 500 CPUs working in parallel and the workload evenly divided amongst those CPUs, a workload of reading 4 billion rows can be completed in the total elapsed time required by a single CPU to read a mere 8 million rows - one half of one percent of the time required by a single CPU working in sequential fashion.

Thus while Structured Query Language is the recognized standard for accessing relational databases, only Teradata, with its unique architecture, can make it perform with the speed required by the major users of today, while at the same time offering the potential for almost unlimited growth tomorrow.

4 Evolution of the Teradata Database

Legend has it that a wet Saturday afternoon in 1978, a canceled football game, two disappointed computer engineers, a problem to solve, one really clever idea, and a six-pack of beer resulted in the concept of the Teradata Corporation. All the most brilliant ideas are simple, and become obvious - after the fact. This particular idea revolved around the concept that if one computer could scan all the rows in a large table in a certain elapsed time-frame, by dividing the rows equally amongst some number (n) of computers working in parallel, the task could be completed in 1/nth the time. The idea of multiple cooperative processors in a single machine was probably not new. However the innovative design of the device to link the multiple processors together, to evenly divide the workload amongst the multiple processors and return the result to the user as a single, sorted, coherent data stream was revolutionary. Known as the *Ynet,* this intelligent interconnect became the single most important component of the world's first massively parallel database machines.

Development of the hardware and software took longer than expected, but the first large-scale production machines were eventually delivered to AT&T, CitiBank and K-Mart in mid-1985, and the Teradata Corporation took its first major steps to unseat the main-frame from its long-held dominant position.

Teradata's last prospectus as a privately owned company for fiscal year 1987, described the enterprise in these words:

"Teradata designs, manufactures and markets a high performance, fault tolerant computer system optimized for relational database management.

Through its proprietary implementation of parallel processing, which incorporates standard microprocessors, the Company's DBC/1012 database computer system offers significant improvements over other database management alternatives in many applications, particularly for large complex databases. The DBC/1012 creates a shared database resource by off-loading the processing and storage of data from one or more host computers, including those manufactured by IBM. This allows users to eliminate the costs of duplicated data storage, and the difficulty of maintaining and manipulating disparate databases. The DBC/1012 is designed to be modularly expandable from three to 1,024 processors by adding small increments of processing capacity and storage, and has been configured as the largest capacity database management system currently available."

By the time of its acquisition by AT&T, and merger with NCR in late 1991, the Teradata Corporation was responsible for better than 70% of the world's very large relational database applications, and drew its customers almost exclusively from Fortune 100 companies and government organizations.

The Concept

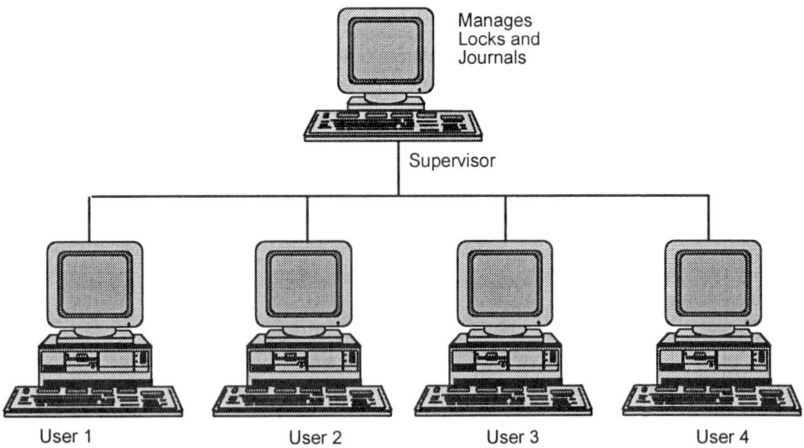

Fig 4-1

Fig 4-1 represents a simple network of Personal Computers with 4 users, each of whom has his/her own data.

Each user can work independently of the others. At some point however User 4 wants to access User 2's data over the network. If we wish to avoid the dangers of multiple uncoordinated copies of the same data and the confusion which can result, certain issues need to be addressed:

> Is User 4 responsible for locking User 2 out of User 2's own data while User 4 is accessing it ?
>
> Is User 2 responsible for locking himself or herself out while User 4 is accessing User 2's data?
>
> In any event who is responsible for rolling back a failed transaction?

One solution might be to add a supervisor to the network. Since the supervisor's sole responsibility is to coordinate the activity of the subordinate processors on an immediate basis and does not involve the storage of data, the supervisor requires a Central Processing Unit (CPU), but no disk.

This, over simplified, was the principle on which the architecture of the first Teradata Database machine the DBC/1012 *(Fig. 4-2)* was based.

The DBC/1012 - Access from a Main Frame

The Teradata DataBase Computer/1012 was known as a "shared-nothing" architecture. Each processor CPU has its own memory. Each IFP processor has the sole responsibility for its own interface with a specific host computer. Each AMP processor has the sole responsibility for management and maintenance of its own dedicated disks.

Fig 4-2 shows multiple users accessing the Teradata Database from the main frame, both interactively from a terminal, and in a batch environment. In addition to the primary program, each User's address space contains 9 Teradata sub-routines known as the Call Level Interface. (CLI).

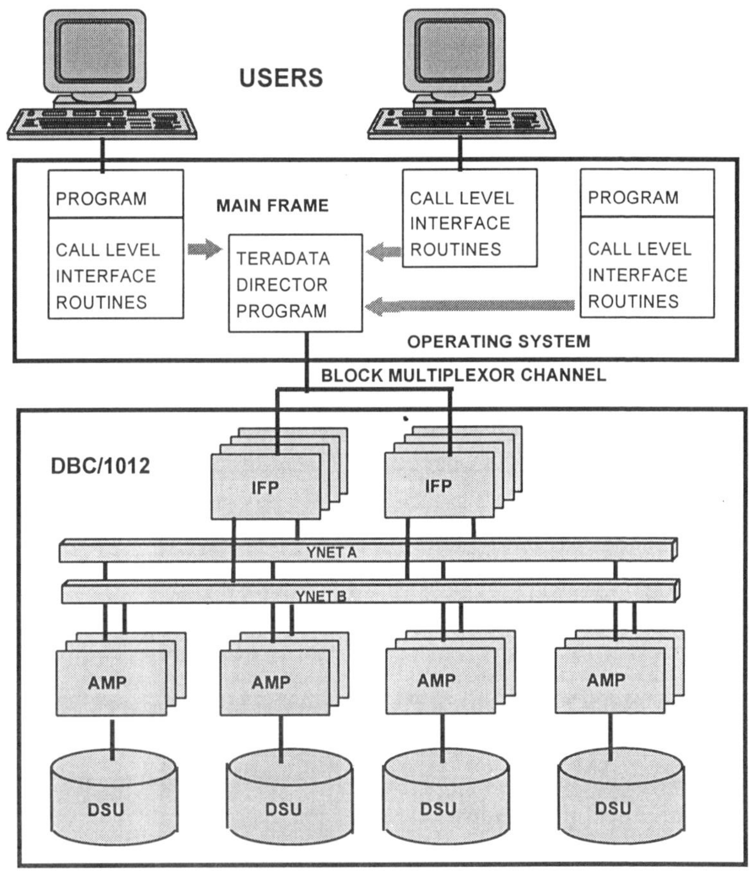

TDP Teradata Director Program
IFP Interface Processor
AMP Access Module Processor
DSU Disk Storage Unit

Fig 4-2

The CLI performs a number of important functions. It:

> Permits a single user to log on to the Teradata Database multiple times (multiple sessions) and send multiple requests at one time. This is particularly useful in a "batch" environment.
>
> Is responsible for keeping track of all requests and ensuring that the results are returned to the user in a coherent order.
>
> Converts the SQL requests into distinct kinds of "parcels" and forwards them to the Teradata Director Program (TDP) using the memory services of the host.

TDP aggregates the parcels from all the users on the main frame into channel blocks up to 32K in length, provides each block with a unique header, and directs it across the block multiplexor channel to a dedicated Interface processor (IFP) on the DBC/1012. The host main frame is now free to attend to other duties.

The Interface Processor (IFP)

Upon receipt of a channel block from TDP, the IFP *(Fig. 4-3)* strips off the block header, resolves it into individual messages. It then parses and optimizes the SQL. After making a decision as to the most efficient way of handling the request, it builds the necessary processing instructions and sends them over the Ynet, to the Access Module Processor(s) (AMP) needed for the database operation.

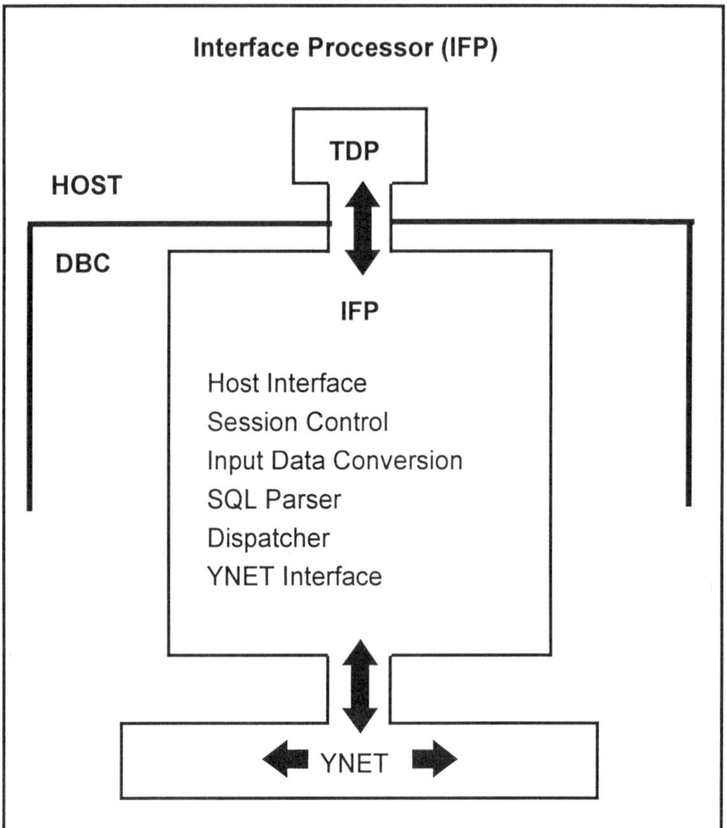

Fig 4-3

The Ynet

The Ynet is the Teradata proprietary high-speed intelligent interconnect which makes the parallelism of the DBC/1012 possible. Its broadcast capability allows it to address one, several or all processors at one time.

Its merge capability permits it to coordinate the response from many individual processors into a single sorted data stream.

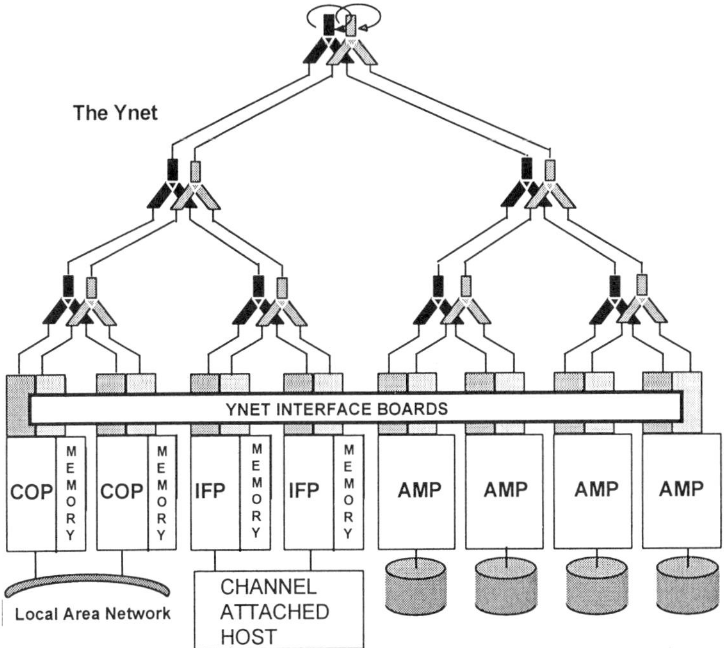

Fig 4-4

In *Fig. 4-4*, the DBC/1012 diagram has been redrawn to accentuate the Ynet, and demonstrate how it functions as a pyramid, with each processor able to direct a message upwards to the apex and broadcast it down to all other processors.

If the processor is powered by an INTEL 486 CPU, it consists of 3 boards. If the processor is powered by an INTEL 386, it consists of 4. In either event, two of these boards are dedicated to the Ynet. Each DBC/1012 has 2 Ynets, A and B, both of which carry an equal amount of traffic during normal processing, but provide redundancy in the event of failure.

With a combined data transfer rate of 10MB per second, the two Ynets, jointly provide high-speed communications between all the processors on the system. They remain however essentially single-threaded and represent the only elements of the Teradata DBC/1012 architecture which are not scaleable. Despite their great speed therefore, it was inevitable that as the number of processors on the system continued to grow, sooner or later the Ynets would become a processing bottleneck.

The Access Module Processor (AMP)

All of the data in the DBC/1012 is distributed apparently randomly but evenly amongst multiple processors called AMPs *(Fig. 4-5).* As an option, a secondary copy of the data can be automatically maintained in such a way that if individual AMPs fail, processing can continue with little ill effect.

Each AMP has its own copy of the Teradata Operating System (TOS), and uses it to access and process the database information required from its own dedicated Disk Storage Units (DSUs). If a large amount of information is to be returned, the results are put into a temporary spool file.

Depending upon the distribution of the data amongst the AMPs, and the nature of the request, each AMP can process its portion of a complex task while other AMPs are processing theirs. This is known as parallel processing.

Finally, when all AMPs have completed their portion of the task, the results are merged on the Ynet, and returned to the requesting IFP which then requests service from the main frame operating system. The response data, aggregated into 32K channel blocks, is returned to the requesting TDP which assumes the responsibility for delivering it to the originating user.

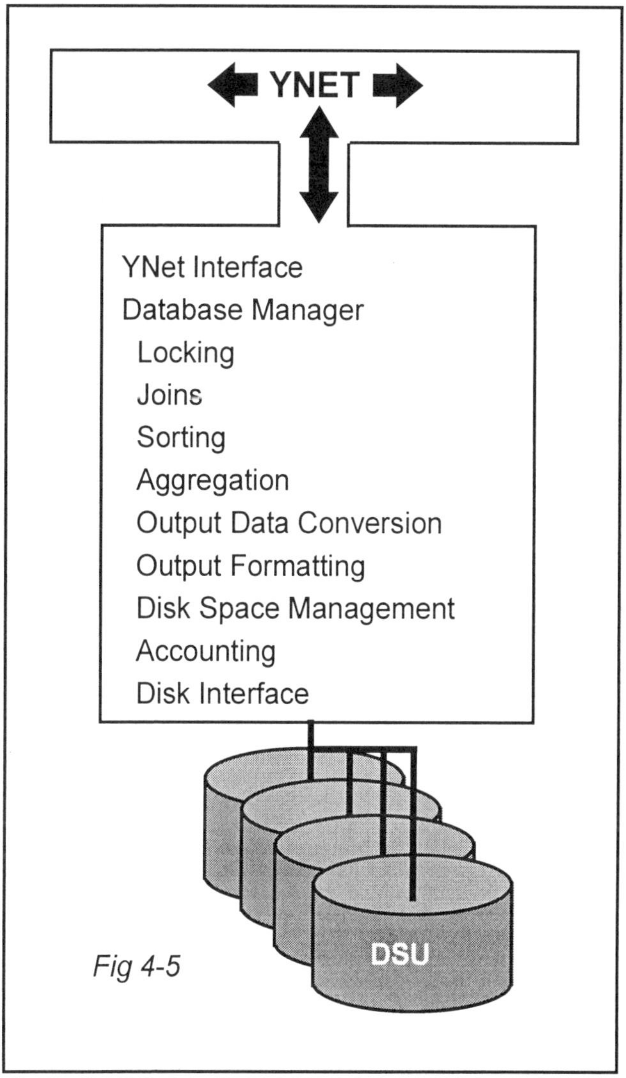
YNET
YNet Interface
Database Manager
Locking
Joins
Sorting
Aggregation
Output Data Conversion
Output Formatting
Disk Space Management
Accounting
Disk Interface
DSU

Fig 4-5

The DBC/1012 - Access from a Local Area Network

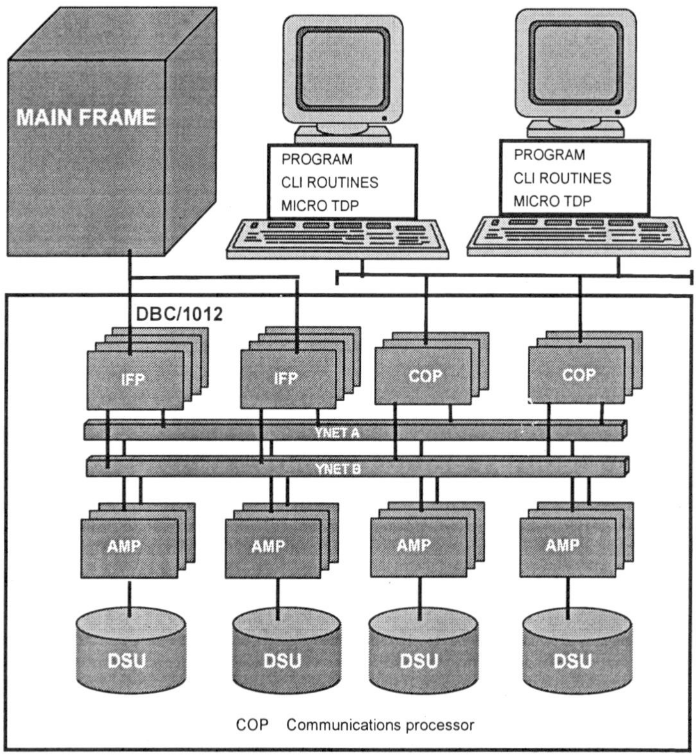

Fig 4-6

Each personal computer or workstation attached to a network is regarded as a host in its own right. It has its own CPU, its own operating system, and usually its own disk. Like any main frame host, it can interface with the Teradata Database *(Fig. 4-6)*. Unlike a main frame, however a personal computer serves one, and only one, user at a time. While each user still requires the CLI routines, the TDP required is a single-user version known as "Micro TDP".

The Communications Processor (COP)

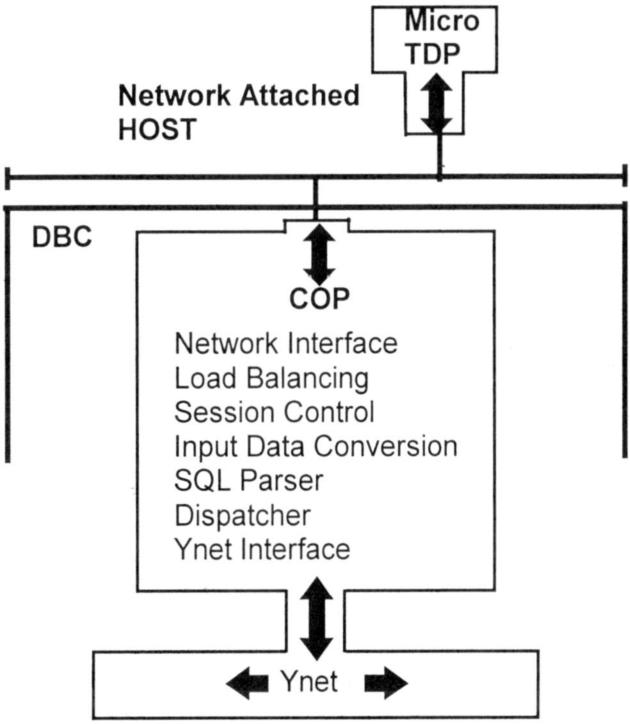

Fig 4-7

The main frame version of TDP serves all users accessing the Teradata Database from that host, and therefore it becomes a funnel through which all requests must pass. As a result the main frame version of TDP is available for the additional duty of balancing the work load amongst its dedicated IFPs.

In a network environment *(Fig. 4-7),* on the other hand, Teradata processors are not dedicated to a specific (single-user) host, and each Micro TDP serves only a single user. The load-balancing function is nevertheless important, and must therefore be performed internally by the DBC/1012. Since IFPs do not perform this function, network connections require another type of processor known as a Communications Processor (COP).

Linear Performance Characteristics

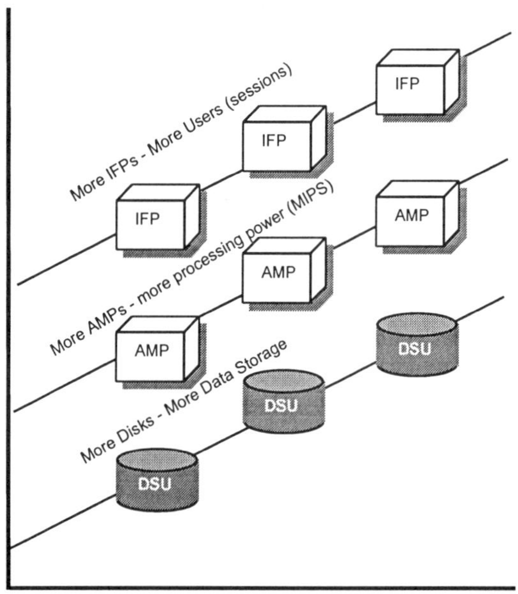

Fig 4-8

Unlike more conventional database systems, the Teradata Database exhibits a near-linear performance improvement by adding more components to the system *(Fig. 4-8).*

More IFPs provide more users with access to the system. Adding AMPs increases the number of MIPS (Millions of Instructions Per Second). Increasing the number of disks permits more storage of data - all as a straight-line graph.

If the number of users remains the same, and we double the number of AMPs - performance doubles. If the number of users doubles, and the number of AMPs doubles, performance remains the same. These linear performance characteristics permit Teradata customers to confidently limit their initial investment to their immediate needs, secure in the knowledge that no matter how large their future data requirements may become, the Teradata system can be expanded to meet them.

The Agreement with NCR

Nature abhors a vacuum. As Teradata's capacity for handling more and more data increased, so did Customer needs. The definition of a "large table" gradually increased from hundreds of millions to billions of rows, and this very success brought with it new challenges.

The DBC/1012 had achieved a high degree of reliability, and could continue to operate with the loss of some number of processors. Nevertheless there was still a need to protect the data against massive failure of some kind, by occasionally archiving the data to a tape drive on the host and storing the tape off-site. As tables grew larger, archiving them required an ever greater share of valuable resources from a main-frame not designed to handle the huge amounts of data typical in a Teradata environment. Clearly this work-load needed to be shifted to the DBC/1012 by adding a tape drive to the database machine itself.

In order to be attached to a host computer as a recognized peripheral, the DBC/1012 was defined to the host computer as a tape drive. It therefore received commands from TDP such as "Read", "Write", "Rewind", "Test" etc. While such a configuration worked well with a main-frame host, one tape drive cannot issue instructions to another and this particular type of configuration was less adaptable to the needs of an ever-increasing number of network-connected users. As a result, the decision was made to incorporate a full UNIX operating system, capable of supporting peripheral devices, into the DBC/1012 to allow it to function as a stand-alone system. This new addition was known as an AP (Applications Processor).

This change of direction represented a major step for a still relatively small company, and having identified NCR as one of the worlds' leaders in UNIX and network technology, Teradata concluded an agreement which would allow NCR to build and market a competitive Ynet-based system, in exchange for financial and technical cooperation in developing a completely new, free-standing, UNIX-based database machine for the mid 1990's and beyond.

In this way, Teradata was able to add the UNIX-based Application Processor to the DBC/1012, and NCR evolved the 3600, which effectively combined the proprietary architecture of the DBC/1012 with a stand-alone UNIX-based host computer not only capable of supporting Teradata, but at the same time running other applications independent of Teradata.

The NCR 3600

The merger of NCR and Teradata in 1991 left the Company with two competing database machines, the DBC/1012 and the NCR 3600, both of which used proprietary hardware and a similar level of technology.

Since the NCR 3600 was a completely redesigned machine, superbly engineered, with all the connectivity of the DBC/1012, a large number of performance-enhancing features, and had been built, ground up, to support stand-alone operations in the UNIX environment, it was positioned as the successor to the DBC/1012. In this way the database expertise of Teradata, and the UNIX/network experience of NCR were effectively combined into a single powerful machine. *(Fig. 4-9).*

With the APs fulfilling the function of a host machine directly connected to the Ynet, there was no longer any need for IFPs and COPs to be specifically dedicated to host or network interface duties. However these processors had also been responsible for parsing and optimizing the SQL requests, and this function was assigned to a new processor, the Parsing Engine (PE).

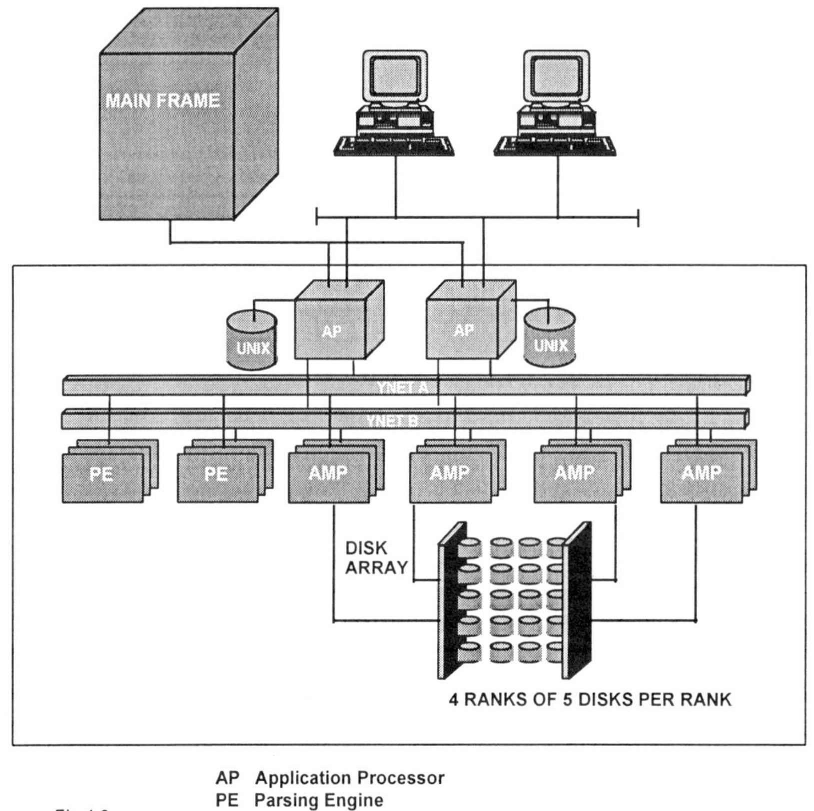

Fig 4-9

The 3600 was additionally advanced by the introduction of Disk Arrays. In the RAID5 (Redundant Array of Inexpensive Disks) implementation, data is written simultaneously to a rank of 5 disks, rather than just 1 in a conventional system. With 8 bits to a byte, this permits 4 disks to be used for *logically* storing 2 bits of data per byte each, with the 5th disk dedicated to 2 parity bits. In the event of failure of any disk in the rank, the data can be reconstructed from the parity bits, and the system can continue to run. Not only do RAID5 disk arrays provide for a high degree of reliability and speed, but in addition they afford protection against a single disk failure for an overhead of only 25% more disk space, compared to the additional 100% needed to maintain fully duplicate (FALLBACK) data.

The 3600 was available with or without the Teradata proprietary hardware connected to the Ynet, and with the introduction of the Oracle Parallel Server, allowed Users to access Teradata and other merchant databases on the same machine.

Teradata Goes Open

In late 1993 the joint logo of AT&T/NCR was abandoned, and with a change of top management, was integrated into AT&T as "Global Information Solutions (GIS)". More than a mere new name, this was a signal for change. While Teradata's innovative architecture had enabled it to provide its customers with all the advantages of massively parallel database machines, as the machines became larger, the high cost of proprietary hardware was becoming keenly felt.

This challenge was eventually met by porting Teradata to a standard UNIX platform as a purely software product known as the "Teradata Database". It was reasoned that by redesigning the Teradata product to run in a tightly-coupled multiple CPU environment, Teradata could duplicate the effect of multiple physical processors as software applications running in parallel. In this way Teradata could retain all the benefits of its proprietary architecture, but as a lower cost software product rather than a more expensive combination of hardware and software.

The NCR 3550

Early in 1995, AT&T GIS proudly announced the Teradata Database as a purely software product running on a near-standard UNIX platform, powered by up to 16 tightly coupled Intel Pentium 90 CPUs (*Fig 4-10)*.

The Teradata Database would logically function much as it had in the past, but instead of hard-wired AMPs, PEs and Ynets, all of these processors would become "virtual" and run as separate programs (Vprocs) on top of the UNIX operating system. This was known as Teradata Version 2.

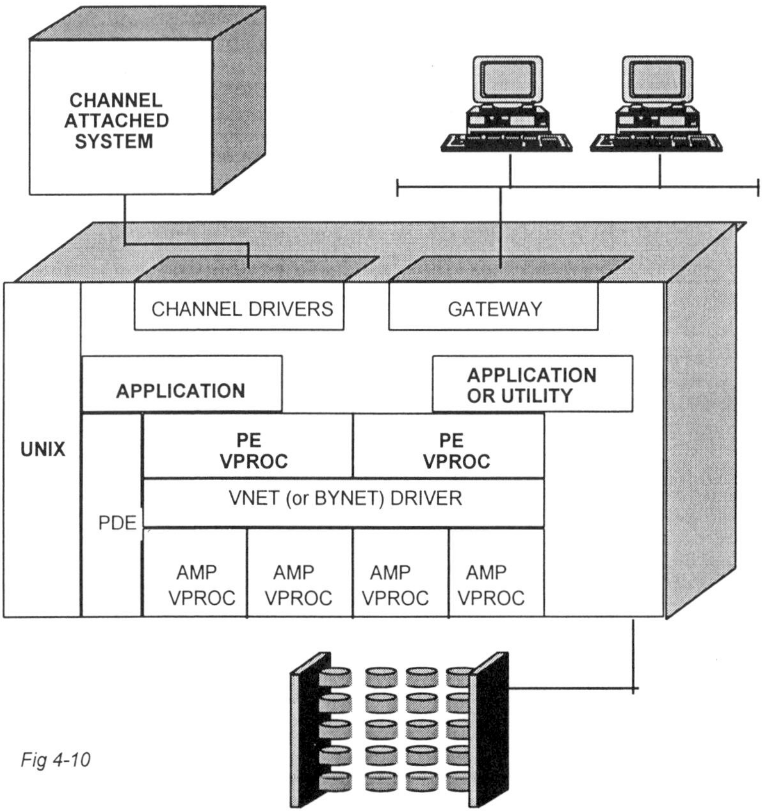

Fig 4-10

The Teradata Operating System (TOS), previously maintained on each AMP, was replaced with a few system-level routines known as Parallel Database Extensions (PDE). Performance was additionally enhanced by a number of other innovative processing strategies and the addition of huge amounts of shared memory.

The hardware-based Ynet was replaced with the Virtual Net (Vnet), an innovative software solution which enabled Vprocs to communicate directly with each other in parallel by placing a message in memory and then re-assigning ownership of that memory to the destination Vproc(s).

The NCR 3550 provides an open, general purpose hardware platform capable of running Teradata Version 2 software and other merchant databases with reduced footprint and improved performance over the NCR 3600, at a fraction of the cost.

The WorldMark 5100

In February 1996, the company, now again named "NCR" announced the long-awaited result of the joint endeavor - the WorldMark 5100 (*Fig 4-11*), supporting Teradata and other merchant Databases such as Oracle and Informix.

If we regard the 3550 as a single Symetric Multi-Processing (SMP) node, the WorldMark 5100 becomes, in effect, a collection of between 2 and 16 such nodes. With 2 nodes per cabinet, each node can be powered by up to 16 powerful Pentium 200 processors, tightly coupled together to behave as a single ultra-powerful CPU.

The Teradata Database however requires no more than eight tightly coupled processors in a single node to deliver its maximum performance. For this reason, a single cabinet of 32 Pentium CPUs can support as many as four Teradata SMP nodes, and this effectively serves to halve the over-all footprint of the system. Each node can support up to eight virtual processors, and each of those is directly connected to all the others by a new, super-fast Bynet which permits as many messages as there are processors to be processed in parallel.

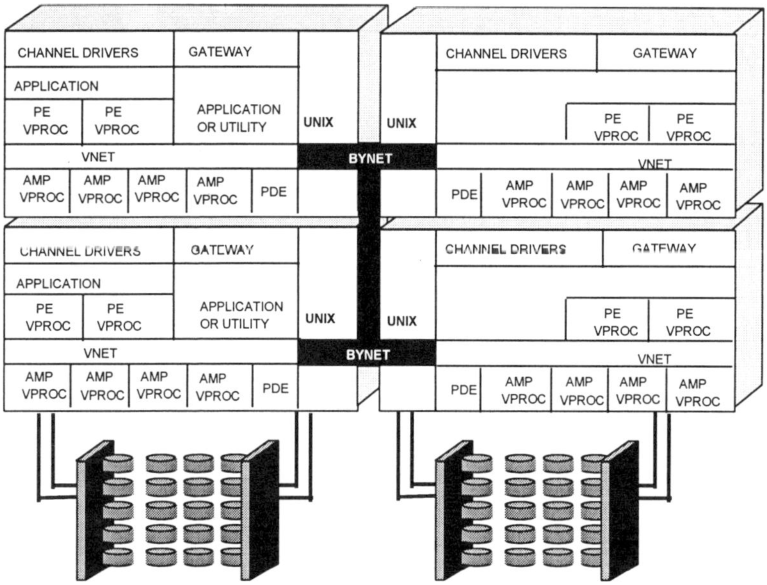

PDE - Parallel Database Extensions
Vproc Virtual Processor

Fig 4-11

The WorldMark 5100 is available in 3 distinct configurations:

5100 TYPE	COMM LAYER	TERADATA SUPPORT
5100 S (Single Node)	Vnet	YES
5100C (Clustered)	Vnet	NO
5100M (Massively Parallel)	Bynet	YES

The Bynet

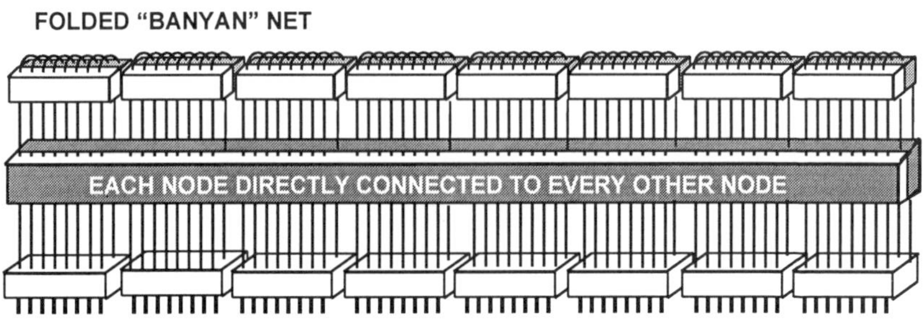

Figure 4-12

Whereas the Ynet is to some degree single threaded, and can only handle one message at a time, the Bynet (*Fig 4-12*) is scaleable in a linear fashion. The structure is described as a "folded banyan tree", in that there are as many possible links between any two SMP units as there are nodes on the Bynet. A bandwidth of 10 Megabytes per second for each node provides the Bynet with all the capability required for handling the heavy demands expected of it in the foreseeable future.

Conclusions

With the WorldMark 5100M as a platform, the Teradata Database is not only ready to defend its title as the world's top performer in complex queries against very large tables, but is now achieving significant success in the competitive worlds of on-line transaction and complex processing. At the same time the low cost and high performance of the WorldMark 5100S now brings the power and speed of the Teradata Database well within the reach of medium sized database users, by providing an entry-level system which can provide them the unique advantages of Teradata, long-term application stability, and the ability to expand to any size as their data needs grow.

5 Parallelism

"Finding a needle in a haystack" is an old adage, but very much today's problem. Simply put, how do you find a single record among billions, in a reasonable period of time? In some cases where the search criteria is not recognized ahead of time, there is often no alternative to searching every record until the target record is found. In other cases some kind of index might be used to reduce the workload. Even with the most ingenious algorithms and clever indexes however, this might still be expected to involve hundreds of thousands of comparisons and, for that reason, take a substantial amount of time. Teradata's parallel access mechanism addresses both these issues in a straight-forward, easy-to-understand way.

Full Table Scan

Some database operations require the system to examine each and every row of a table. This is known as a "Full Table Scan", and can often overwhelm the resources of a single processor. As a result, the number of rows which can be efficiently scanned in this way generally becomes the limiting factor to maximum table size for most database vendors.

The Teradata Database, on the other hand, was built ground-up to perform full table scans of very large tables efficiently by dividing the workload amongst multiple processors, and allowing each processor to function in parallel with the others. In this way the full scan of a large table using multiple processors can be efficiently completed in a fraction of the time required by one.

Since, by axiom, the entire system cannot complete a task until all of its component parts have finished, the total elapsed time to completion is determined by the processor with the largest amount of work to do. Optimum performance of this kind of a system therefore depends heavily upon an even distribution of the workload amongst the multiple processors (AMPs), and this is accomplished in the Teradata environment by using a "hashing" algorithm.

The Hashing Algorithm

One definition of the word "hash" is "chop into pieces", and it might be said that one major function of the hashing algorithm is to "chop" or separate a large amount of input data into individual records, and divide those records into logical groupings or "buckets".

Any piece of data on a computer is represented as a binary number, and arithmetic can be performed on it. If we take any number therefore, large or small, negative or positive and, using integer arithmetic, divide it by some number, the resulting remainder will always be in the range of zero to the divisor minus 1.

In Version 2 (where the Teradata Database was ported to an open systems platform), all input data - whatever the value, is assigned to one of 65,636 hash buckets. The hash buckets in turn, are divided as equally as possible amongst the total number of AMPs on the system, based on "hash maps" maintained on the AMP's Communications Layer Interface (Ynet, Vnet or Bynet). The major function of the hashing algorithm therefore is to distribute the data records amongst the AMPs in as even a way as possible.

In *Fig. 5-1*, data records are being sent to Teradata in random sequence. Each record is subjected to the hashing algorithm and a hash bucket value is calculated. The Communications layer then consults its hash maps and directs the record to the AMP responsible for that hash bucket.

Dividing the workload evenly amongst multiple AMPs provides the Teradata Database with the ability to perform full table scans on large tables with a speed and efficiency unmatched by any other database vendor. The larger the table, the greater the advantage. Even so, the full table scan of a large table generally involves high utilization of resources, and may be slower than other alternatives when searching for a small number of rows.

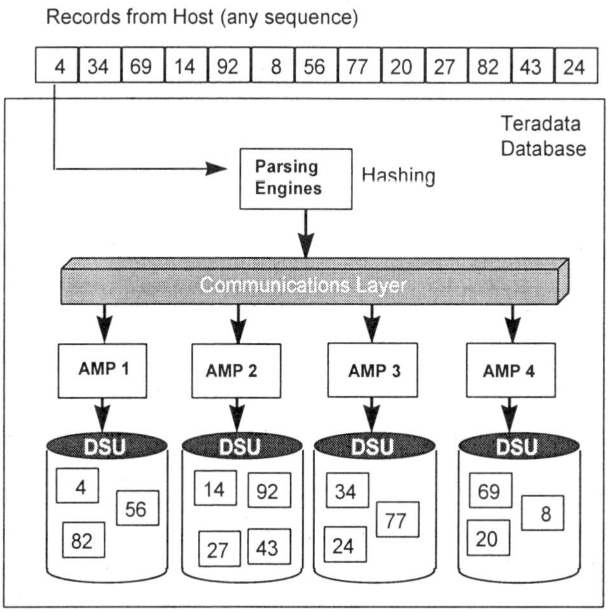

Figure 5-1

Search by Index

Any item temporarily mislaid is easy to find if you know where to look for it. On that basis, if whenever we place a row in a table, we keep a record of where we put it, we should be able to find it again with no trouble whatever. An index on a table is nothing more than another table dedicated to locating a row or rows based on the input of some specific value. Thus if we are searching for one employee amongst thousands, we we will probably give each employee a unique employee number and maintain an sorted index subtable which contains that number and "points" to the row we are looking for *(Fig. 5-2)*.

The Index subtable is smaller and easier to scan than its parent table, and often provides an attractive alternative to a full table scan. It does however have certain disadvantages:

INDEX SUBTABLE

EMPLOYEE NUMBER
1856
1925
2013
3111
4312
4315
4411
4500

TABLE EMPLOYEE

EMPLOYEE NUMBER	LAST NAME	FIRST NAME	BIRTH DATE	SALARY AMOUNT
3111	Benson	Thomas	10/17/69	35000.00
1856	Davis	Paul	04/10/60	43000.00
4312	Lopez	Raoul	06/15/71	28000.00
1925	Lee	Robert	07/31/72	39000.00
2013	Waters	Jackson	12/10/66	40000.00
4315	Chong	Kim	05/11/71	24000.00
4411	Adams	Peter	08/31/70	27000.00
4500	Cousins	Anne	11/11/73	30000.00

Figure 5-2

Subtables require additional storage space,

Locating rows probably involves multiple reads of the subtable in addition to at least one read of the parent table.

Changes to the base table require additional maintenance of subtables.

Primary Index

Almost all tables, however have some column or combination of columns by which they are most frequently accessed. The Employee table, for example, will generally be accessed by the Employee Number more frequently than by Last Name, and the Department table will generally be accessed more frequently by Department Number than by Department Name.

The particular column or combination of columns most frequently used to access the table is designated as the "Primary Index". If the Primary index value is used to initially store the row, the same value (where provided) can also be used to locate the row, using the hashing algorithm. In this way the overhead involved in maintaining a separate index subtable can be avoided for the majority of access.

It is the Primary Index value then, which is subjected to the hashing algorithm and:

Determines the location of the row on the disk.
Is required to evenly distribute the workload amongst the AMP processors.

Primary Indexes may be unique or non unique. If the primary index value is unique or nearly unique there is no conflict. The hashing algorithm guarantees an even distribution of the rows. Thus designating the primary **key** (which must be unique) as the primary **index** will guarantee an even distribution of the rows. On the other hand, if the primary key column or columns are seldom used for retrieval, the advantage is lost. The choice of a primary index is therefore based on two equally important but occasionally conflicting criteria:

Uniqueness for distribution.
Fast access to data.

Using the Primary Index to Locate or Place a Row

The Primary Index value for the incoming row is put through the hashing algorithm *(Fig. 5-3)*. The result is a 32 bit value composed of:

A Hash Bucket
A Remainder.

In Version 2, the Hash Bucket is a value between zero and 65,535, and the 16 bit remainder is added to improve uniqueness.

The AMP Communications Layer Interface contains hash maps which determine the AMP is responsible for a given bucket.

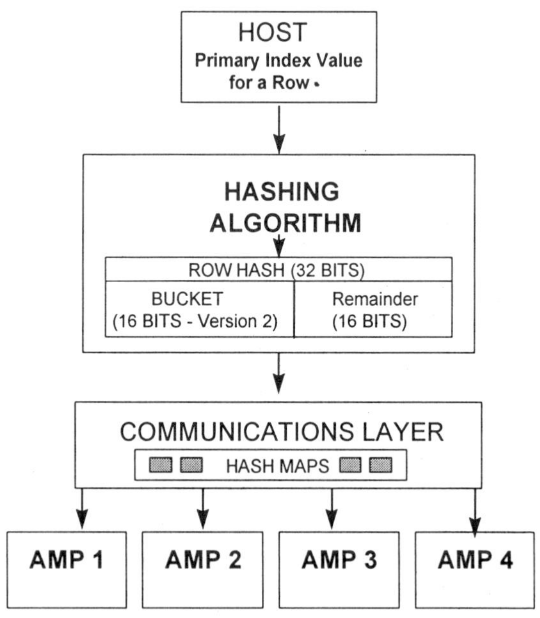

Figure 5-3

In *Fig. 5-4*, the Primary Index value of 7550 is hashed, and results in a hexadecimal bucket number of 001A, and a 16 bit remainder.

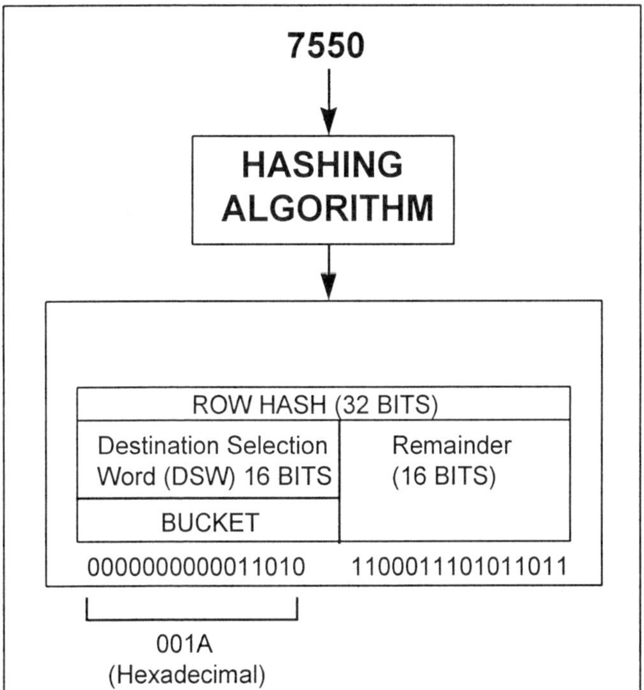

Figure 5-4

Identical values input to the hashing algorithm will produce the same hash bucket number and remainder. Hence rows with duplicate primary index values cannot, *at this point*, be uniquely identified.

The resulting bucket number is referred to the hash map in the AMP's Communications Layer Interface which identifies the AMP responsible for that hash bucket.

In *Fig 5-5*, the hash bucket 01A is assigned to AMP 3.

EACH AMP'S COMMUNICATIONS INTERFACE

HASH MAP

	0	1	2	3	4	5	6	7	8	9	A	B	C	D	E	F
00	01	02	03	04	05	06	07	08	01	02	03	04	05	06	07	08
01	01	02	03	04	05	06	07	08	01	02	03	04	05	06	07	08
02	01	02	03	04	05	06	07	08	01	02	03	04	05	06	07	08
03	01	02	03	04	05	06	07	08	01	02	03	04	05	06	07	08
04	01	02	03	04	05	06	07	08	01	02	03	04	05	06	07	08
05	01	02	03	04	05	06	07	08	01	02	03	04	05	06	07	08

AMP 1 **AMP 2** **AMP 3** **AMP 4** .... **AMP 5**

Figure 5-5

Hash Collisions and Duplicates

Although a 32 bit numerical field can store a very large number, it is still finite, and sooner or later duplicate results will occur for different input values. This is known as a "hash collision". Identical hash values can also result from duplicate Non Unique Primary Index values (NUPI Duplicates). To enforce uniqueness of each distinct row, therefore an additional 32 bit "uniqueness" value is assigned

The Uniqueness value is calculated by the system as a row is inserted into the table. If a row hash value is unique, it will be assigned a uniqueness value of 1. Otherwise the system will calculate the maximum uniqueness value previously assigned to that row hash value and increment it by one *(Fig 5-6)*.

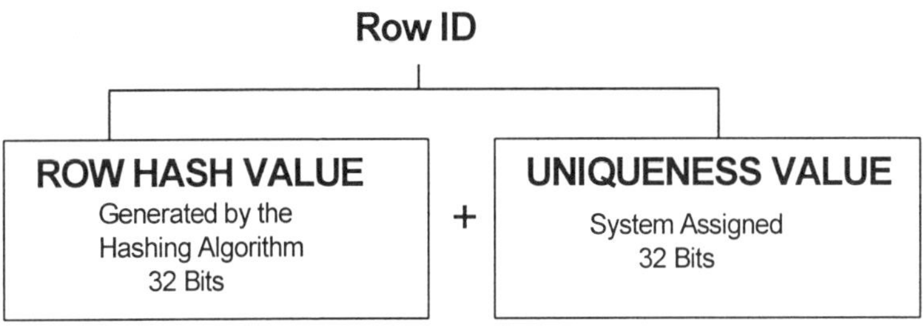

NUPI Duplicate and Hash Synonyms

Index Value	Symbolic Row Hash	Uniqueness Value	
933	52345	1	Duplicate
933	52345	2	Duplicate
904	33391	1	
721	52345	3	Synonym

Figure 5-6

The combination of the 32 bit Row Hash Value plus the 32 bit Uniqueness value is known as the "Row ID" which is appended to the beginning of the row *(Fig 5-7)*. Each row therefore has a unique 64 bit Row ID composed of:

The 16 bit Bucket Number
The 16 bit Remainder
The 32 bit Uniqueness Value.

In this way the Row ID becomes a "header" for the user data, since rows are stored on the disk sorted ascending by Row ID, the entire row becomes, in effect, self-indexing. This avoids the overhead required to maintain and access an additional subtable. In addition to the Row ID, each row has a leading and trailing 2 byte row length, which facilitates reading the row in either direction.

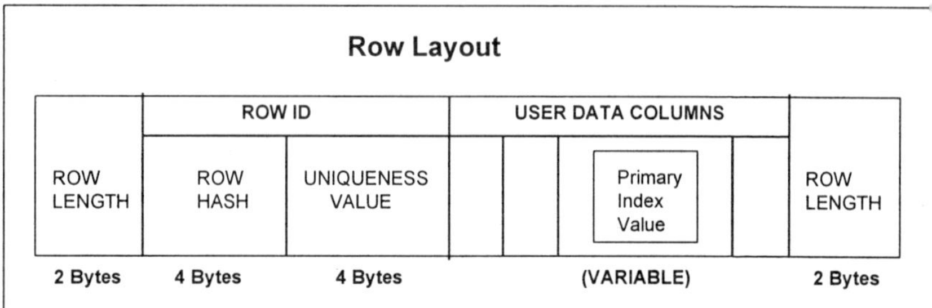

Figure 5-7

The Data Dictionary/Directory (DD/D)

Each User, database, table, view or macro is assigned a unique numeric ID by the system. This information is maintained as a series of relational tables in a system-owned User with a name of "DBC", referred to as the Data Dictionary/Directory (DD/D)".

With more than 70 tables, the DD/D accumulates information about:

Users and ownership,
Access rights and Security rules,
Accounting and Space Management,
Resource usage,
Data demographics,

The DD/D is updated automatically by the system, and is used by the SQL Parser (located in the Parsing Engine) to obtain information needed to process SQL statements.

Locating a Row using the Primary Index

In *Fig. 5-8*, the Parsing Engine builds a 3-part message consisting of:

Table ID from DD/D).

32 Bit Row Hash.

Bucket Number.

Remainder.

Index Data Value.

The Bucket number is used to identify the responsible AMP.

The AMP's file system uses the Table ID and 32 Bit Row Hash to locate the Data Block.

The Row is located using a 3-part pointer array which is built at the end of each data block and consists of:

Row ID + Byte Offset + Row Length.

Rows are stored in data blocks of up to 32K bytes in length using the following criteria:

Rows are sorted ascending by row hash.

All rows in a block are from a single table.

Wherever possible rows which hash to the same value will be accommodated in the same block.

Rows never span blocks.

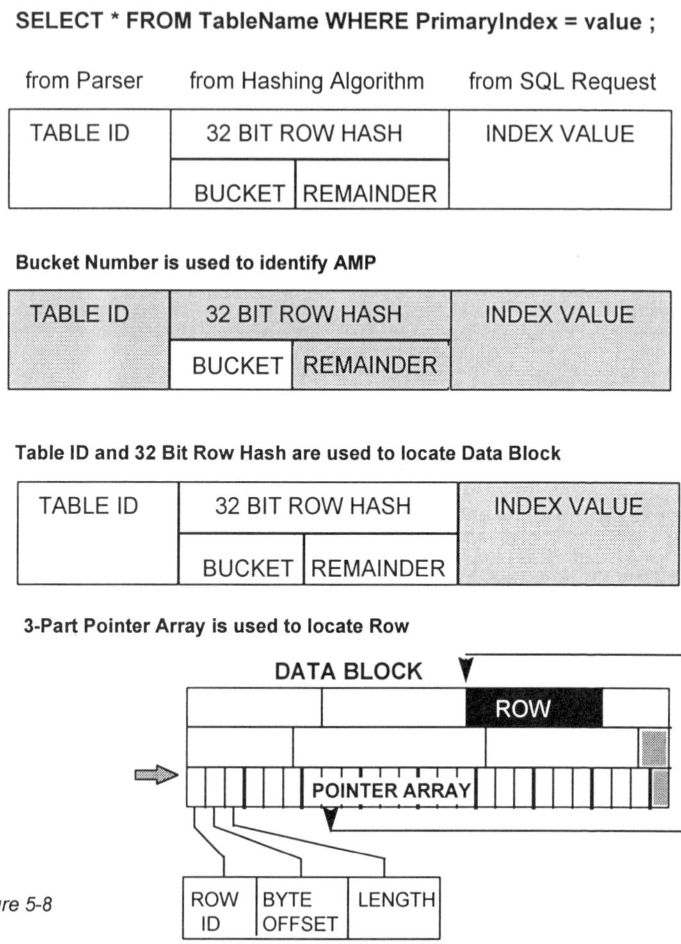

Figure 5-8

Example:

```
SELECT Last_Name
        ,First_Name
        ,Hire_Date
        FROM Employee
        WHERE Employee_Number = 3250
;
```

Each AMP maintains a Master Index permanently in memory *(Fig. 5-9)*.

TABLE ID	ROWHASH	VALUE
100	1000	3250

MASTER INDEX

TABLE ID	STARTING HASH	CYLINDER NUMBER	CONTINUED HASH FLAG
.	.	.	.
.	.	.	.
.	.	.	.
078	58234,1	204	0
100	00107,1	037	0
100	00823,1	(169)	0
100	01361,2	777	0
100	02937,1	802	0
100	03662,1	117	0
100	04123,1	888	1
100	05974,1	753	0
100	07353,1	477	0
123	00543,1	529	0
.	.	.	.
.	.	.	.
.	.	.	.

FREE CYLINDER LIST	FREE CYLINDER LIST
.	.
.	.
.	.
045	761
059	780
100	895
101	896
107	914
124	941
125	935
126	1012
183	1234
189	1375
.	.
.	.
.	.

TO CYLINDER INDEX

Figure 5-9

The Master Index lists, in ascending order, the lowest hash value for each Table ID occurring on each cylinder. There is therefore only one cylinder reference per table.

Each table ID, and each starting hash and uniqueness value are maintained in ascending sequence. Therefore cylinder 037 will hold row hash values of table 100 equal to or greater than 00107,1, but less than 00823,1.

The Master Index also contains a "Continued Hash Flag". This flag is set to "1" if there is at least one row with the starting hash value in the previous logically adjacent (on the Master Index) cylinder. Thus if we were searching for table 100 with a starting row hash value of 04123, we are directed to cylinder 888. However the continued hash flag is set to 1, which indicates that there is at least one row with that hash value on the previous (logically adjacent) cylinder 117. We must therefore begin reading on cylinder 117 and continue from there to cylinder 888.

In our example, we are searching for table 100, Row Hash 1000 which is greater than 00823 and less than 1361. (The uniqueness value is not known at this time). We are therefore directed to the index for Cylinder 169.

The Master Index also contains a list of cylinders not currently in use. Teradata never stores PERMANENT data and SPOOL on the same cylinders. Hence when a cylinder previously used for SPOOL is no longer required, it is simply returned to the Free Cylinder List. Since the Master Index is always in memory this involves no costly I/Os to the disk.

Each Cylinder Index *(Fig 5-10*) is permanently maintained on disk, but has about a 50% chance of being in memory at any given time. It is organized in a similar way to the Master Index, and lists, in ascending order, the lowest hash value for each data block by Table ID. Thus, if row hash 1000 exists, it will be found in the data block beginning at sector 0789 for 6 sectors.

The data block represents the standard Input/Output (I/O) unit. Since the Master Index is always maintained in memory, and the Cylinder Index may or may not be in memory at this time, the search for this row by primary index value probably consumed no more than a single access to the disk *irrespective of the total number of rows in the table.*

TABLE ID	ROWHASH	VALUE
100	1000	3250

CYLINDER INDEX -CYLINDER 169

TABLE ID	STARTING HASH	SECTOR NUMBER	SECTOR COUNT	CONTINUED HASH FLAG
.	.	.	.	.
.	.	.	.	.
078	02523,1	1010	9	0
100	00998,1	0789	6	0
100	01035,1	0530	4	0
100	01185,3	0056	5	1
100	01221,1	1138	5	0
.	.	.	.	.
.	.	.	.	.
.	.	.	.	.

FREE BLOCK LIST

SECTOR NUMBER	SECTOR COUNT
.	.
.	.
.	.
0305	2
0307	8
0320	5
0470	4
0401	6
.	.
.	.
.	.

TO DATA BLOCK

Figure 5-10

In changing the SQL from a read to a write transaction, we perform exactly the same series of steps through the Master Index and Cylinder Index 169 to locate the row.

Example:

```
DELETE from Employee
        WHERE Employee_Number = 3250
        ;
```

Having retrieved the data block containing the row, the system calculates that only 5 sectors are required to re-write the block after the row has been deleted. Teradata never updates in place. It searches the Free Block List for the first block with sufficient free contiguous sectors to accommodate the new block. In this example it finds sector 307 which is the first of 8 contiguous sectors and is large enough to write the 5 sectors required.

CYLINDER INDEX -CYLINDER 169				
TABLE ID	STARTING HASH	SECTOR NUMBER	SECTOR COUNT	CONTINUED HASH FLAG
...	...	...	...	...
078	02523	1010	9	0
100	00998	0307	5	0
100	01035	0530	4	0
100	01185	0056	5	1
100	01221	1138	5	0
...	...	...	...	...

FREE BLOCK LIST	
SECTOR NUMBER	SECTOR COUNT
...	...
0305	2
0312	3
0320	5
0470	4
0481	6
0789	6
...	...

Figure 5-11

The new block is written to the 5 sectors beginning 0307 *(Fig 5-11), and* the remaining 3 sectors beginning 0312, together with the now-unused 6 sectors beginning with 0789, are returned to the Free Block List.

If the transaction involves the INSERT of a new row, the maximum uniqueness value of any pre-existing rows with the same row hash value is incremented by one. This becomes the uniqueness value for the new row and both the Master and Cylinder indexes are updated accordingly.

By avoiding updating in place, Teradata performs, in effect, a minor REORG with every write, and in this way effectively avoids the need for major REORGs - ever!

Conclusions

Whether a table has three rows or three billion rows, locating a row in the Teradata environment using a unique primary index takes exactly the same amount of time - one elapsed I/O. Add this to the awesome power of its full table scans, and with parallel wizardry, Teradata has truly mastered the art of finding the metaphorical needle in an electronic haystack!

6 Choosing a Primary Index

Of all tasks and duties which face the Teradata Database administrator, the choosing of Primary indexes is by far the most important. In the earlier epoch of the hierarchical database, where the drill-down path to the detail data was pre-set and immutable, the question was moot. For many relational database products today, the difference between primary keys and primary indexes is indistinct. Teradata's unique multiple-processor environment, however, requires that the primary index column or columns are chosen, not purely on the basis of being unique, not null and never changed, but more importantly, on the basis of data distribution and access. Performance of the Teradata Database therefore requires that the differences between primary keys and primary indexes are well understood.

Keys vs Indexes

Every table must have a column or combination of columns designated as the Primary Key which are:

Unique.
Not NULL (must have a value).
Never changed.

Relational tables must also have a defined single or multiple-column Primary Index which:

May be unique or non unique.
May be NULL (NULL is treated as if it were a value).

May be changed, although this is considered an unreasonable update, and is discouraged.

It must be recognized however that while Primary Keys and Primary Indexes have a certain similarity of appearance, they serve very different objectives.

The Primary Key is a logical modeling construct which serves merely to uniquely identify each instance of a person, place or thing of interest to the organization. In relationships with Foreign Keys, Primary Keys are used to ensure referential integrity amongst tables.

The Primary Index is input to the hashing algorithm, and is initially used to physically determine where a row should be written to disk. If the Primary Index is unique or nearly unique, the hashing algorithm guarantees an even distribution of rows amongst all the AMPs. If the same value is later supplied in the SQL, *in its entirety*, the same method used to place the row can be used to locate it. If the primary index is based on multiple columns, this method can only be effective if a value is supplied for each of those columns in the SQL. Teradata cannot hash on a partial or incomplete value.

Distribution of the Rows

The total amount of disk space (PERMANENT SPACE) allocated to a database or user is equally divided amongst all the AMPs in the system, and AMPs are never permitted to borrow space from each other. Unevenly distributed data can therefore result in "out of space" conditions on heavily populated AMPs, even though less populated AMPs may still have a significant amount of unused capacity available. Uneven or lumpy distribution of data caused by a poor choice of Primary Index results in inefficient utilization of one of the system's most expensive resources - *disk space.*

Examples:

In *Fig. 6-1*, we have chosen Order_Status as a non-unique Primary Index (NUPI). This column has only 2 distinct values, "C" and "O". Since similar values passed through the hashing algorithm will always yield the same result, and similar values will always hash to the same AMP, only 2 AMPs receive rows. If the system had 100 AMPs, 98 would have no rows at all - *poor distribution.*

ORDER

ORDER NUMBER	CUSTOMER NUMBER	ORDER DATE	ORDER STATUS
PK			
			NUPI
1011	32	10/12/96	C
1012	27	10/13/96	O
1013	32	10/15/96	C
1014	32	10/16/96	C
1015	25	10/16/96	C
1016	32	10/17/96	O
1019	35	10/17/96	O
1020	32	10/17/96	O

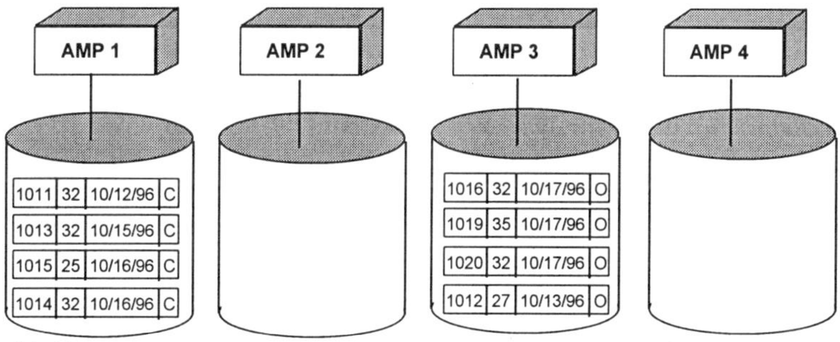

Figire 6-1

Re-assigning the Primary Index to Customer Number utilizes more AMPs, but it is still not unique, and since some customers place disproportionately more orders than others. This results in very uneven distribution *(Fig. 6-2)*

ORDER

ORDER NUMBER	CUSTOMER NUMBER	ORDER DATE	ORDER STATUS
PK			
	NUPI		
1011	32	10/12/96	C
1012	27	10/13/96	O
1013	32	10/15/96	C
1014	32	10/16/96	C
1015	25	10/16/96	C
1016	32	10/17/96	O
1019	35	10/17/96	O
1020	32	10/17/96	O

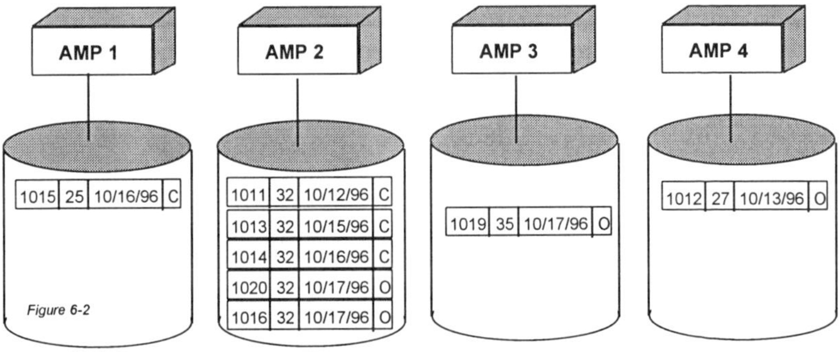

Figure 6-2

In Fig 6-3, Order_Number is unique. The Teradata hashing algorithm guarantees apparently random but even distribution of rows amongst the AMPs if the Primary Index is unique or nearly unique. A Primary Index based upon this column therefore guarantees an even distribution of the rows amongst the AMPs.

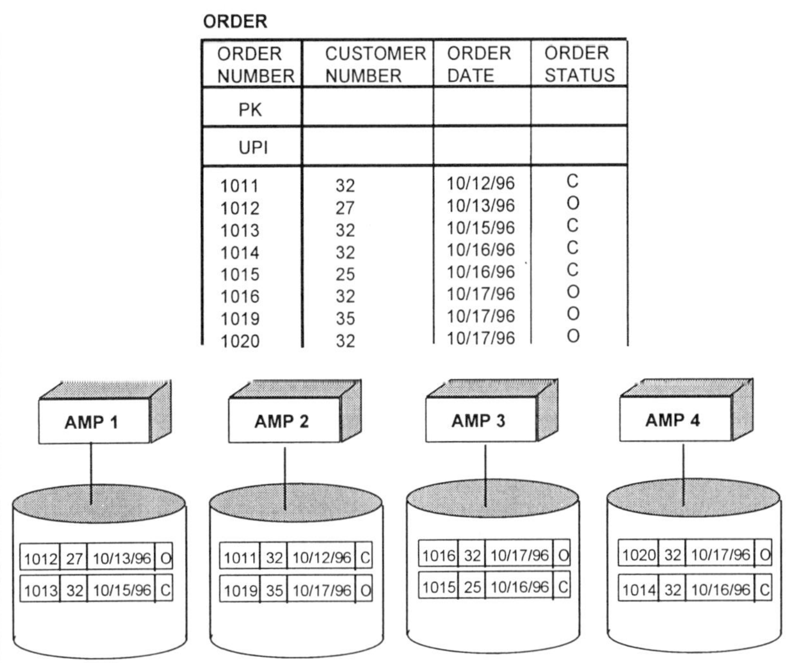

Figure 6-3

Primary Index Access

The majority of tables in any data model are classified as "Prime Entities" and have a single column Primary Key. These may be subdivided into "Major" and "Minor" and "Sub" Entities.

Major Entities are the dynamic, important tables which become the focus of the applications. They tend to be few in number, have a significant number of columns, and a fairly large number of rows. Major Entities are usually assigned a numeric Primary Key, which is frequently the column by which the rows are most commonly accessed. The Primary Index of a major entity is generally based on the Primary Key (or some other nearly-unique column) which conveniently addresses the issues of both distribution and access without conflict.

Sub Entities, as the name implies, are used to sub-divide the rows and columns of a major entity into more manageable units. Sub entities have the same Primary Key and the same Primary Index as the parent entity.

Minor Entities are frequently described as validation tables. Minor entities are small static tables with typically fewer than 100 rows, and seldom more than 2 or 3 columns. The Primary Key of a minor entity may be numeric or a short alpha code, which is generally the column most frequently used for access, and therefore the optimal choice for Primary Index.

In order to successfully locate a row by a hash of the Primary Index value, the SQL must supply all components of the Primary Index. If some, but not all, of the Primary Index components are supplied, the hashing algorithm cannot be used to locate rows, and a less efficient access method may be required as a result.

All the remaining tables in the database have multiple column Primary Keys. Since such tables are rarely accessed by supplying all the Primary Key components in the SQL, the Primary Index is generally based on the single *non-unique* column most frequently used for access.

Example:

The ORDER PART table *(Fig. 6-4)* models a many-to-many relationship between orders and parts, such that one order could be for many parts, and one type of part could appear on many orders. It is known as an "associative" table. Associative tables always have a multiple column primary key (PK), each component of which will be a Foreign Key (FK).

The Order Part table might be used in one of two ways. It might be used to identify the parts on a specific order (Order Department), or it might equally well be used for identifying the orders to which specific parts are committed (Warehouse). Either way we will generally be supplied with one of the two values in order to resolve the other.

ORDER PART

ORDER NUMBER	PART NUMBER	ORDER QUANTITY
PK		
FK	FK	
NUPI		
1011	1032	50
1011	1027	288
1012	1032	40
1012	2021	400
1012	1027	144
1013	2021	350
1014	2021	200
1014	1027	144

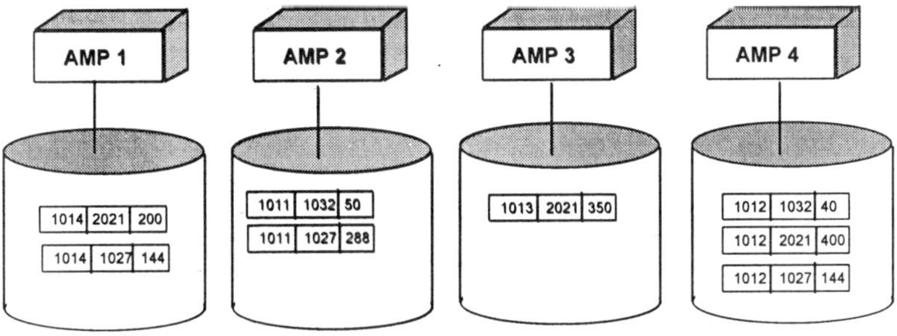

Figure 6-4

A primary index on both the Order Number *and* Part Number columns would provide excellent distribution amongst the AMPs, but rarely (if ever) would *both* values be supplied in the SQL to access rows. Thus a single-column Primary Index based on the Order Number might well serve the Order Department, but it would, at the same time, inhibit the Warehouse application. Since the choice must inevitably be made, it requires a thorough understanding not only of how the table will be used, but how often access is made by supplying the Order Number compared to the frequency of access by the Part Number.

In *Fig. 6-5*, customers place orders for parts, and need to know the status of their orders. There can be multiple parts on an order. If the parts are available in inventory, they are immediately shipped to the customer and the event is recorded in the ORDER PART SHIPPED HISTORY table.

CUSTOMER

CUSTOMER NUMBER	CUSTOMER NAME	PHONE NUMBER
PK		
		NUPI
25	WILLIAMS	541-2296
27	LEE	327-9912
32	LOPEZ	445-6623
35	BROWN	445-6977

PART

PART NUMBER	PART DESCRIPTION	ON HAND QUANTITY
PK		
UPI		
1032	REDWOOD STUDS	750
1027	6 IN. WOOD SCREWS	1440
2021	4 X 8 PLYWOOD	0
2029	1 X 12 X 96 PINE	200

ORDER

ORDER NUMBER	CUSTOMER NUMBER	ORDER DATE
PK	FK	
UPI		
1011	32	10/12/96
1012	27	10/13/96
1013	32	10/15/96
1014	32	10/16/96
1015	25	10/16/96
1016	32	10/17/96
1019	35	10/17/96
1020	32	10/17/96

ORDER PART

ORDER NUMBER	PART NUMBER	ORDER QUANTITY
PK		
FK	FK	
NUPI		
1011	1032	50
1011	1027	288
1012	1032	40
1012	2021	400
1012	1027	144
1013	2021	350
1014	2021	200
1014	1027	144

ORDER PART SHIPPED HISTORY

ORDER NUMBER	PART NUMBER	SHIPPED DATE	SHIPPED QUANTITY
PK			
FK			
NUPI			
1011	1032	10/12/96	50
1011	1027	10/12/96	288
1012	1032	10/13/96	40
1012	1027	10/13/96	144
1014	1027	10/17/96	144

Figure 6-5

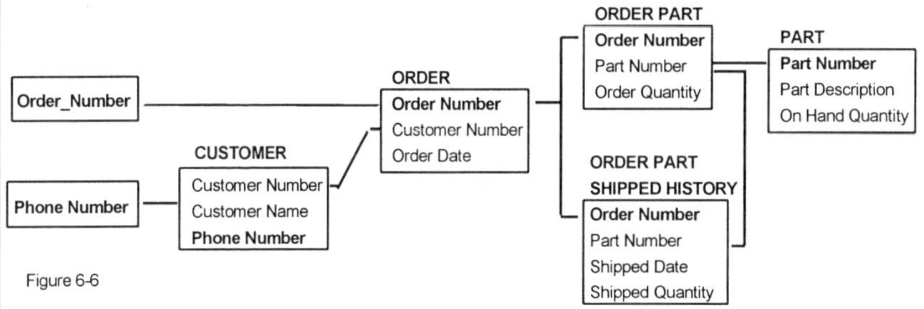

Figure 6-6

Fig. 6-6 demonstrates the path by which the order and part information is derived from the Order_Number provided by the customer. It clearly shows why Order_Number might be chosen as the unique primary index of the ORDER table, and the non-unique primary index of the ORDER PART and ORDER PART SHIPPED HISTORY tables on the basis of frequent access. Since the PART table can only be accessed from the other tables by Part_Number, this becomes the uncontested candidate for unique primary index.

The reason why the Phone Number is chosen as a non-unique primary index for the CUSTOMER table over the more obvious unique Customer Number, becomes clearer when we recognize that, while a customer may or may not be aware of the number assigned by our system, that same customer is unlikely to forget his or her own telephone number.

Having chosen the primary index columns on the basis of frequent access, it is interesting to note that of the five tables:

ORDER and PART have UPIs based on the primary key.

ORDER PART and ORDER PART SHIPPED HISTORY have NUPIs based on part of the primary key.

CUSTOMER has a NUPI based on a non-key column.

Conclusions

If we assume the above example to be fairly typical, we can draw a number of interesting conclusions which become a *rule-of-thumb.*

Major and minor entities (40% to 60% of the tables in the model) with a single column Primary Key will generally end up with a Unique Primary Index based on the Primary Key column.

Tables with multiple column Primary Keys (40% to 60% of the tables in the model) will usually be assigned a Non-Unique Primary Index based on one of the Foreign Key components of the Primary Key.

A small number of tables, generally with single column primary keys, might require a primary index based on a column other than the primary key or any part of it.

Thus while the above rules-of-thumb might prove helpful in identifying most primary index candidates on the basis of their association with the primary key, they are of little assistance in identifying those primary index candidates based on columns other than the primary key. Since overall performance of the Teradata Database depends almost exclusively on the correct choice of primary indexes, much more information about the full impact of all applications and the data is required. The Teradata-designed Activity Transaction Modeling (ATM) process provides all the rules and guidelines needed to generate *enterprise-wide* statistics and demographics on:

The number of rows in each table (present and future).

The number of distinct values in each column.

The maximum and typical number of rows per value.

The maximum number of nulls in each column.

The approximate frequency of change for each column.

The frequency of applications which change those values.

How many times in the course of a year the table is accessed by supplying a literal value for each specific column.

The number of columns involved in each distinct operation.

How many times annually the table is accessed by way of a join on each specific column.

The number of columns involved in each distinct operation.

The collection of these vital statistics is a time-consuming but necessary task. While the precise details of the ATM process go well beyond the aspirations of this present work, it must be well recognized that *only when this information is at hand* can the *correct choice* of primary indexes for the tables be made, and Teradata's impressive performance potential realized.

7 Secondary Indexes and Full Table Scans

In the Teradata environment, the primary index value is based on the column or columns most frequently used for access, and is used to store and locate rows. As an integral and required part of the table, the primary index value is used to construct the Row ID which is appended to the data row by the file system. Each row in a table therefore becomes self-indexed, and the primary index itself can be considered to have no additional cost in terms of system resources.

Secondary indexes are optionally employed to facilitate access to the data using less frequently used paths. Secondary indexes may be created and dropped by the User as and when needed, to improve performance of the Teradata Database. For example:

```
CREATE UNIQUE INDEX Customer_Number ON Customer;
DROP INDEX Customer_Number ON Customer;
```

They can be up to 16 columns wide and not more than 32 indexes per table.

Each secondary index requires the maintenance of a subtable *(Fig. 7-1)* - another table which has as its primary index column, the secondary index value. The secondary index subtable records Row ID(s) including the uniqueness value, of the base table row(s).

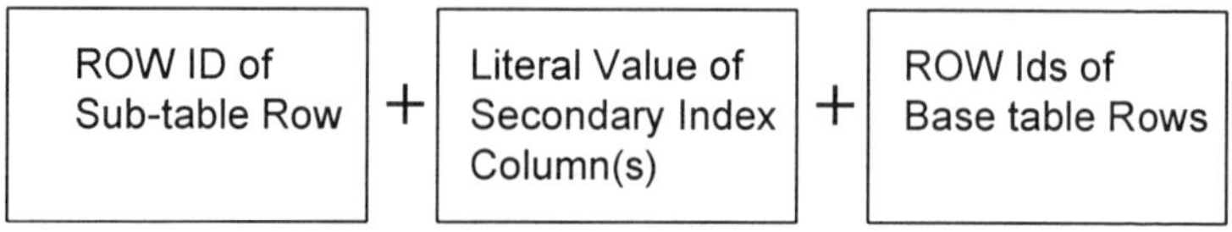

Figure 7-1

Secondary index subtables are built and maintained by Teradata. They are transparent to the user, and can be changed only by changing the base table row(s) to which they refer.

Like other tables in the Teradata system, secondary index subtables require storage space, and additional processing for write transactions. As a result, the resource cost of a secondary index should always be carefully weighed against its processing advantage.

Secondary Indexes may be unique (USI) or non-unique (NUSI), and in addition to their alternate-path access role, may also be used to facilitate aggregate operations, and avoid costly duplicate row checks where the Primary Index is non-unique.

Revisiting the example from *Figs. 6-5 and 6-6*, we will now add Unique Secondary Indexes (USI), and Non-unique Secondary Indexes (NUSI) *(Fig. 7-2):*

> The CUSTOMER, ORDER PART and ORDER PART SHIPPED HISTORY tables all have non-unique primary indexes. In order to perform a duplicate row check for the table the system would have to compare each full row to every other. This is a costly operation which can be avoided by the simple expedient of assigning a USI to the primary key column(s).
>
> *Any unique value concatenated to any other value will always produce a unique result.*

At the same time, the USI forces the uniqueness or *integrity* of the primary key itself.

CUSTOMER

CUSTOMER NUMBER	CUSTOMER NAME	PHONE NUMBER
PK		
USI	**NUSI**	NUPI
25	WILLIAMS	541-2296
27	LEE	327-9912
32	LOPEZ	445-6623
35	BROWN	445-6977

PART

PART NUMBER	PART DESCRIPTION	ON HAND QUANTITY
PK		
UPI		
1032	REDWOOD STUDS	750
1027	6 IN. WOOD SCREWS	1440
2021	4 X 8 PLYWOOD	0
2029	1 X 12 X 96 PINE	200

ORDER

ORDER NUMBER	CUSTOMER NUMBER	ORDER DATE
PK	FK	
UPI		
1011	32	10/12/96
1012	27	10/13/96
1013	32	10/15/96
1014	32	10/16/96
1015	25	10/16/96
1016	32	10/17/96
1019	35	10/17/96
1020	32	10/17/96

ORDER PART

ORDER NUMBER	PART NUMBER	ORDER QUANTITY
PK		
FK	FK	
NUPI		
USI		
1011	1032	50
1011	1027	288
1012	1032	40
1012	2021	400
1012	1027	144
1013	2021	350
1014	2021	200
1014	1027	144

ORDER PART SHIPPED HISTORY

ORDER NUMBER	PART NUMBER	SHIPPED DATE	SHIPPED QUANTITY
PK			
FK			
NUPI			
USI			
1011	1032	10/12/96	50
1011	1027	10/12/96	288
1012	1032	10/13/96	40
1012	1027	10/13/96	144
1014	1027	10/17/96	144

Figure 7-2

Since the CUSTOMER table is occasionally referenced by the Customer_Name as an alternate access path, a NUSI is used to avoid a full table scan.

The Unique Secondary Index (USI)

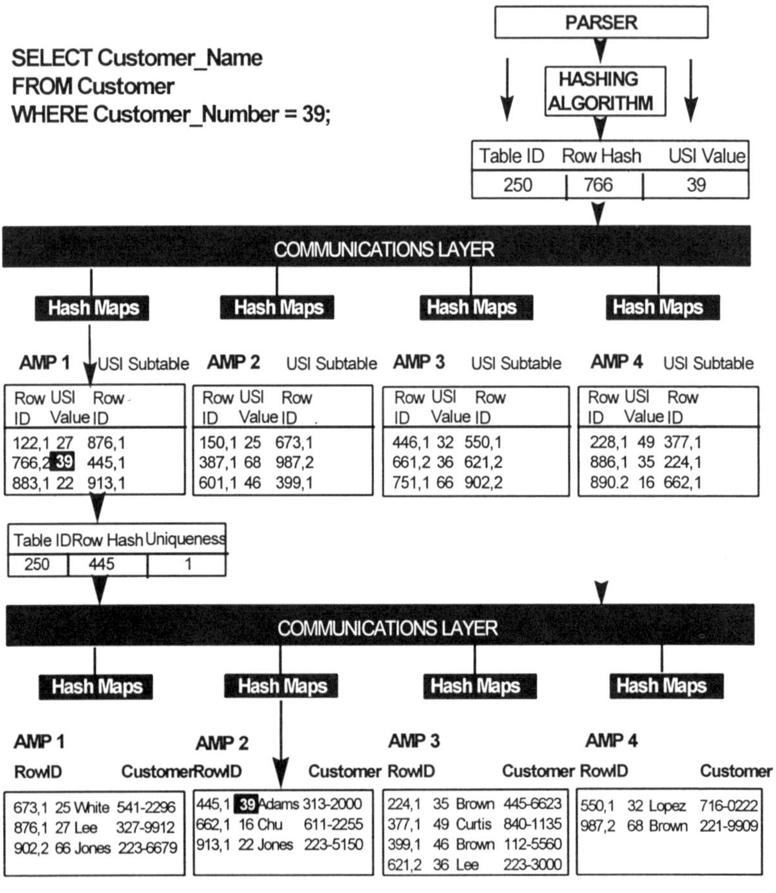

Figure 7-3

In *Fig. 7-3*, the CUSTOMER table is being accessed by a literal value for Customer_Number.

The Parser (in the Parsing Engine) obtains the table ID from the Data Dictionary. It identifies the Customer_Number column as a unique secondary index, and hashes on the value of 39. It then builds a 3-part message containing the table ID, the Row Hash of 39 and the literal value of 39, which it dispatches to the Communications Layer (Ynet, Vnet or Bynet).

The Hash maps on the Communications Layer identify the AMP responsible for the appropriate subtable row, and the AMP locates the row using the Master Index, Cylinder Index and a forward read through the data block.

After checking the literal value to ensure against hash collision, the Row ID and the *Uniqueness value* of the appropriate Customer Table row are used to build another 3-part message, which is then returned to the Communications Layer.

The Hash Maps identify AMP2 as the AMP responsible for the Customer table row, and the Master Index and Cylinder Index are used to locate the data block. Since the uniqueness value is now supplied, the row can be accessed without the additional overhead of a forward read through the data block.

Unique secondary index retrievals are extremely efficient and typically involve no more than 2 disk-read operations.

The Non Unique Secondary Index (NUSI)

NUSI retrievals frequently return a large number of rows. Locating these rows by way of the Master Index and Cylinder Index method would often involve searching the same data block multiple times and result in a large number of expensive but relatively unproductive read operations. Teradata therefore decided to travel another route.

Unlike unique secondary indexes (USI), where the index value is hashed and the bucket number is used to determine the responsible AMP, NUSI subtables are maintained on the same AMP as the base table row. The index value is still hashed, but the bucket number component is ignored, and the request is broadcast to every AMP. Each AMP then proceeds to search its portion of the non-unique secondary index subtable to determine if it has any qualifying rows. Every non-unique secondary index transaction becomes therefore an all-AMP operation. While at first glance, having each AMP access its NUSI subtable might appear to be expensive in terms of system resources, the actual index search process generally involves one read on each AMP. Since these reads occur in parallel, the net cost becomes *one elapsed read I/O.*

The structure of the NUSI subtable is identical to that for the USI subtable except that instead of "pointing" to a single base table row, the NUSI subtable contains multiple sorted Row IDs which "point" to all of the qualifying rows on the same AMP:

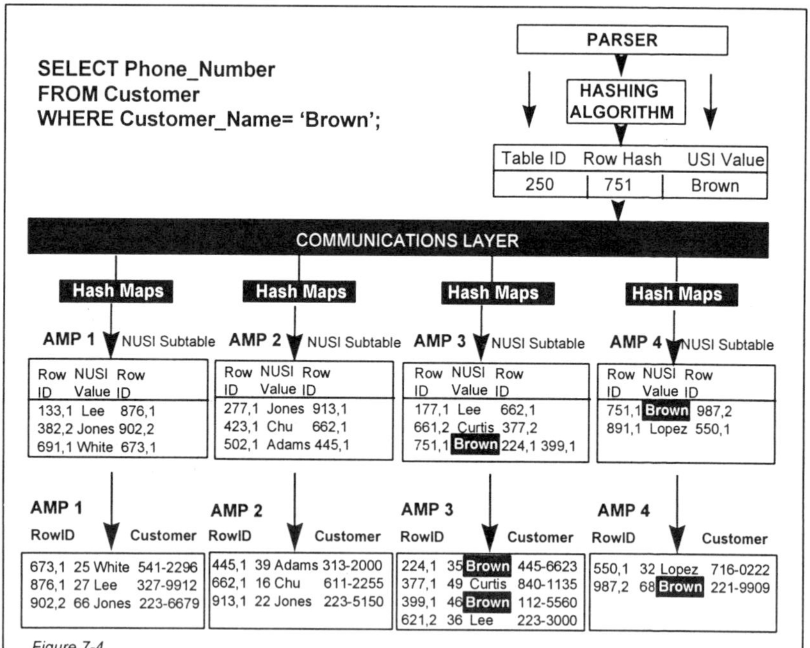

Figure 7-4

In Fig. 7-4, the SQL Parser recognizes the column of Last_Name as a NUSI, hashes on the value of "Brown" and puts all-AMP instructions on the communications layer. Each AMP uses the hashed value to locate the NUSI row (if any) for "Brown".

AMPs 3 and 4 both have NUSI rows for that value and, using the base table Row IDs, retrieve the rows using the Master and Cylinder Indexes.

While Primary and USI retrievals are always highly efficient in the Teradata environment, the over-all utility of a NUSI depends heavily on the selectivity of the index. An index which returns a large number of rows is said to be "weakly selective", while an index which returns a small number of rows is referred to as "strongly selective". The determination of the selectivity of an index is made by the OPTIMIZER, a major component of the Parser charged with the responsibility of ensuring the SQL is processed by Teradata in the most economical and efficient method possible.

Primary and unique secondary indexes are usually strongly selective and involve a small number of costly I/Os. Access using primary or unique secondary indexes is always preferred by the optimizer.

On the other hand, while full table scans are often considered the access method of last resort by other vendors, the Teradata Database was built ground-up to perform this type of transaction with elegance and ease. As a result, the optimizer might well consider a full table scan to be faster and more efficient than a weakly selective NUSI.

The Full Table Scan (FTS)

Of all its outstanding contributions to the world of relational database management, Teradata's major achievement probably still lies in its incredible ability to perform highly efficient full table scans. While the FTS performance of most other database vendors tends to deteriorate in direct proportion to the volume of data being scanned, Teradata's performance depends only on the capacity of the hardware and the number of physical or virtual processors employed.

In selecting all the rows from the Customer table, we leave the optimizer with no alternative other than a full table scan *(Fig. 7-5):*

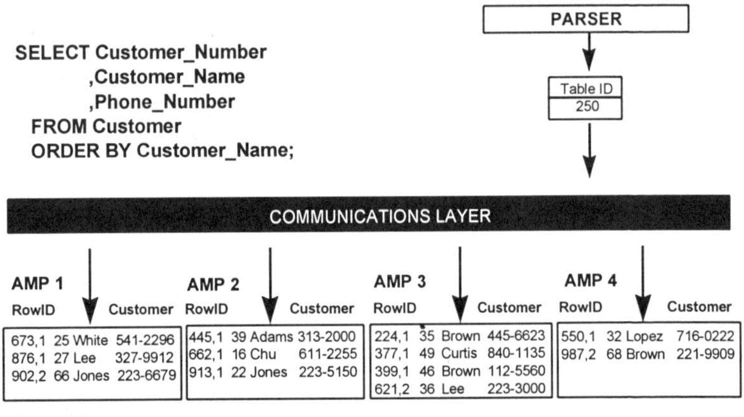

Figure 7-5

Each AMP consults its Master Index and identifies all the cylinders which have data blocks for Table ID 250. The Cylinder indexes identify all the relevant data blocks.

The reader will recall that Teradata:

> Never mixes rows from different tables in the same block and
>
> Rows never span blocks.

This permits each AMP to scan up to 32K bytes of the table for each block read. Thus, in the total *elapsed time required for a single read I/O*, all of the AMPs working in parallel can scan up to (32K * the number of AMPs) bytes of data.

Summary

Primary Index transactions require the services of one AMP *(Fig. 7-6)*

USI transactions require 2 AMPs.

NUSI and full table scans are always ALL AMP operations

ACCESS METHOD	NUMBER OF AMPS USED	NUMBER OF RESULT ROWS
UPI	1	0 - 1
NUPI	1	0 - MANY
USI	2	0 - 1
NUSI	ALL	0 - MANY
FULL TABLE SCAN	ALL	0 - ALL

Figure 7-6

Secondary Indexes are used to improve performance of the Teradata Database in locating rows by less frequently used access paths *(Fig. 7-7).*

Primary and Secondary indexes can be up to 16 columns wide.

Indexes are automatically maintained by Teradata although secondary indexes require additional space for their subtables.

INDEX	PRIMARY	SECONDARY
Affects Performance	YES	YES
Number of Columns	1 - 16	1 - 16
Multiple Data Ttypes	YES	YES
Unique	UPI	USI
Non-unique	NUPI	NUSI
Required	YES	NO
Number per Table	1	0-32
Affects Distribution	YES	NO
Unique vs Non-Unique	Function Similarly	Function Differently
Subtable Required	NO	YES
Extra Processing Overhead	NO	YES

Figure 7-7

While the difference in performance between a unique primary index and a nearly-unique primary index is negligible, the performance of unique and non-unique secondary indexes differs greatly. As the demographics of a table change over time - as additional rows are inserted, as others are deleted, and as the column values change, so will the Optimizer's dynamic execution plan. It therefore becomes the responsibility of the User to re-evaluate the choice of secondary indexes from time to time to ensure that they are still useful to the application, and have not become, in effect, expensive and unnecessary excess baggage.

8 Sending the SQL To Teradata

Teradata provides a wide variety of ways to send the SQL from a host system to the Teradata Database. Host systems might include:

Main-frame computers.

UNIX-based systems.

Network-attached work stations

Personal computers.

As will be discussed in Chapter 10, the mission-critical applications confidently assigned to Teradata by many of the largest data-processing organizations in the world, tend to be both innovative in concept and wide in scope. As a result, a well-stocked toolbox of application tools is required, with each tool designed to address some compelling need or other.

In this chapter we will review a number of these Teradata host-based tools, which divide into two major groups *(Fig. 8-1)*.

Programming Interfaces:

The Call Level Interface.
The C, COBOL and PL/I Preprocessors
The Teradata ODBC Driver

Application Utilities:

BTEQ.
BulkLoad.
FastLoad.
MultiLoad.
FastExport.

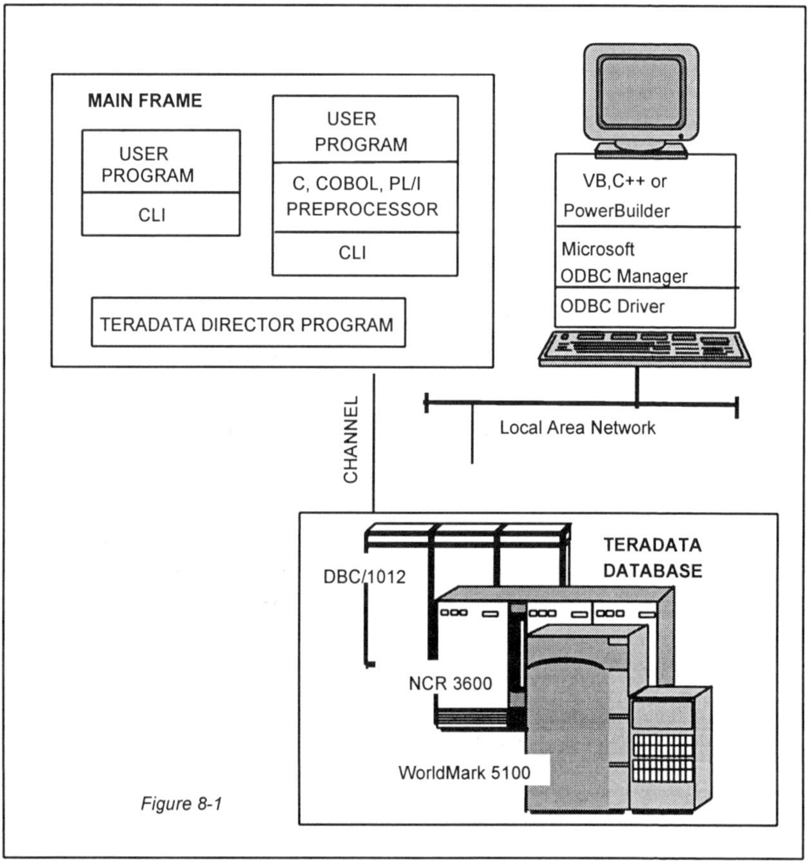

Figure 8-1

Programming Interfaces

Call Level Interface (CLI)

CLI, was introduced in Chapter 4. It is a series of 9 medium-level callable sub-routines, which reside in each User's address space, and is the low-level interface to the Teradata Database. Its primary function is to keep track of the User's SQL requests, and make sure the response is delivered back to the user in coherent fashion. Since these requests may involve multiple SQL statements sent to Teradata in parallel, CLI is an innovative and sophisticated device.

CLI programs are written in a compilable 2nd or 3rd Generation Language (2GL or 3GL). Applications which access the CLI directly can be extremely flexible in scope, and speedy in execution, but require a high-level of programming skill, and tend to be difficult to maintain.

The Teradata Pre-Processor

Teradata pre-processors provide users with the ability to imbed SQL within a C, COBOL or PL/I program. In this way they can combine the power of SQL with the flexibility of a 3GL procedural language. In addition, the pre-processors provide a number of additional high-level benefits including:

> Multiple Cursors (multiple simultaneous threads)
>
> 2-Phase Commit (synchronized interface with other database applications)
>
> *Compatibility* with other major database vendors.

Programs written using the pre-processor provide the ability to access data from multiple vendor database systems in a single program, but still rely heavily on the design, coding, debugging and maintenance skills of the user.

The Teradata ODBC Driver

As the main focus of modern data-processing moves more and more towards the Windows environments, as an ever growing number of users see Windows NT as a possible successor to UNIX, vendors have become increasingly aware of the need to provide sophisticated powerful and attractive Graphical User Interfaces (GUI).

No longer need we present management with lengthy reports, which provide volumes of data, from which it is difficult to derive meaningful information. With a GUI we can interface with other database applications in a transparent way, and produce attractive full-color charts and graphs that make the important points clear to everyone in the organization at a glance - and the price for this advantage is remarkably affordable.

In recognition of the computer industry trend away from the limitations of the main-frame, the Teradata Corporation had developed a remarkable innovative Widows-based Call Level Interface (WinCLI). WinCLI becomes the engine for such powerful developments as the Teradata Manager - a highly functional interface which permits Teradata administrators to monitor and control multiple Teradata machines from a single station. Despite the many benefits it has brought to the Teradata product however, WinCLI remains proprietary and may fall victim to future open standards.

For several years, a representation of major database vendors, known as the SQL Access Group (SAG), had been trying to reach agreement on Open Database Connectivity (ODBC) standards. As is typical of large groups, there was a great deal of discussion and very little real progress. Finally, becoming impatient, Microsoft took it upon itself to unilaterally develop ODBC standards tied to the Windows environment, and subsequently endeavor to secure the approval of the other vendors.

ODBC programs are required to make standardized calls to the Microsoft ODBC Manager, which are then passed to a vendor-developed interface (ODBC Driver) which translates, and perhaps optimizes the calls into the particular dialect of SQL supported by that specific vendor.

In this way the user is able to build windows-based, vendor-transparent, portable front-end database programs in such attractive media as Microsoft Visual Basic, Visual C++ and PowerBuilder *(Fig. 8-2):*

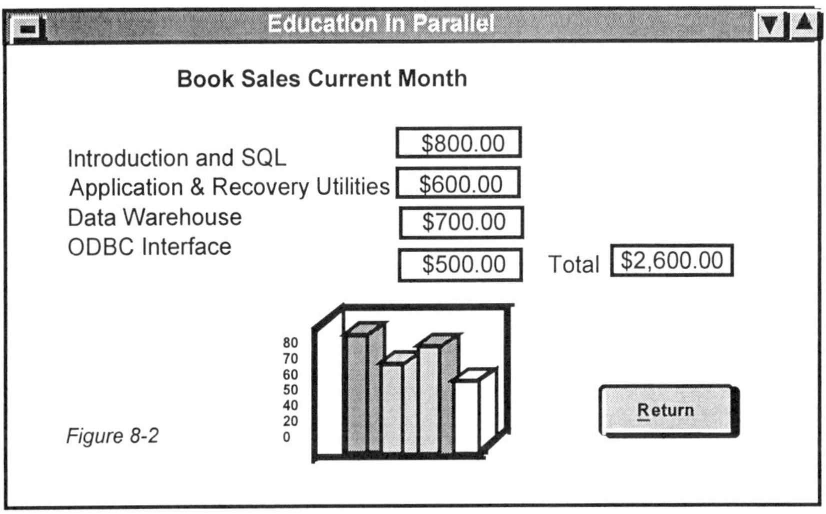

Figure 8-2

The Application Utilities

The Application Utilities are primarily provided for large-scale data loading and maintenance in the Teradata environment. Like the programming interfaces, they are host-resident *(Fig. 8-3)* and communicate with the Teradata Database through the CLI.

With the exception of BulkLoad, which is only available in an IBM channel connected environment, the application utilities are available from every host platform, network and main frame, supported by Teradata.

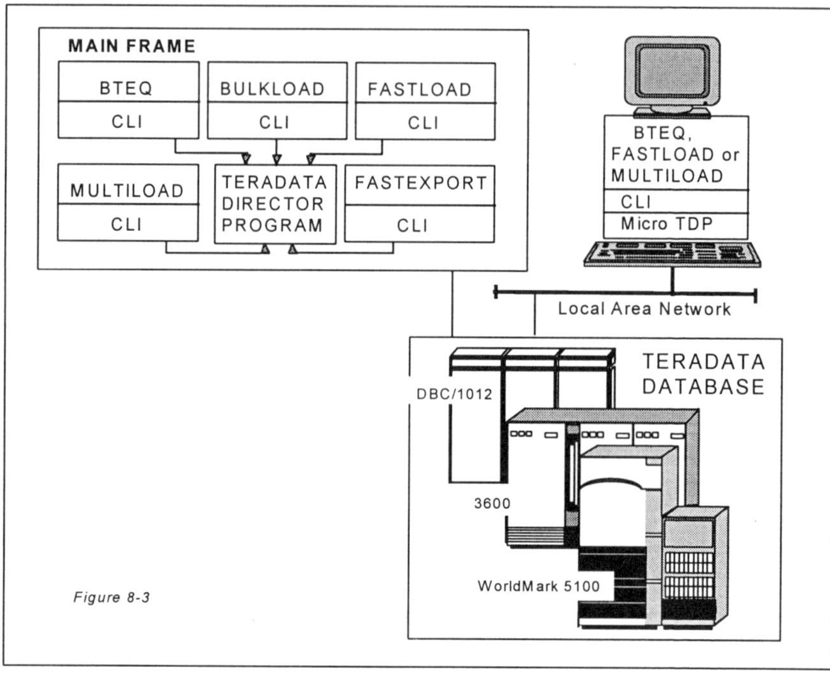

Figure 8-3

The application utilities accept input commands from a "script" and data from a host-based data set or file. The input commands are SQL-like in nature, and enable applications to be designed, prepared and tested in a fraction of the time required by other database access methods.

The application utilities were not designed as end-user tools. They are intended to be used by application designers, developers, data maintenance personnel and administrators.

As we examine these utilities in greater detail, we will become aware of inconsistencies in both syntax and function. These are minor in nature, but likely to trap the unwary. They occur as a result of one of the most prominent development maxims of the Teradata Corporation that "Our last customer is more important than our next".

Teradata believed, rightly or wrongly, that the needs of existing customers who had already invested in this technology had precedence over the needs of any possible future customers. As a result there was a perceived need to protect any existing customer applications against future development, which might at some time in the future, cause them to become obsolete and fail. Utility enhancements and improvements likely to have such a negative effect on existing applications were, for that reason, consigned to a new utility rather than interfere with the status quo. Each new utility was therefore developed in response to a recognized customer need for a feature which was seen as incompatible with the current product.

The first application utility to be developed was BTEQ.

Basic Teradata SQL (BTEQ)

BTEQ is the major work-horse of the Teradata Database. Although it is the ancestor of all later application utilities, it remains the most functional and widely used of all the utilities. It provides:

User interactive or file-based SQL access to Teradata.

A simple but functional report writer.

An EXPORT function for returning large amounts of data to the host as a report, or as flat-file data suitable for input to another application.

An IMPORT function for reading large amounts of input data from a host-based file and processing it as a series of inserts, updates or deletes.

Conditional processing based on a test of the Error code, number of rows returned, or user-defined error severity.

Performance statistics.

A comprehensive HELP facility.

BTEQ scripts are free-form, and contain BTEQ commands such as ".logon", ".logoff" or ".quit", (identified as beginning with a period ".") as well as regular SQL statements.

Fig. 8-4 is an example of a BTEQ multiple request transaction, which logs on to Teradata, reads input data described by the USING clause and processes:

An insert to the Acct table,
An update to the Custr table, and
An insert to the Acct_Custr table

for each input record. The incoming fields are identified in the "USING" clause and are substituted in the SQL for the similar field name preceded by a colon. Thus the incoming value for "AcctNo" is substituted at execution time for ":AcctNo" in each of the INSERT statements. It is important to note that the "USING" clause describes the input file layout, but the variables may be applied multiple times and in any order. Since the example shows a multiple statement request, a single "USING" clause may be used to fuel the entire transaction.

```
.SESSIONS 8;
.Logon username,password;
.Repeat * ;
 USING      AcctNo        (INTEGER)
          , Street        (CHAR(30))
          , City          (CHAR(20))
          , State         (CHAR(2))
          , CustNo        (INTEGER)
          , CName         (CHAR(20))

   INSERT  INTO       Acct
        (   Account_Number
          , Street
          , City
          , State_Code)
          VALUES (
          :AcctNo
          ,:Street
          ,:City
          ,:State )

;    UPDATE        Custr
       SET Last_Name = :CName
           WHERE Customer_Number
         =:CustNo;

;    INSERT  INTO       Acct_Custr
        (      Customer_Number
             , Account_Number )
        VALUES (
               :CustNo
             , :AcctNo )
;

.quit ;
```

BTEQ Commands

Describes Input File Layout

SQL Insert

SQL Update

SQL Insert

BTEQ Logoff/Quit

Figure 8-4

The user is guaranteed that even if the job itself is interrupted by a power failure, each three statement transaction will completely succeed or completely fail, but will never be permitted to partly succeed nor partly fail.

The ".REPEAT *;" command instructs BTEQ to continue reading records until end-of-file.

Multiple Sessions (See Fig. 8-4)

The Customer_Number column is the primary index of the Custr table. (This information does not appear in the script, but it is known to the developer). Inserts are always, by their nature, primary index requests, and so all three data manipulation language (DML) statements are primary index requests and single-AMP operations.

Each DML statement requires only one AMP, and if Teradata is running with four AMPs, the capacity exists for each AMP to be handling one DML request in parallel with all the others. In other words, the system could handle (best case) four DML requests in the total elapsed time required for one.

In order to permit each of the four AMPs to work on a different request simultaneously, it becomes necessary to supply Teradata with at least four requests at a time. The reader will recall that rows are distributed amongst the AMPs based on the row hash of the primary index value. The likelihood of any four consecutive items in an input file, happening by chance, to hash one to each of the four AMPs is perhaps only slightly better than the possibility of winning the Lottery.

One way to improve the chance of winning the Lottery is to buy more tickets. If instead of sending Teradata four pieces of data, and hoping that each of the four will happen to hash to one and only one AMP, if we sent twice as many, we more than double the chances that of the eight possibilities, each AMP will find one of them on which it can work.

Since the data is being supplied by an input file, we can control how the file is read and the data sent to Teradata. In this example the ".SESSIONS 8" statement instructs BTEQ to logon to Teradata eight distinct times. Each logon is seen by the Teradata Database as a single and distinct user, and the Call Level Interface assumes the responsibility of managing the response.

The maximum throughput is achieved when, on average, each AMP is fully employed all of the time. Thus the maximum number of transactions which can run in parallel is determined by the type of query and the total number of AMPs in the system.

Type of query	Number of AMPs
Primary Index	1
Unique Secondary Index	2
Non-Unique Secondary Index	ALL
Full Table Scan	ALL

Although BTEQ takes advantage of multiple sessions to improve performance, and guarantees full transaction integrity, it does not provide a restart log in the event of system failure. BulkLoad was therefore developed primarily to provide a reliable restart functionality for long-running IMPORT or "batch" type programs.

BulkLoad

BulkLoad is only available from a channel-connected IBM host and is optimized to process large numbers of DML statements on the Teradata Database, based on input from a data set or file. It also provides restart logic in the event of host failure. While relatively narrow in purpose, BulkLoad does not need all the rich functionality of BTEQ.

Nevertheless its features include:

Multiple sessions.

Progress checkpoints to a host-based restart log.

Automated restart capability under most conditions.

Error reporting and maintenance of error files.

User-specified error information.

Support of INMODs (User-written input modification routines for pre-processing data before it is passed to the utility).

Operational statistics and time stamps.

BulkLoad supports each of the four DML statements:

SELECT
INSERT
UPDATE
DELETE

but does not support multiple-statement transactions.

Fig. 8-5 illustrates a BulkLoad INSERT operation:

The User Logs on to the database, reads input data described by the "DEFINE" clause from "Datafile", and sends INSERT SQL to the Teradata Database. As the job progresses, BulkLoad will write checkpoints to a log file defined in the JCL and maintained on the IBM host, which will be used for re-positioning in the event of restart.

While BulkLoad offers significant advantages over BTEQ for batch-type operations, it exhibits similar performance characteristics. Both BTEQ and BulkLoad make at least one write to disk for each DML statement processed. It is this one disk write per DML which becomes the limiting factor of overall performance and throughput.

```
LOGON  Username,Password;                    BulkLoad LOGON
DEFINE
        AcctNo            ( INTEGER )
        ,Strt             ( CHAR(25) )       Input Data Layout
        ,Cty              ( CHAR(20) )
        ,Stat             ( CHAR (2) )
DDNAME = DataFile ;

INSERT   INTO Acct (
        Account_Number                       SQL INSERT
        , Street
        , City
        , State_Code )
        VALUES (
        , :ActNo
        ,:Strt
        ,:City
        ,:Stat )
        ;
                                             BulkLoad LOGOFF
  LOGOFF ;
```

Figure 8-5

As Teradata evolved, however, it became apparent that its particular market niche was to be found in complex queries against tables with billions of rows. As impressive as Teradata's performance might be handling complex queries against very large tables, it would amount to little unless the means for initially building those very large tables within a reasonable time-frame were readily available in the first place.

FastLoad

FastLoad was developed with only one thing in mind - *speed!* It was reasoned that if the throughput of the system was largely limited by the time it took to write to the disk, fewer writes would result in greater throughput. Fewer writes could be achieved if, instead of writing data to disk a *row* at a time, data were written a *block* at a time.

Again we should remember that Teradata stores rows in blocks of up to 32K bytes in length. Each block contains complete rows from a single table, and the rows are sorted within and between the blocks ascending by row hash value. With an initially empty table, therefore a complete file of INSERT transactions could be hashed, sorted and blocked in AMP memory before being written to disk.

The objectives of FastLoad were well-defined. Teradata needed:

> A “Batch” mode utility for loading new tables to the Teradata database.
> Availability from all host platforms.
> Full checkpoint / restart capability throughout.
> Error limits, error capture and error reporting.
> Performance Statistics.
> Support of Input Modification Routines (INMODs).
> *Faster than any other utility.*

Fig. 8-6 represents a simple FastLoad script. The table being loaded (target table) must exist, but be completely unpopulated at the start of the FastLoad. The best way to ensure that both these conditions are met is to first drop the table (which also deletes any rows which may be present), and then recreate it. (“DROP TABLE” will fail if the table is not present, but the FastLoad will be permitted to continue).

FastLoad data errors are captured in Teradata tables which are created by FastLoad and automatically dropped at the end of the FastLoad, if they are empty. As a fail-safe device against the premature discard of populated error tables, which might still exist from a previous load, FastLoad will terminate if it detects that the error tables already exist.

```
LOGON UserName, Password;
DROP TABLE ACCT;
DROP TABLE ACCT_ERROR1 ;
DROP TABLE ACCT_ERROR2 ;
CT   ACCT (
        Account_Number    INTEGER
      , Street            CHAR(25)
      , City              CHAR(20)
      , State             CHAR(2))
  UNIQUE PRIMARY INDEX (Account_Number) ;
  BEGIN LOADING ACCT
  ERRORFILES Acct_Error1, Acct_Error2
        CHECKPOINT 1000000 ;
DEFINE
        AcctNum       (INTEGER)
      , Strt          (CHAR(25))
      , Cty           (CHAR(20))
      , St            (CHAR(2))
    FILE = DataIn ;

INSERT INTO Acct VALUES (
        :AcctNum
      , :Strt
      , :Cty
      , :St ) ;

END LOADING;
LOGOFF ;
```

Drop and Recreate the table to ensure it is empty.

Identify targetTable end error tables

Describe input data layout

INSERT with substitutable variables

Build data blocks in memory and write to disk

Figure 8-6

This provides the user with the opportunity to monitor the situation before important information is irretrievably lost.

The "Checkpoint 1000000" statement causes a restart checkpoint record to be written to the restart log file (for an IBM host) or restart log table (for any other platform) for each million-or-so records processed. The actual value is recalculated by FastLoad to avoid splitting a channel block. Although minor changes to the script might be required, a FastLoad operation is fully restartable under all conditions.

Finally, the "END LOADING" statement notifies Teradata that all data has been processed on the host and permits it to begin building the sorted blocks and block-writing the data to disk.

The performance of FastLoad depends heavily on the length of the rows being loaded, but if we assume the rows to be between 50 and 100 bytes in length, FastLoad generally exceeds the performance of SQL insert operations by a factor of 20 or more.

FastLoad provides the means of loading large tables on the Teradata Database at high speed, has full restart capability, but is limited in function to a single INSERT operation against an initially-empty table.

BTEQ is extremely functional, but runs at SQL-type speeds and offers little opportunity for automatic restart in the event of a host failure.

It was probably not surprising therefore, that the next application utility development was an attempt to marry the speed and restartability of FastLoad to the functionality of BTEQ. The result was MultiLoad.

MultiLoad

The development of MultiLoad proved to be the largest single software development project to that time, in Teradata's history, but the result was spectacular.

MultiLoad and all future utilities would not be called directly by the user, but by way of a standard front end known as the "Support Environment", which would give each future utility the same look and feel. At the same time, the *Support Environment* would provide a number of sophisticated new features including:

Completely automatic restart from any failure *with no human intervention.*

Full SQL support (except for the SELECT).

Preliminary syntax checking prior to execution.

Conditional processing of commands with full .IF, .ELSE, .ENDIF capability.

Support of user-defined and system variables.

The Design Specification for MultiLoad required that it should use FastLoad-like logic to perform between 5 and 10 times faster than BulkLoad, and at the same time offer a wide range of new features:

Support of up to 20 Inserts, Updates or Deletes against a maximum of 5 *populated* target tables in a single operation with full transaction integrity.

Conditional processing of statements or groups of statements.

Support of multiple layouts in the input file with (COBOL-like) redefinition capability.

Although the syntax of MultiLoad is quite different in form to that of its predecessors, it is similar in function. To illustrate this point, let us re-introduce the tables from Chapters 6 and 7 *(Fig 8-7),* and consider an application:

Customers place orders (INSERT in Order table).

Orders are for parts (INSERT in Order Part).

If the part is available in inventory, it is immediately shipped to the customer. This is determined by whether or not the field "Shipped" in the input record has the value "Y". (Conditional UPDATE to Part, INSERT to ORDER PART SHIPPED HISTORY based on the value of "Shipped").

CUSTOMER

CUSTOMER NUMBER	CUSTOMER NAME	PHONE NUMBER
PK		
USI	NUSI	NUPI
25	WILLIAMS	541-2296
27	LEE	327-9912
32	LOPEZ	445-6623
35	BROWN	445-6977

PART

PART NUMBER	PART DESCRIPTION	ON HAND QUANTITY
PK		
UPI		
1032	REDWOOD STUDS	750
1027	6 IN. WOOD SCREWS	1440
2021	4 X 8 PLYWOOD	0
2029	1 X 12 X 96 PINE	200

ORDER

ORDER NUMBER	CUSTOMER NUMBER	ORDER DATE
PK	FK	
UPI		
1011	32	10/12/96
1012	27	10/13/96
1013	32	10/15/96
1014	32	10/16/96
1015	25	10/16/96
1016	32	10/17/96
1019	35	10/17/96
1020	32	10/17/96

ORDER PART

ORDER NUMBER	PART NUMBER	ORDER QUANTITY
PK		
FK	FK	
NUPI		
USI		
1011	1032	50
1011	1027	288
1012	1032	40
1012	2021	400
1012	1027	144
1013	2021	350
1014	2021	200
1014	1027	144

ORDER PART SHIPPED HISTORY

ORDER NUMBER	PART NUMBER	SHIPPED DATE	SHIPPED QUANTITY
PK			
FK			
NUPI			
USI			
1011	1032	10/12/96	50
1011	1027	10/12/96	288
1012	1032	10/13/96	40
1012	1027	10/13/96	144
1014	1027	10/17/96	144

Figure 8-7

This entire operation can be performed by MultiLoad in a single seamless operation. Once the script has been tested and determined to be syntactically and functionally correct, MultiLoad provides the additional benefit that recovery *from any failure for any reason* is accomplished by simply resubmitting the job. *MultiLoad takes care of the rest:*

```
.LOGTABLE  Restart_LogTable;
.LOGON  UserID, Password ;
.BEGIN IMPORT MLOAD
   TABLES    Order, Part,  Order_Part ,Order_Part_shipped_History;
.LAYOUT  Orders_Layout;
.FIELD     Cust        *  INTEGER ;
.FIELD     Ord         *  INTEGER ;
.FIELD     Part        *  INTEGER ;
.FIELD     Qty         *  INTEGER ;
.FIELD     Ord_Date    *  DATE;
.FILLER    Shipped     *  CHAR(1);
.DML       LABEL Label1;
INSERT     INTO     Order         VALUES    (:Ord, :Cust, :Ord_Date);
INSERT     INTO     Order_Part    VALUES    (:Ord, :Part, :Qty );
.DML       LABEL Label2;
INSERT     INTO     Order_Part_Shipped_History
                                  VALUES    (:Ord, :Part, :Qty, :Ord_Date);
UPDATE              Part           SET Qty = Qty - :Qty
                                   WHERE Part = :Part  ;

.IMPORT   INFILE   OrdersInput
                   LAYOUT Orders_Layout
                   APPLY Label1
                   APPLY Label2 WHERE (Shipped = 'Y') ;
.END MLOAD ;
.LOGOFF;
```

Identify Restart Log and Logon to Teradata

Identify Target tables

Describe input data

Group and Label SQL

APPLY statements in Label1 with no conditions.
APPLY statements in Label2 only if "Shipped" = "Y"

Figure 6-8

FastExport

FastExport has been described as a "reverse FastLoad", in that it uses multiple sessions to return data to the host in 32K blocks. It should be recognized however, that FastExport was not designed to make Teradata perform faster. The Teradata Database was already optimized to perform SELECT operations in a highly efficient manner. FastExport was designed primarily for larger systems connected to the host with multiple channels, to take full advantage of the additional bandwidth provided by those multiple channels. As such, while it is available from all supported platforms, the full benefits of FastExport are only realized by larger systems exporting millions of rows.

FastExport uses syntax similar to MultiLoad and enjoys all the advantages provided by the Support Environment, including the ability to be restarted after any failure condition, by simply resubmitting the job.

```
.LOGTABLE RestartLog                ;
.RUN      FILE Logon                ;
.BEGIN    EXPORT
          SESSIONS 12               ;

.LAYOUT   UsingLayout               ;
.FIELD    Cty      *  CHAR(20)      ;

.IMPORT   INFILE   DataIn
          LAYOUT   UsingLayout        ;
.EXPORT   OUTFILE  DataOut            ;
SELECT A.Account_Number
        , Last_Name
        , First_Name
        , Balance_Current
  FROM  Acct A
        , Custr C
        , Acct_Custr AC
 WHERE  A.Account_Number   = AC.Account_Number
   AND  C.Customer_Number =   AC.Customer_Number
   AND  City       = :Cty
   ORDER BY 1                       ;
.END      EXPORT                    ;
.LOGOFF                             ;
```

DEFINE RESTART LOG

LOGON FILE

NUMBER OF SESSIONS

DEFINE INPUT DATA FOR THE SELECT

OPTIONAL INPUT FILE AND LAYOUT

DESTINATION FILE

SEND REQUEST TO TERADATA

Figure 8-9

In *Fig. 8-9*, the data is returned to the host using multiple sessions and 32K data blocks. The response rows are sorted both in and between blocks which requires the data to be sorted twice. The Communications Layer was designed to perform a single merge of the data from multiple AMPs into a single sorted stream, and was not intended to perform additional sorts. As a result, much of the sort activity must be assigned to the AMPs, which results in substantial additional overhead. The performance of FastExport returning sorted data therefore is significantly less efficient than its performance with unsorted data.

Fig. 8-10, documents the results of a series of tests which compared the total elapsed time required by BTEQ and FastExport to successfully deliver between 1 and 20 million sorted and unsorted rows from the Teradata Database to an IBM main frame host.

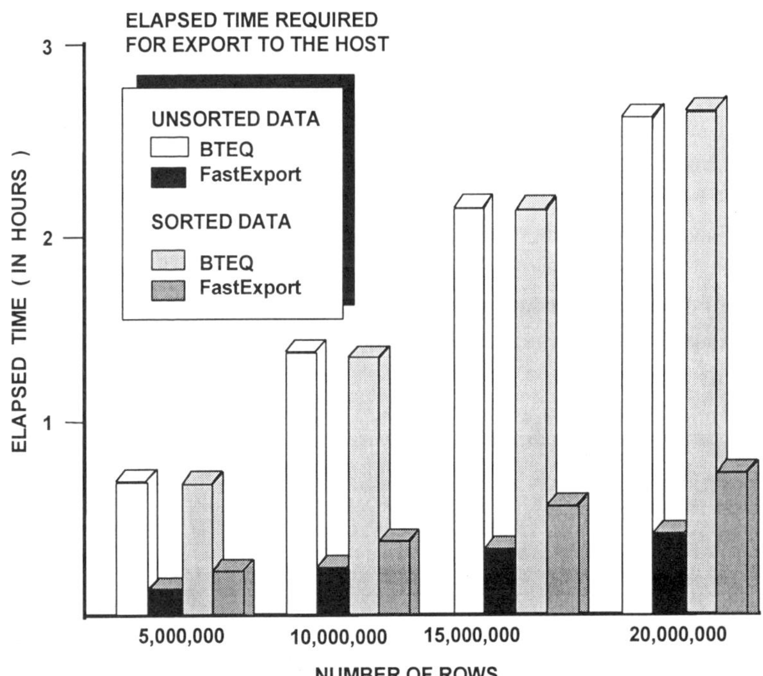

Figure 8-10

These tests used a Teradata Database Computer configured with 18 IFPs, 104 AMPs and used 36 parallel sessions to take full advantage of the additional bandwidth provided by 3 block multiplexor channels. Rows were 100 bytes in length.

While *Fig. 8-10* clearly evidences the additional cost of sorted output to FastExport, it also dramatically demonstrates how FastExport outperforms BTEQ, even for relatively small volumes of data, and how its advantage tends to increase as the volume of data grows.

Continuing Utility Development

Teradata had initially believed that the speed and functionality provided by MultiLoad would render the need for BulkLoad obsolete. However this subsequently turned out not to be the case.

MultiLoad owes much of its performance to its ability to process multiple DML transactions to the target table with a single read and a single write of the target table data block, thereby effectively eliminating large numbers of expensive disk-write operations.

BulkLoad, on the other hand, is restricted to writing data to disk a *row* at a time. Thus, the performance of MultiLoad largely depends on the *density* of DML transactions per target table data block. As the number of transactions per block approaches unity, BulkLoad often out-performs MultiLoad.

As a result, while BulkLoad continues to be the utility of choice where a relatively small number of INSERTS, UPDATES and DELETES need to be applied to very large tables, it is only available to users with a channel-connected IBM host.

In addressing this need, Teradata is currently developing a new utility, known by the rather unappetizing development name of "TPump", which is designed to be faster and more functional than BulkLoad, which will support multiple statement requests using a dynamically tunable number of sessions, and will be available for all supported host platforms.

Conclusions

We have examined just a few of the many application tools available to Teradata users. Add to these a rich selection of other vendor-developed interfaces and the tool box is comprehensive indeed. As a result Teradata users seldom find a need to re-train their end-users, already comfortable with some established front-end product. These end-users will simply become aware that the computer seems more reliable than it used to be, and much, much faster.

9 Data Protection and Recovery

"We agreed to ship goods to a customer on an emergency basis, but the transaction failed, and we don't know who ordered them. In any event somebody else was updating the Inventory at the same time as I was, and we don't have the items in stock. Not only that, but while we were deciding what to do about it, the system had a disk failure, and now we cannot be sure of the status of any of our orders. About the only thing worse that could happen would be for lightning to strike the data center and fry the entire computer system to a crisp!"

Clearly, this is going to be a bad day for two people in particular- the DBA (Database Administrator), responsible for application failures, and the System Administrator charged with the over-all availability of the system.

In the Teradata environment all these problems and many others, are preventable by a combination of good coding practice and the protection built into the system against all reasonable hardware and software failures.

1. Protection from Unauthorized Users

The Teradata Database qualifies *in all known respects* for the US Government's "C-2" security rating - the highest in the industry for all existing relational databases. Any user who wishes to access the Teradata system must successfully negotiate a number of security barriers, both on the host and on the Teradata Database.

Teradata Logon

Having successfully negotiated the various security implementations on the host, a potential user must supply a valid User ID and password for entry to the Teradata Database.

The System Administrator may require Teradata users to change their passwords on a regular basis. The password, together with the date and time of last change is maintained in the Data Dictionary/Directory as a one-way encrypted value. Adding the date and time renders it difficult for a potential hacker to create an encrypted dictionary and attempt to match across.

Once the Teradata RDMS (Relational Database Management Software) has validated the User ID and password, it then has the opportunity to review the source, date and time of attempted entry and any other conditions imposed by the System or Security Administrator. Unauthorized entry to the Teradata Database itself therefore becomes difficult.

Access Rights

Availability of the data in the Teradata Database is strictly controlled by Access Rights stored in the Data Dictionary. Teradata security and access rights are scrupulously checked for each separate attempt to access the Teradata Database. If the user has the rights necessary to perform a specific function, the operation is permitted to proceed, otherwise permission is denied. Access rights are generally tightly controlled by the Security Administrator and may be extremely wide or narrow in scope. On the one hand, the system administrator will require a sweeping range of privileges to oversee all activity on the system. A department junior, on the other hand, may merely need to generate or update an employee telephone list from time to time. Depending on the degree of security required by the organization, access rights can ensure that no data can be viewed or changed by anyone without prior approval.

Locks and Priorities

The Teradata Database may have thousands of users trying to access the same tables at the same time. Clearly it would be unwise to allow one user to read the same information that someone else is trying to update, since erroneous information might easily result. Each user of the system needs to be insulated from all other users by a system of locks which effectively protect against the simultaneous, and possibly contradictory, activities of all the others. At the same time, some applications may be more mission-critical than others and therefore require a higher level of priority. The Teradata Database provides a comprehensive system of lock management and user priorities to address these important issues.

The examples below illustrate that the database management software will immediately grant any lock request, subject to the system of priorities detailed below, provided the lock is fully compatible, or does not conflict with pre-existing locks. Any lock request which is not immediately compatible must wait in a queue until the non-compatible lock is released. There are 4 levels of locks (Fig 9-1). In ascending order of magnitude they are:

ACCESS — Read the data even if another user has a WRITE lock, and may be updating the same data at the same time. Access may be granted more speedily, but may result in unreliable information. An ACCESS lock is never queued except for a pre-existing EXCLUSIVE lock.

READ — Read data unless someone else has a WRITE or EXCLUSIVE lock. Multiple users may *read* data at the same time.

WRITE — Write to disk. No other User read or write activity permitted, except for reads using an ACCESS lock.

EXCLUSIVE Used for changing the structure of a database, table view or macro. This lock prevents any other user access to the data and is obliged to wait in the queue behind any other pre-existing lock request.

LOCK REQUEST	LOCK TYPE HELD NONE	ACCESS	READ	WRITE	EXCLUSIVE
ACCESS	Granted	Granted	Granted	Granted	Queued
READ	Granted	Granted	Granted	Queued	Queued
WRITE	Granted	Granted	Queued	Queued	Queued
EXCLUSIVE	Granted	Queued	Queued	Queued	Queued

Fig 9-1

In Fig 9-2, a READ lock is held on the data, and a WRITE lock is waiting in the queue. The WRITE lock cannot be granted until the READ lock is removed. A new request for a READ lock is received. This READ lock cannot be granted until the WRITE lock has been satisfied. The new READ lock is therefore queued behind the WRITE lock.

On the other hand, had the new request been for an ACCESS lock rather than a READ lock, it would have been immediately granted.

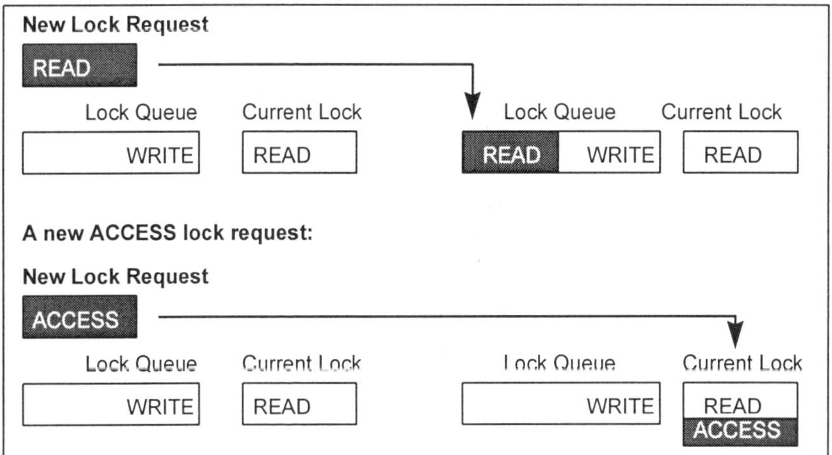

Fig 9-2

Automatic Locks

The Teradata Database attempts to lock objects at the least restrictive level necessary to preserve data integrity *(Fig. 9-3).* The level of lock depends on the type of SQL statement being processed. If the SQL supplies a Primary Index or Unique Secondary Index value, the data is locked at the row level (Row Hash). If the access is by other than a primary or unique secondary index, the entire table must be locked.

ROW HASH	The least restrictive lock. Locks all rows in a table which hash to one and only one specific value. Other rows, even in the same data block are available to other users.
TABLE	Locks all rows in the table.
DATABASE	Locks all tables in the database including secondary index subtables.

SQL STATEMENT	TYPE OF LOCK		
	ACCESS TYPE		
	PRIMARY OR USI	**NUSI OR FTS**	
SELECT	Row Hash	Table	READ
INSERT	Row Hash	N/A	WRITE
UPDATE	Row Hash	Table	WRITE
DELETE	Row Hash	Table	WRITE
CREATE, DROP OR ALTER TABLE	N/A	Table	EXCLUSIVE
CREATE, DROP OR MODIFY DATABASE	N/A	Database	EXCLUSIVE

Figure 9-3

While Users are permitted to upgrade locks to a higher level (READ to WRITE, WRITE to EXCLUSIVE or READ to EXCLUSIVE) by using the SQL "LOCKING FOR" command *(Fig. 9-4)*, downgrade of locks is only permitted from a READ lock to an ACCESS lock:

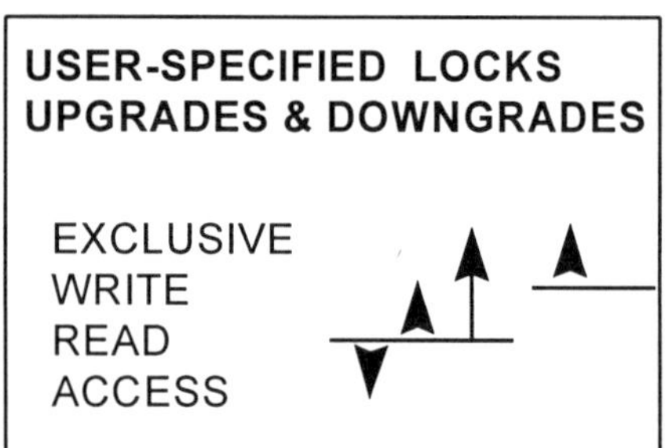

Fig 9-4

Teradata will not abort a transaction which attempts to write to the tables with an ACCESS lock, but it will recognize that such a transaction might have a negative effect on the integrity of the data, and apply for a WRITE lock.

Priorities

CPU service is provided for the user based on one of four assigned priorities:

LOW,
MEDIUM,
HIGH and
RUSH.

Each of which is provided with one fourth the service of the priority above.

In this way a user running at HIGH priority may expect to receive 16 times the number of CPU services allocated to a LOW priority user, or 4 times the number of CPU services allocated to a MEDIUM priority user. RUSH priority is usually reserved for the system administrator.

Each User of the Teradata system may be provided with up to 200 distinct account strings, one of which is required for each logon. The account strings are used to identify the assigned priority level for the session:

For Example:

```
.LOGON TDPId, UserName, Password, $L_AName;
```

Account strings can be given any name permitted by the normal naming convention. If the first two characters of the assigned name are a dollar sign ($) immediately followed by the letters “L”, “M”, “H” or “R”, this denotes the priority level. If not, the priority level defaults to MEDIUM.

Priority Level	Account String Prefix	Description
Low	$L	Lowest priority
Medium	$M	4 times the priority of LOW.
High	$H	16 times the priority of LOW or 4 times the priority of MEDIUM.
Rush	$R	4 times the priority of HIGH, 16 times the priority of MEDIUM, or 64 times the priority of LOW.

Additionally, each account string name may include a variable date or time suffix which is resolved at logon time, and provides the System Administrator with the ability to:

> Control the overall workflow by assigning user priorities based on job or time-of-day.
>
> Measure each individual's use of the system CPU and disk resources on a logon-by-logon or application-by-application basis.

Combined with the disk space accounting, provided by the Data Dictionary/Directory, System Administrators are provided with a number of highly accurate tools and criteria for measuring and controlling user use of the resources.

Transaction Boundaries

A transaction can be defined as "one or more SQL statements which take a database from one consistent state to another". The recognition of transaction boundaries therefore become extremely important, and generally result in a loss of database integrity whenever they are violated.

For example, suppose the bank is transferring $500 from your savings account to your checking account. This requires an update to savings and another update to checking. If both transactions succeed, the mission is accomplished. If both fail, no harm is done. On the other hand, if the $500 is successfully taken from the savings account, but for some reason, not applied to the checking account, you have lost $500, and the bank has made an instant profit at your expense.

Unless otherwise instructed, each single SQL statement is treated by Teradata as a single and separate transaction. Teradata recognizes multiple SQL statements as a transaction under the following circumstances:

Environment	Method
Pre-processors	SQL statements are enclosed between a "BEGIN TRANSACTION" (BT) and "END TRANSACTION" (ET) pair of statements.
BTEQ	Multiple statement requests. BTEQ continues to read SQL statements as a single transaction until it encounters a semi-colon followed by blanks to the end of the line of script. (Revisit the BTEQ .IMPORT example in Chapter 8).
Teradata Macros	All statements within a Teradata macro are guaranteed to succeed as a unit or fail as a unit. They will never partly succeed nor partly fail.

Deadlocks

Teradata never downgrades a lock during a transaction, but always maintains the "high-watermark" lock. Deadlocks usually occur when one user is prevented from completing a task because another user already holds a lock on the data. At the same time, the second user is also prevented from continuing because of a lock being held by the first user.

Although most deadlocks can be avoided by observance of strict programming standards, they can still trap the unwary.

For Example:

Users first select a row before updating it in a single transaction.

User 1 begins a transaction with a BT statement and selects a row from the table. User 1 gets a READ lock on the row.

User 2 also begins a transaction with a BT statement and selects the same row. Since multiple users are permitted to read a row at the same time, User 2 is also granted a READ lock on the row.

User 1 now attempts to update the row and requires the READ lock upgraded to a WRITE lock. User 1 is obliged to wait in the queue until User 2's READ lock has expired. Unaware of User 1's plight, User 2 similarly attempts to update the row and acquire an upgraded lock from READ to WRITE, but must wait behind User 1 in the queue. Neither User can move, and we have a classic case of a deadlock.

Deadlocks occurring within a single AMP are detected in seconds, and quickly resolved by the simple expedient of rolling back the youngest transaction and returning a message to the application. Deadlocks occurring between AMPs must be resolved by a background task running in the Parsing Engine which looks for deadlocks at user-defined intervals.

The deadlock example on the previous page could have been prevented in one of two ways:

> Each User could have selected the row using an ACCESS lock instead of a READ lock, although this might result in misleading data or
>
> The Select could have been treated as a single transaction, and the row updated using a "WHERE" clause.

2. Protection against Transaction Failure

The Transient Journal

The Transient Journal is system-maintained in the Data Dictionary /Directory and is used to protect transactions in flight against:

> Power outage.
> Host failure or abend.
> Teradata hardware or software failure.
> Deadlock.

For each single or multiple statement transaction, the Transient Journal captures a copy of the data row(s) before any change has occurred. In the event of transaction failure, the "before-change" copy of the row is super-imposed over any new value, and change is effectively nullified. Once the transaction successfully completes, the rows are automatically removed from the journal.

The Before-Change Image (BEFORE IMAGE) Journal

While the Transient Journal is automatically provided and maintained by the Teradata Database, the BEFORE IMAGE journal is optional and permanent, in that rows are only captured or discarded by specific User command. BEFORE IMAGE journals are user-created on a table-by-table basis and, in connection with the SQL CHECKPOINT statement, can be used to roll badly corrupted tables back to some earlier consistent point in time. This has the net effect of undoing all changes to the table made since the checkpointed time. Permanent journals are discussed in more detail under "Archive and Recovery".

3. Protection from Hardware Failure

Any hardware component is guaranteed to fail, sooner or later. Electronic components such as boards fail rarely, and seldom, if ever, permanently compromise data when they do. Mechanical components, such as disk drives, tend to fail more frequently, and may result in loss of data. The obvious way to protect data against loss is to maintain a second copy, and this option, known as "FALLBACK" is offered by the Teradata Database.

FALLBACK Protection.

Tables in the Teradata Database may be declared as "FALLBACK" or "NO FALLBACK" when the table is initially created, or may be changed at some later time with an "ALTER TABLE" SQL statement. If a table is not provided with FALLBACK protection, any disk failure is likely to result in some data loss, and will almost certainly involve a time-consuming recovery procedure of some kind. With FALLBACK protection however, the data remains available and processing can continue largely uninterrupted.

Fig 9-5 illustrates a system where each primary row (represented by numbered squares) is protected by a duplicate row on some other AMP/DISK. Imagine that the system has 100 AMPs.
If the Disk on AMP3 became unreadable, a copy of each row on that disk is maintained by another AMP in the *system.* (Row 12 is protected on AMP 5, and Row 2 on AMP 7). All the data is still available, but 99 AMPs are now doing the work of 100. Over-all performance of the

system is therefore expected to degrade by 1/99th - less than one percent, a negligible amount.

On the other hand, if in addition we were to lose AMP 7, we could no longer be certain that all rows were still protected. (Row 2 would have been lost). Thus we can say that while FALLBACK protects against a the loss of a single disk in the system, a failure of *more than one* results in missing data. Since the chances of any *two disks out of one hundred* failing at the same time is probably quite high, this is considered an unreasonable degree of risk.

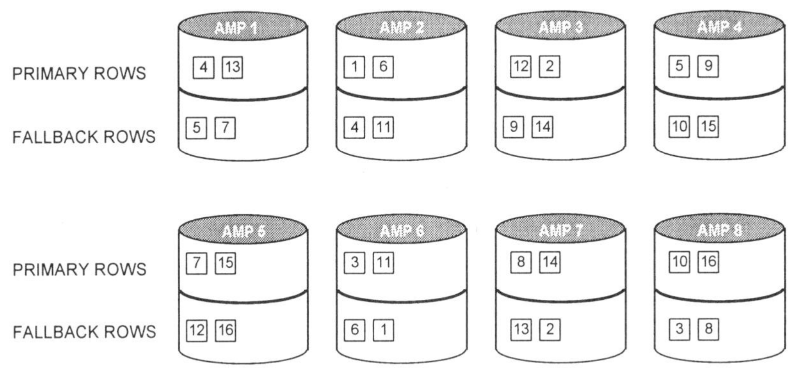

Figure 9-4

A better plan might be to organize the AMPs in groups or *clusters* with some small number of AMPs to a cluster, in such a way that the primary rows of each group would be protected on another AMP in the same cluster. This would permit a failure of one (*and no more than one*) AMP per cluster and still allow full access to data. On the other hand, any single failure would be expected to have a significantly greater impact on over-all performance of the system:

AMPs per Cluster	Total Tolerated Failures	Performance Degradation
5	20%	25%
4	25%	33%
3	33%	50%
2	50%	100%

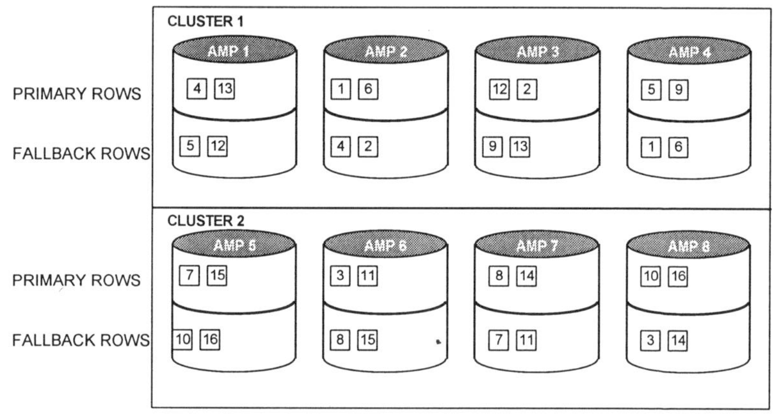

Figure 9-6

The determination of the optimum number of AMPs per cluster clearly involves a trade-off between level of protection needed and the maximum degree of performance degradation which can be tolerated in the event of failure.

Teradata users generally agreed that 4 AMPs per cluster *(Fig 9-6)*, and 33% degradation represented an acceptable compromise. Thus a 100 AMP system would now have 25 *clusters*, with primary data rows protected, not on another AMP in the *system*, but on another AMP in the *cluster*. *At this point, while we would still lose access to data if two disks failed in the same cluster, each cluster could have a single disk failure (a total of 25 for the system) at any one time and still allow full access to the data.*

While FALLBACK provides data protection at the hardware level, it does of course require double the disk space to accommodate twice the data, and additional CPU workload for write transactions. This was largely solved by the introduction of Disk Array technology in 1995.

Disk Arrays

Disk Arrays *(Fig. 9-7)* are supported in the NCR 3600 and NCR 3500 environments, but are standard for the WorldMark 5100.

There are five individual disks in an array, known as a "rank" and 4 ranks to an array unit:

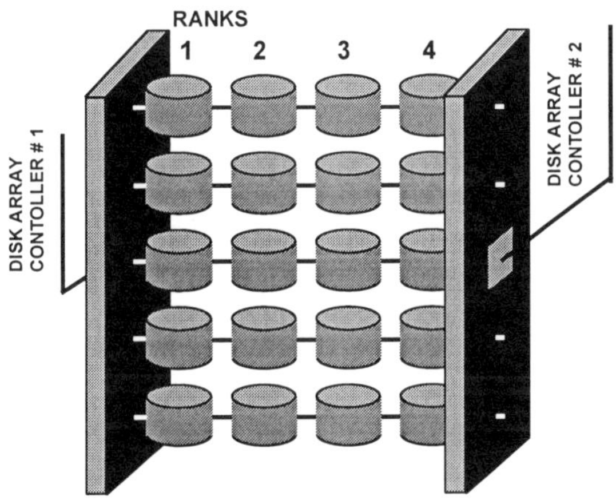

Figure 9-7

Each 4-rank array has 2 disk array controllers (DACs), one active and one passive. These disk array controllers are usually housed in different SMP (Symmetric Multi-Processor) units and, if possible, in different cabinets, to provide protection in the event of a single SMP failure. If the active disk array controller fails for any reason, the passive controller is promoted to active status and assumes double duty. While this double duty has, to some degree, a negative effect on performance, access to the array is not compromised.

There are two disk array data protection mechanisms supported by the Teradata Database:

RAID 1 (Redundant Array of Inexpensive Disks).

A mirror copy of the data from one physical disk is maintained on another. This requires twice the disk space, but ensures that little or no performance is sacrificed in the event of failure of either disk.

RAID 5

Data is spread amongst each of four of the disks in a 5 disk bank (analogous to 2 bits per byte). The fifth disk is used to maintain parity using a machine instruction known as an "XOR" (Exclusive OR) calculation:

Each of the four data bits are compared top to bottom:

If the numbers of 1s or 0s are even (0000 or 1111 or 1001 or 0011 etc.), the parity bit is 0.

If the bits are odd, (1110, 0001, 0111 etc.), the parity bit is 1.

For Example:

Disk 1	0101	0100	**T**
Disk 2	0100	0100	**D**
Disk 3	0100	0001	**A**
Disk 4	0101	0100	**T**
	EEEE	**EOEO**	(**E**=Even, **O**=Odd)
Disk 5	0000	0101	**Parity**

In the Teradata environment, data is distributed among the disks in a rank by data block rather than by byte, but the principle is the same. In the event of a single disk failure, the data on that disk can be deduced by calculating its parity.

This requires only 25% more space, and a minor reduction in performance in the event of a single disk failure, but ensures that data is always fully available.

Cliques

When the Teradata Database is running on a multiple-node system such as the WorldMark 5100, nodes are grouped into *cliques (Fig. 9-8)* - a collection of individual nodes with shared access to disk arrays using SCSI interfaces.

Notice that *each node has access to every disk array.* This shared access provides a powerful level of hardware protection and permits the system to continue operating even with the loss of:

> One disk in every rank,
> One controller in every array,
> One Bynet and three nodes.

The system not only continues to operate, but in addition, automatically reconfigures itself for transparency.

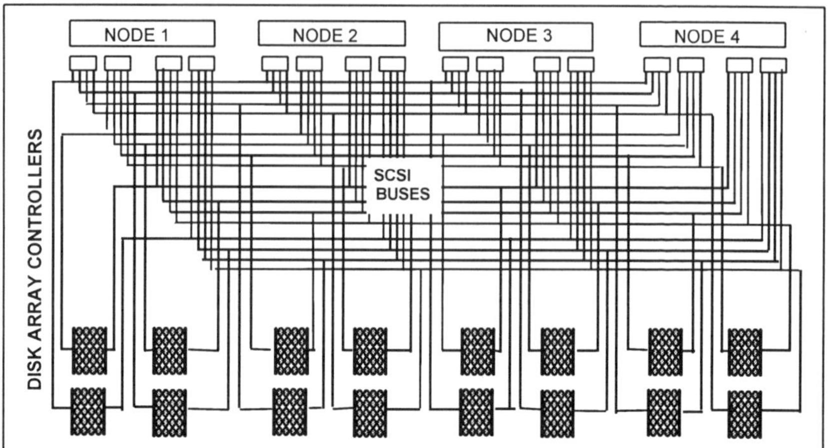

Figure 9-8

While disk arrays and cliques provide a high degree of data protection, a possibly slight yet important risk of double-disk failure in the same rank remains. At this point the parity disk can no longer be used to reconstruct the data. For this reason, many large users of the Teradata Database continue to define their mission-critical tables as FALLBACK.

Archive and Recovery of Data

No matter how much protection is intrinsically built into the hardware and software, we must always allow for the complete loss of a system due to some kind of major catastrophe. In this event we are faced with the prospect of rebuilding the data from a previously archived copy stored off-site. As the typical tables maintained by Teradata users expand from hundreds of millions to billions of rows, the challenge of initially capturing the archived data, in direct competition with the ever-increasing demands of the production environment, becomes more and more difficult with each passing day. Very large tables take a significant amount of time to load, and a substantial amount of time to archive to tape.

Notwithstanding the difficulties however, the challenge must be met, and even though the Teradata Database provides a fast Archive/Recovery utility supported on every host platform, it still becomes the most pressing duty of the System Administrator to devise and implement a recovery policy which subordinates the workload to the limited resources available.

The majority of tables in the database are most likely *minor entities* - small static tables which seldom change. These can generally be archived once, and refreshed only as the need occurs.

Tables used for decision support are often down-loaded to the Teradata Database from an original tape on the Host. Many users rely on being able to repeat this operation from the original source medium.

Tables which are subject to frequent insert, update or delete generally require archive protection. Since these tables may be very large, the Teradata Archive/Recovery Utility needs to offer a high degree of flexibility to archive:

> A complete Teradata system (with a single command),
>
> A database (including tables, views and macros) and its descendants,
>
> A table with or without indexes, in full, or partitioned over multiple archive sessions.
>
> Day-to-day changes to data using Permanent Journals.

and be able to efficiently restore this data to the same or another hardware platform.

Permanent Journals

Permanent Journals are an optional feature of the Teradata Archive/Recovery utility, and provide the User with the ability to capture *changes to data* (rather than the data itself) as:

> After Image journals, which protect against a hardware failure
>
> Before Image journals permitting a time-oriented rollback following an application failure.

For Example, a very large table involving many millions of rows, which is subject to a few hundred thousand updates each evening needs to be protected against hardware failure. The amount of time needed to archive the complete table to tape each evening exceeds the amount of time available to do it. The following strategy was therefore employed:

> Once a week, on a Sunday evening when the system is not busy, a copy of the complete table (millions of rows) is archived to tape (see *Fig. 9-9).*
>
> Each evening during the week, an After Change Journal is used to quickly capture the daily changes to the data.
>
> In this way the complete table is protected with one lengthy, (but off-peak) procedure once per week, supplemented by a short daily procedure, which effectively avoids the need for a lengthy daily procedure during peak processing hours.

ARCHIVE

SUNDAY

```
ARCHIVE DATA TABLE DB.Sales
            ,RELEASE LOCK
            ,INDEXES
FILE = ARCHIVE.DAT;
```

MONDAY

```
CHECKPOINT DB.Sales_Jnl
            ,WITH SAVE;
ARCHIVE JOURNAL  TABLE DB.Sales_Jnl
            ,RELEASE LOCK
            FILE = JNL1.DAT;
```

TUESDAY

```
CHECKPOINT DB.Sales_Jnl
            ,WITH SAVE;
ARCHIVE JOURNALS TABLES DB.Sales_Jnl
            ,RELEASE LOCK
            FILE = JNL2.DAT;
```

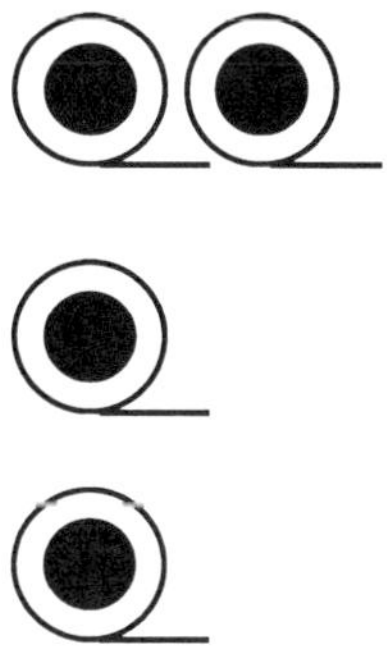

ETC.

Figure 9-9

On the week in question:

The full archive was taken as usual on Sunday.

On Monday evening we book-marked (checkpointed) the after-change journal was checkpointed and the changes committed to tape.

On Tuesday evening, the procedure was repeated for Tuesday's changes.

Prior to start of business on Wednesday, a user dropped the table in error resulting in a complete loss of data.

It therefore became necessary to recover the table from the archive copy, using the procedure described in *Fig. 9-10.*

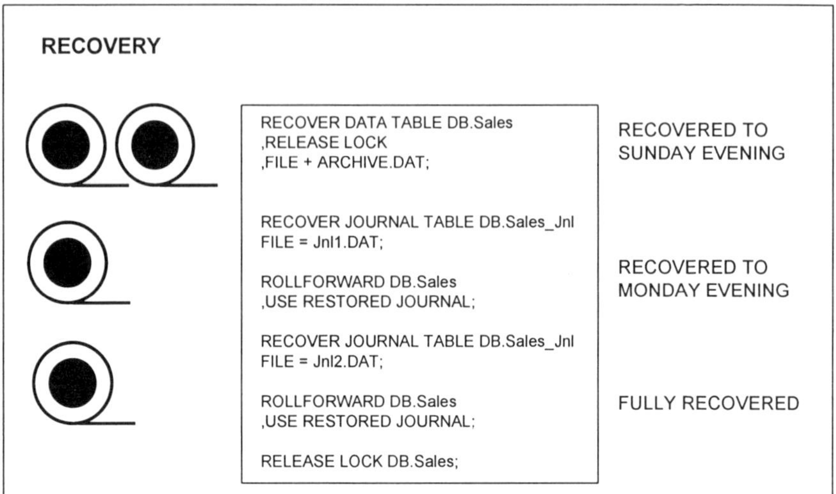

Figure 9-10

The recovery involved a script containing the following steps:

1. The complete table is recovered from the full data archive taken on the previous Sunday.

2. The journal rows captured on Monday evening are recovered, and the changes reapplied to the table (rollforward).

3. The journal rows captured on Tuesday evening are recovered, and the changes reapplied to the table (rollforward).

4. Since the table is fully recovered, it is unlocked and made available to other users.

Conclusions

Although the Teradata Database provides a high level of protection against most reasonable hardware and software failure scenarios, Murphy's Law, which states that, " Whatever can go wrong, will go wrong," continues to apply. The best time to fix a problem is before it occurs. Thus, the implementation and maintenance of carefully crafted recovery procedures becomes the most pressing and immediate responsibility of the System Administrator.

10 Who's Using Teradata?

Teradata supports the *biggest databases (Fig10-1)*, the *largest tables (Fig 10-2)*, and the *largest number of users* accessing the database at any one *time (Fig 10-3)* - this according to the survey conducted by the Winter Corporation at their US Very Large Database Conference in 1996.

The Biggest Databases:

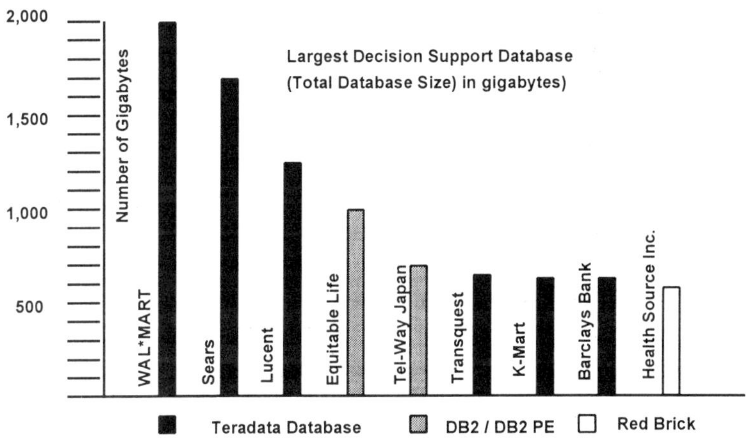

Figure 10-1

The Largest Tables:

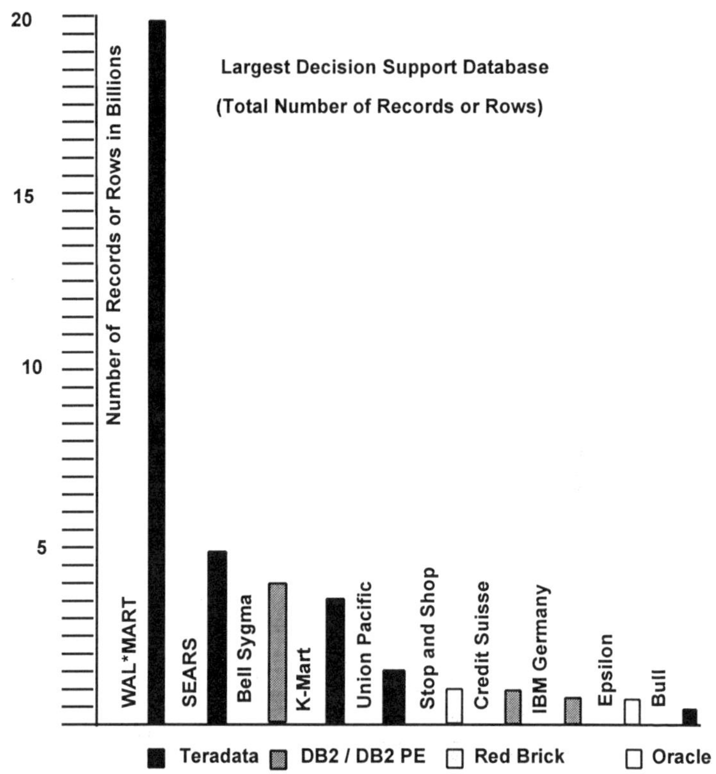

Figure 10-2

The Largest Number of Concurrent Users:

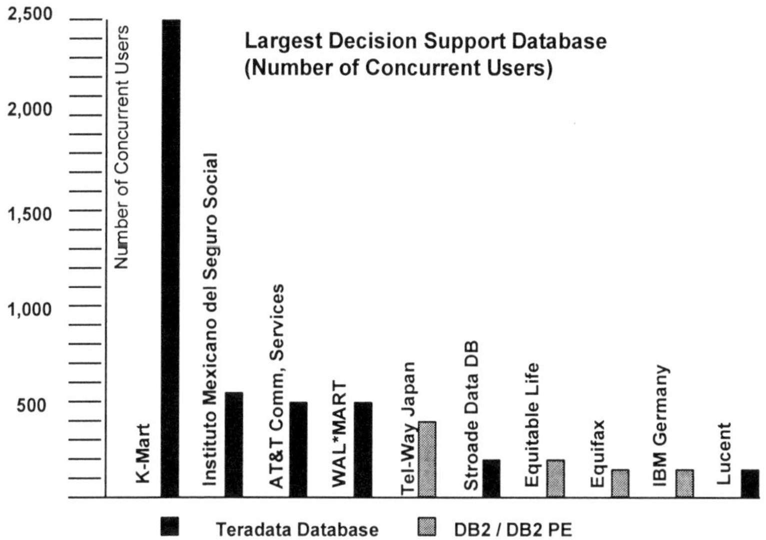

Figure 10-3

The Teradata Database Massively Parallel Processing (MPP) and Data Warehouse is delivering real and measurable benefits to industries around the world. Its true value lies not only in speeding up existing processes, queries and reports, but in providing fast and reliable answers to business questions never before possible.

The largest Teradata currently in operation is a 48 node Worldmark 5100M with a total of 384 Pentium pro 200MHz CPUs, 192 GB of memory and 8 TB of disk storage and supports more than 16,000 queries per day. Another system exactly double that is due to be installed in a customer site in June, 1997.

Although the Teradata Database permeates every segment of modern industry and society, its Users may perhaps be divided into nine main major groups:

1. Retail
2. Consumer Goods / Retail Supply
3. Cargo Transportation
4. Passenger Transportation
5. Telecommunications
6. Health Care Insurance
7. Banking and Financial
8. Public Sector
9. Other

1. Retail

Checkout scanner data from hundreds or thousands of stores world-wide has resulted in huge amounts of historical data available to assist in the key areas of:

Purchasing, pricing and inventory management
Store configuration
Sales promotions and coupon offers.

Clothing trends and other fads are carefully tracked, analyzed and managed to maximize profit and avoid carrying costs. Inventory is quickly moved between stores and regions based on local market demand to minimize loss on excess inventory and provide warehouse space for new items coming in.

Contrast the fortunes of *Wal*Mart and Sears*, the top retailers in the United States. Sears was the number one retailer for decades up to the late 1980's, when Wal*Mart began investing heavily in Teradata. From 1986 Sears revenues grew by only 4.3% annually, and its operating margins dropped from 4.9% to 1.2%. During this same period,

Wal*Mart averaged an incredible 28% growth and 4% margins. This might well be attributed to coincidence, except that after investing in Teradata in 1985, Sears has experienced what "The Economist" called, "the biggest comeback in history."

Other major retailers include Kmart, Meijer, Kohl's, American Stores (Jewel, Lucky, OSCO, Sav-On, ACME, SuperSaver), Mervyns, Buttrey Food and Drug, QVC, Canadian Tire, WH Smith Books (UK), Great Universal Stores (UK), Casino Supermarkets (France), Migrosgenossenschaftsbund (Switzerland), Otto Versand (Germany) and Pacific Dunlop (Australia).

2. Consumer Goods/Retail Supply

This industry functions as a wholesaler, and supplies massive quantities of goods to the Retail industry above. Since they do not get paid until the products are actually sold to the consumer, goods are shipped to the retailers "on consignment".

Teradata provides the Consumer Goods / Retail Supply Industry with the crucial intelligence needed to discover:

> How much product will sell at a particular price point.
>
> How much needs to be manufactured to ensure just-in-time delivery.
>
> Measure the effect of marketing campaigns, advertising blitzes and coupon promotions.

Major retailers and suppliers use Teradata to share information and thus enable retailers to take over inventory replenishment, the stocking of store shelves, and pass the savings to the consumer.

In the summer of 1993, engineers at *Whirlpool*, the global appliance manufacturer, detected a faulty hose clamp on hundreds of washing machines that had already been sold. Mechanics were quickly dispatched, thereby avoiding any costly property damage resulting from water leaks. This was possible because Whirlpool not only recognized the importance of customer service to their success, but *had the all the data they needed available* on Teradata.

Other major Teradata users in this category include Coca-Cola, Nike, Procter & Gamble, Hallmark, Maybelline, Helene Curtis, 3M, Owens Corning Glass, Karsten Ping, and Walt Disney Home Video.

3. The Cargo Transportation Industry

The Cargo Transportation industry uses Teradata to facilitate huge shipments of cargo between the major retailers and their suppliers in semi-trailer sized containers via truck, ship and train. Years of data regarding:

> Millions of shipments, capacities and delivery times,
> Costs, revenues, and profits,
> Equipment, way-bills and bills-of-lading

are kept by:

> Railroads,
> Airlines,
> Ocean shippers,
> Trucking companies.

Thus MPP enables:

> Just-in-time delivery of raw materials to factory sites,
> Just-on-time manufacturing,
> Just-in-time inventory replacement.

Conrail claims that Teradata has been instrumental in winning back business for the railroads, previously lost to the trucking industry. At the Teradata Users Conference in 1994, Jim Horgan, Conrail's Director of Customer Logistics, was quoted as saying, "Today we're answering questions that three years ago we couldn't even imagine asking". Teradata helps them to set up accurate long-distance train schedules, coordinate trade between various modes of transportation, and allows them to reroute trains quickly in case of bad weather and natural disasters, such as the Great Mississippi Flood in the summer of 1993.

On a typical day, Conrail must keep track of 100,000 individual rail cars, 1,237 trains and an enormous number of containers. It is keenly aware that one late shipment can bring a manufacturer's assembly lines to a screeching halt. Being on time is no longer a goal - it has become a requirement.

The demand for manufactured Goods is expected to continue to grow rapidly with the advent of the GATT/WTO global trade agreement, together with regional pacts such as NAFTA, the EU and the emerging markets of China and the former Soviet block.

Other major Teradata Users include Burlington Northern Santa Fe, Union Pacific, Norfolk Southern, American President Lines, and the cargo units of major airlines including Delta, QANTAS, British Airways, American Airlines, and Canadian Airlines.

4. The Passenger Transportation Industry

With years of customer and reservations data on hand, the Passenger Transportation Industry relies heavily on Teradata for:

Market Research and Frequent Flyer Promotion,
Capacity Planning,
Yield management, revenue and cost accounting,
Purchasing, inventory management and distribution,
Quality Programs and Customer Service.

American Airlines was the first carrier to introduce a frequent-flyer program. This grew to 1 million members in 1981, 3 million by 1986 and 26 million by 1994. Its "Aadvantage" data originates in SABRE, American's legendary real-time reservations system, which runs on twelve of IBM's biggest mainframes running "in parallel" in Tulsa, Oklahoma. This system processes 1.5 million transactions and adds 8,000 new members each day. Once per week approximately 35 gigabytes of data is down-loaded to Teradata and is used, amongst other things, to select high-profile candidates for mass-mailing. Over the years, American has originated more than 150 million direct mail pieces and, (a marketeer's dream), customers complain if their mailing fails to arrive. Not only that, but American claims it has saved more than $100 million by cutting back on expensive mass-media campaigns.

Other Users in this category include Delta, Lufthansa, QANTAS, British Airways, Canadian Airlines, and the SNCF French National Railway.

5. The Telecommunications Industry

The telecommunications industry uses Teradata to compete in an ever-increasingly competitive and deregulated global market that is undergoing sweeping technological changes with the introduction of cellular phones, fiber optics and the internet. Huge volumes of data involving:

Millions of customers,
Circuits and network configurations,
Monthly bills and call volumes,
Services used and equipment sold,
Revenues, profits and costs.

are required for:

Target Marketing
Revenue Accounting,
Government Reporting and Compliance,

Purchasing and Inventory,
Network Management.

AT&T has been the world's largest user of Teradata for the last 10 years, and relies so heavily on Teradata that it purchased the company in 1992. As one of the oldest Teradata customers, AT&T has helped Teradata evolve through 5 distinct generations of parallel-processing hardware, numerous releases of software, and provided more than 65% of the Teradata Corporation revenues during the recession of the early 1990's. AT&T's 29 distinct Teradata systems consist of many thousands of Intel processors and more than three times as many disk drives.

By being able to react quickly in a complex and rapidly changing global industry, AT&T posted 1994 profits of $4.7 billion on $75 billion in sales, and thus regained everything it had lost by deregulation and break up.

AT&T's Teradata applications include:

Sales and Marketing
Purchasing and Inventory
Leasing and Leased Lines
Accounting, Finance and Capital Management
Manufacturing and Distribution
Voice and Data Network Configurations
Customer Databases
Universal Card Services

Other Telecommunications Users include Ameritech, NCR, Belgacom (Belgium), Bell Atlantic, Bell South, British Telecom, GTE, Motorola, New Zealand Telecom, Sprint, Telecom Italia, Telestra Australia, Telecom Ireland, Televerket (Sweden), Unitel (Canada) and U S West.

6. The Health Care Insurance Industry

This industry uses Teradata to implement "managed care" and "capitulation" programs. Many years of data regarding the "seven P's" of healthcare, Patients, Providers, Procedures, Prices, Performance, Plans and Premiums are used to create profiles of diseases. These profiles are then used to guage whether various treatment patterns fall within certain norms.

"Capitulation" plans involve covering an entire company for a set price regardless of how much care is provided, and creates a strong incentive to provide the best service for the lowest price.

Health Care Services Corporation relied on a number of massive claims databases resident on an IBM main frame, which was difficult to update. Obtaining answers to questions often took two to four days, and answers sometimes differed substantially depending on how the question was phrased and which specific data base was accessed. This was inclined to infuriate their corporate customers who need accurate and timely information in order to control costs.

With Teradata, HCSC now gets accurate information in about 3 minutes, and is able to routinely provide its corporate customers with the accurate reports they need on a timely basis. For example, HCSC is able to report on:

> How often Doctors recommend hospitalization vs. out-patient care.
>
> The length and frequency of office visits for various ailments.
>
> How often a Doctor refers a patient to a specialist.
>
> Which Doctors perform unnecessary surgeries.
>
> The frequency and volume of diagnostic tests.

A case in point, the cost of treatment for breast cancer can be held down if mammograms are offered to women over 50 on a regular basis. HCSC can identify which of its corporate clients are not doing this, and ask why it is not being done. *The insurer is not afraid to pay for quality - provided that the doctor shows results.*

Other major Teradata users include Anthem Blue Cross Blue Shield (Community Mutual), Mutual of Omaha, Health Alliance Plan, Baxter Travenol, Merck's Medco Containment, and Blue Cross Blue Shield of Illinois, Kentucky, Pennsylvania and Ohio.

7. The Banking and Financial Industry

The Banking and Financial industries use Teradata for "relationship" banking, whereby customer account information from a variety of sources is merged on Teradata for cross-segment marketing. In this increasingly competitive and deregulated market, banks need to achieve large economies of scale in order to effectively compete.

Recent years have seen a number of large bank mergers. Teradata enables its customers to quickly find and evaluate take-over targets. If acquired or merged, account information from the subsidiary can be rapidly assimilated into the general data warehouse.

Bank of America uses Teradata to analyze trends in its relationships with customers to determine those most likely to purchase a particular bank product or service. Information regarding the bank's $28 billion mortgage-loan portfolio also resides on Teradata, and these loans may be sold as securities to Fannie Mae, Ginnie Mae, Freddie Mac or other private investors. This system proved invaluable in the aftermath of the devastating Los Angeles earthquake of January 17th, 1994. The residential lending group was able to discern within minutes its potential losses. Mr. Charles Griffin, a Vice President at the bank's Concord, California facility described how, "They were able to go in and see by zip-code how many and what type of real estate loans we had in those areas where the earthquake hit".

Citicorp, the largest bank in the USA, was not only an early investor in the Teradata Corporation, but was also its first large customer. Over the years, Citicorp has acquired 11 subsidiaries, each with its own system. Getting a simple report that listed all the checking and savings accounts, credit cards, loans and mortgages for any specific household was not only difficult, but was frequently out-of-date. With no fewer than nine parallel processing machines running the Teradata Database, Citibank can not only call on an accurate customer profile in seconds, but can also use that information to identify new business opportunities.

In October of 1988, a hurricane swept through Southern England. At the time Royal Insurance had been setting up a motor vehicle insurance application on Teradata, but quickly decided to load its property and casualty histories instead. Using the power of Teradata, Royal quickly discovered its maximum exposure by listing all the policies and their value. By analyzing the history of similar catastrophic events in the past, Royal was able to project precisely when and how much they would need to borrow to cover potential claims. As a result, Royal paid its first claim within one week, and received front-page acclaim in the London Financial Times - a prestigious organ which does not permit advertising on the front page.

Other Users in this category include Chemical, Chase Manhattan, Banc One, Nationsbank, Dime Savings of New York, Lloyds Bank, Barclays Bank, National Westminster Bank, Abbey National, Trustee Savings Bank, Royal Bank of Canada, Bawag (Austria), Credit Commercial de France, Caisse d'Epargne (France), National Bank (Australia), Advance Bank (Australia). Reuters News Service (UK), Merrill Lynch, Kemper Financial, Transamerica Insurance Group, TRW Credit, Fidelity Investments, Capital Group, Chicago Board of Options Exchange, Federal Home Load Mortgage (Freddie Mac), Central Provident Fund Board (Singapore) and Canadian Tire Acceptance.

8. The Public Sector

Teradata is heavily employed in the public sector to save taxpayer money by ensuring that benefit checks only go to those who qualify. It is used to increase taxpayer compliance, track underfunded company pension plans, and identify fraud and money-laundering schemes.

The Australian Department of Social Security maintains a national database on Teradata, and is used to detect, prevent and deter overpayments and fraud. The Australian DSS paid out more than $27.8 billion to more than 5 million entitlement recipients during 1991/2. The installation of Teradata is credited with savings of around $100 million during 1992/3 and is expected to save double that amount *annually* in the foreseeable future.

The Italian State Police and Carabinieri use Teradata to warehouse and access passport, vehicle and other data. The elimination of most border checks and passport controls in the European Union (EU) has created many interesting challenges in the areas of:

Immigration,
Missing and Wanted Persons,
False Documents,
Firearms,
Automobile Theft and Registration.

For example, a person may enter France, travel for many weeks, enter Italy and depart for some non EU country. France would be aware someone entered, Italy would be aware somebody left, but until Teradata was installed there was no way to match the two events.

Other major Teradata sites include the US Air Force, Internal Revenue Service, US Department of Justice, Central Intelligence Agency, Centers for Disease Control, Michigan Social Security, Texas Department of Health, Teale Data Center (California) and La Poste (France).

9. Other Industries

The University of California at Irvine uses Teradata for clinical research at the school's Alzheimer's Disease Research Center. Data is gathered from sources at UCI and other state and national programs and is used to explore complex relationships between brain function and brain physiology. Investigators are able to find specific cases that meet certain criteria and relate their findings to those of other researchers throughout the world.

McDonnell Douglas estimates the financial savings from using Teradata, to be about $20 million per year. It is used to support:

Manufacturing and Assembly and Bill of Materials
Scheduling and workload forecasting
Engineering
Operations
Fabrication Management Tracking.

Assembling an aircraft requires thousands of specialized parts, and it is critical to have the right parts available at the right time. Previously the tooling and scheduling analysts would spend days sifting through voluminous reports to get the answers they needed, and all too often those answers would be out-of-date by the time they were discovered. With Teradata the process has been streamlined to just a few hours.

Other Industries served by Teradata include:

Utilities	*Electricite de France, Ontario Hydro,*
Entertainment	*Walt Disney,*
Publishing	*Shepard's / DRI, McGraw Hill, Americtech Publishing,*

Automobiles	*Ford, Volkswagen*
Oil & Gas	*Chevron,*
Defense & Aerospace	*Boeing, McDonnel Douglas, Lockheed Martin,*
Pharmaceuticals	*Baxter Travenol, Merck's Medco Containment, BASF Chemicals (Germany),*
Industrials	*3M, Thyssen Steel (Germany), and Sumitomo Metals (Japan).*

Conclusions

Teradata's future looks even brighter than its past. The decade of the millennium promises to be even more frantic than the recession-prone decade of the 1990's. With the headlong rush for new technology, business and industry will face greater challenges than ever before. With a logarithmic expansion in the amount of data available for analysis, the need for highly detailed market intelligence will soar to Olympian heights, and it is the Teradata Database that shows the most promise of becoming the primary power source needed to drive this dynamic new era.

With every television set in every home shortly tuned to the Internet, the quiet whisper of the Information Revolution has already become an audible murmur, and the murmur will soon crescendo into a roar. The machines which transform raw data into useful intelligence are operating at high speed, and getting faster every day. So kindly return your seats to the upright position. Whatever happens now is going to change your life.

The Teradata Database

SQL

Brian Marshall

1 Teradata SQL

"To boldly go where no-one has gone before". Gene Roddenbury's mission statement might be said to have applied as much to the real-life Teradata Corporation as to the fictional StarFleet Command.

In 1978, armed only with the rules of the relational data model as defined by Dr. Edgar Codd and Dr. Chris Date, the newly developed computer micro-chip, and an unconquerable resolve to succeed, the fledgling Teradata Corporation embarked on a fascinating odyssey which, nearly twenty years later, would find them still the only mature parallel processing product capable of supporting the data warehousing needs of the world's largest companies.

Teradata's vision involved the design and creation of a unique combination of computer hardware and software, operating in massively parallel fashion, to build, maintain and analyze the colossal volumes of data needed to fuel the furious economic and social advances of the late 20th century.

Although it did not coin the phrase, Teradata was perhaps the first vendor to truly embrace the concept of the "data warehouse" - a huge repository of data which can be accessed on demand by any or all applications, regardless of the host (source computer) on which they might be running.

User requests to access the Teradata Database must observe the syntax requirements of Structured Query Language (SQL) - the industry standard for relational databases. Although SQL was developed by IBM during the 1970s, few standards were in evidence at that time, and each vendor tended to develop its own particular dialect. Unlike most computer languages, SQL uses a very English-like syntax, and avoids the

the need for complex "compile and link" operations. Often described as "Fourth Generation", SQL has been described as a "sub-language" since its only purpose is to interface with the database. It differs from earlier languages like COBOL, Fortran and C in that it is non-procedural. It does not tell the computer what to do - it simply provides information about the nature and location of the data it requires, and allows the computer to do the rest. As a result, SQL does not recognize such concepts as "Open File", "GO TO", "FOR/NEXT" loops etc., but instead provides the user with a set of extremely powerful tools for maintaining and using data to obtain quick, reliable answers to important business questions.

The SQL can be generated from a multiplicity of sources, perhaps IBM VM or MVS using CICS or some third party interface such as FOCUS, NOMAD or INTELLECT. It might originate from UNISYS or a LAN (Local Area Network) *(Fig. 1-1).* By whatever means the SQL is generated, it is transmitted to the Teradata Database as plain English text, and is consequently not subject to the vagaries or eccentricities of any specific compiler. Thus the same (textual) SQL query applied to the same data can be expected to deliver the same result, *regardless of the source of the query.*

As an early explorer of a mysterious new frontier, it was inevitable that Teradata would frequently encounter situations for which the rules had yet to be formulated. As a result, in order to proceed, it would find itself obliged to commit to a specific path or course of action, with the risk that this action might, at some future point in time, prove to be non-standard.

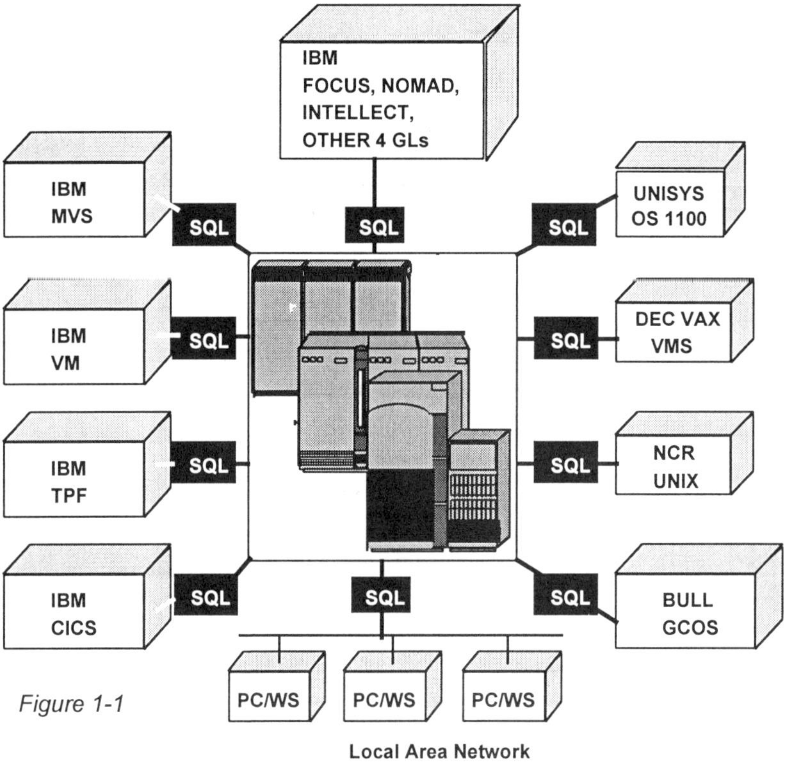

Figure 1-1

In 1978 the rules and mathematics of the relational database were well known. Yet to be developed were the syntax, structure and standards of SQL on which the American National Standards Institute (ANSI) were to agree in 1986, and again in 1992. The Teradata Corporation's first major *production*, massively parallel database machine, the DBC/1012, was delivered to AT&T in the summer of 1985 using Teradata's own version of SQL known as "Tequel" (Teradata SQL). The winner of the prestigious Fortune Magazine award for technical excellence, the DBC/1012 was quickly identified by a large number of Fortune 500 corporations as the primary information vehicle for the 1980s and beyond. As a result, Teradata was catapulted into the somewhat enviable position of unchallenged world leader of very large database applications running on a massively-parallel architecture.

By 1986, a number of other now-major database products, including IBM DB2, ORACLE, INFORMIX etc., had matured, each with its own particular dialect of SQL. As a result, the need for well-documented standards was being keenly felt. With the exceptions of Britton-Lee (whose parallel architecture was better suited for small-to-medium databases) and Teradata, all of the other major Relational Database Management Systems (RDBMS) ran on more traditional sequentially-processing main frame computers, and the ANSI standards of 1986 tended to reflect the needs of the majority.

The most important rule of the relational database, rigidly endorsed by Teradata, prohibits duplicate rows in a table. Imagine the confusion which might occur if we were unable to tell the difference between two employees having the same name, or which shipment needed to be delivered to which customer. Nevertheless the ANSI standards of 1986 called for the support of duplicate rows in a table. It should be emphasized however, that while ANSI standards mandate the *support* of duplicate rows, they do, at the same time, permit the definition of unique keys and indexes which effectively prevent their accidental occurrence.

Nevertheless, the Teradata Corporation found itself in a quandary. On the one hand, newer users were calling for standardization of SQL and portability of code from one vendor to another. On the other hand, as a result of its pioneering efforts, Teradata had invented an impressive number of powerful non-standard extensions to SQL upon which its pre-existing customer base had come to rely. Teradata developed a policy therefore, which attempts to provide each of them with the best of both worlds:

Where there is no major conflict between Teradata SQL and ANSI standards, ANSI syntax prevails, although previous syntax continues to be supported for a limited time.

Where a major conflict exists between Teradata and ANSI, users can choose to log on as "Teradata" or "ANSI", either as a system default or on a session-by-session basis.

New enhancements are required to conform to ANSI standards.

In this way, Teradata hopes to provide new customers with all the benefits of standard SQL, while at the same time protecting the investment of its pre-existing customer base.

Teradata's Version 2 Release 2 (V2R2) software includes most of the 1992 entry-level ANSI SQL. In addition, this software release provides Teradata users with a number of long-requested, major new features, including:

Built-in automatic referential integrity checking using Primary and Foreign Keys and the "CHECK" option.

Expanded outer-join support,

The "GRAPHIC" data type for Kanji support.

Expanded date handling.

Support of the Correlated Subquery.

In adopting ANSI standards, Teradata has sacrificed little but gained much. As a result Teradata users continue to benefit from Teradata's rich experience in the past, while at the same time being reassured by the promise of tomorrow.

2 The Database

The Relational Database is beyond doubt the most powerful, and yet the simplest known way of storing huge amounts of data in clear, concise and unambiguous fashion. Its building blocks are two-dimensional tables composed of horizontal rows, each of which represents a real world person, place thing or idea, and vertical columns, each of which contains a single item of information which describes the subject of the row itself.

Information maintained in tabular form has been widely used by every civilization which left written records, since the dawn of human history. Tables, in one form or another, are amongst the first things taught to children in grade school. As a consequence, use of tabular data is generally so well understood that it becomes almost second nature.

A relational database consists of a number of tables which together describe some kind of business, social or scientific enterprise. Relational tables are required to conform to certain rules. *For Example:*

Each table must have a unique name.

Each column must have a unique name within a table.

Each row must be unique within a table.

Each column in a row must contain no more than a single "atomic" item of information.

The order of rows within a table, or columns within a row must be independent of their meaning.

In searching for a suitable database (or data model) to demonstrate the principles outlined in this and the following chapters, we must confess to having become somewhat bored with the run-of-the-mill examples of Employee and Department, Order and Part type tables generally served to students as gourmet fare. The "Classics" database, which we have created instead, models events in the life of the author, Charles Dickens, his stories, the characters in his stories, their relationships to one another and recent publishing of his books. The tables are capable of eventually supporting other authors as well. All the information is factual, except for telephone numbers, prices and sales information, and might stand the student in excellent stead, should such questions arise during a "Jeopardy" session.

The "Classics" Database

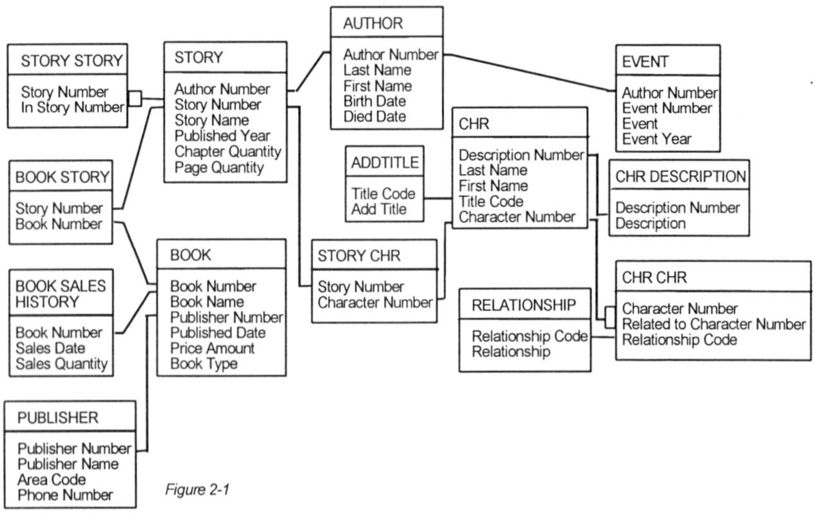

Figure 2-1

Fig. 2-1 is an "ER" (Entity-Relationship) diagram of the "Classics" database. In a relational database, real-world persons, places and things of interest to the enterprise are known as "ENTITIES". Each table describes a single entity. Information (Rows) contained in multiple tables can be cross-matched, based on a column or columns in each table which have similar meanings and data values. Columns used for cross-matching are known as "KEYS", and keys represent relationships between the tables.

In the ER diagram, each box represents a single named entity (upper-case) and contains a list of the column names for that specific table. The lines which join the various tables together identify the key relationships between the tables. Notice how columns which participate in key relationships are given identical names.

Such diagrams however can only deliver a relatively narrow spectrum of information about the tables. They cannot, for example, provide samples of the data itself, nor do they supply much of the information crucial to application success. For that, we must turn to a representation of the tables themselves.

Figures 2-2 and 2-3 show diagrams of each table in the "Classics" database (in alphabetical order) together with a short description, column names, key identifications (PK, FK), indexes (UPI, NUPI), and a small number of sample data rows.

ADDTITLE
Description: Address mode

Title Code	Add Title
PK	
UPI	
MR MRS MSTR	MR MRS Master

AUTHOR
Description: Writer of Stories

Author Number	Last Name	First Name	Birth Date	Died Date
PK				
UPI				
101	Dickens	Charles	1812-02-07	1870-06-09

BOOK
Description: Published Volume

Book Number	Book Name	Publisher Number	Published Date	Price Amount	Book Type
PK		FK			
UPI					
1002 1003 1004	Christmas Tales Great Expectations Our Mutual Friend	104 103 103	950430 940120 951030	6.99 5.95 10.95	P P H

BOOK_SALES_HISTORY
Description: Sales by Book

Book Number	Sales Date	Sales Quantity
PK,USI		
FK		
NUPI		
1001 1001 1001	961215 961220 961210	1 2 1

BOOK_STORY
Description: Associative

Book Number	Story Number
PK,USI	
FK	FK
NUPI	
1001 1002 1002	101 112 102

CHR
Description: Fictional character in story

Character Number	Last Name	First Name	Title Code	Description Number
PK			FK	FK
UPI	NUSI			
1001 1002 1003	Scrooge Marley Scrooge	Ebenezer Jacob Fan	Mr Mr Mis	101 102

CHR_CHR
Description: Associative

Character Number	Related to Character Number	Relationship Code
PK,USI		
FK	FK	
NUPI		
1001 1002 1001	1002 1001 1003	PAR PAR BRO

CHR_DESCRIPTION
Description: Character description in story

Description Number	Description
PK	
UPI	
101 102 103	Grasping covetous old man Deceased Apprentice at Fezziwigs'

Figure 2-2

EVENT

Description: Event in author's life

Event Number	Event	Event Year	Author Number
PK			FK
UPI			
101	Born at Landport, Portsmouth	1812	101
102	Family moves to Chatham	1817	101
103	Family moves to Camden Town,London	1822	101

PUBLISHER

Description: Book Publisher

Publisher Number	Publisher Name	Area Code	Phone Number
PK			
UPI			
101	Washington Square Press	212	2232000
102	MacMillan Publishing	212	3355100
103	Oxford University Press	213	5247000

STORY_CHR

Description: Associative

Story Number	Character Number
PK,USI	
FK	FK
NUPI	
101	1001
101	1002
101	1003

STORY

Description: Fictional story

Story Number	Story Name	Published Year	Chapter Quantity	Page Quantity	Author Number
PK					FK
UPI					
101	A Christmas Carol	1843	5	63	101
102	The Seven PoorTravellers	1861	3	22	101
103	Doctor Marigold	1859	2	5	101

RELATIONSHIP

Description: Character associations

Relationship Code	Relationship
PK	
UPI	
PAR	Partner
BRO	Brother
SIS	Sister

STORY_STORY

Description: Associative

Story Number	InStory Number
PK,USI	
FK	FK
NUPI	
104	103

Figure 2-3

SQL Naming Convention

SQL object names may be composed of upper or lower case alpha, numeric, or certain special characters ("#", "$" or "_"):

Names may be up to 30 characters in length (no spaces).
Names may not start with a numeric character.
User names and database names must be unique.
Table names must be unique within a database.
Column names must be unique within a table.
Column names and table names may be "qualified" using the period (".") as a separator, to avoid ambiguity:

[databasename] . tablename . columnname

Keys

Keys are a relational data modeling concept and come in two flavors:

Primary Keys (PK)
Foreign Keys (FK).

Primary Keys

Every relational table is required to have a Primary Key. This may be one or a combination of columns for which the value, or combined value, must be:

Unique (no duplicate values permitted).
Not Null (must have a value).
Never changed (not subject to update).

Primary keys serve the single purpose of uniquely identifying a row. For large or frequently accessed tables ("Major" entities) the value is generally numeric. Certain smaller tables which typically have fewer than one hundred rows and are seldom subject to change are known as "Minor" entities whose primary key may consist of a two or three character alpha code. Tables which have a single column primary key are known as "Prime" entities. Apart from the Book_Sales_History table, which reflects recent book sales, all the other tables in this database with two column primary keys are "Associative" tables used to model a many-to-many relationship between two prime entities.

Foreign Keys

If a column or combination of columns is marked "FK" (for Foreign Key), it implies that the column or columns have a relationship to another column or group of columns identified as "PK" elsewhere in the database.

For Example, in Fig. 2-2, the CHR table has 2 columns marked "FK":

Title_Code refers to PK of ADDTITLE table.

Description_Number refers to PK of Chr_Description table.

Unlike PK columns, which must be unique, never null and never changed, values in columns marked "FK" need not be unique and may be null. At the same time, note that each value which does appear in a FK column must be a valid value in the PK column of the table to which it refers. Values in FK columns may also be changed. We might hope that the Description_Number of Scrooge as 101 ("a grasping covetous old man") might one day be changed to some other number for which the description is, "a kindly benefactor to Tiny Tim".

From this we can derive the rules for columns marked "FK":

Column values may be non-unique.

They need not have a value (may be null), but any value which does exist must be a valid value in the PK column of the same or another table.

FK values may be changed.

Referential Integrity

As long as the relationship between PK columns and FK columns is properly maintained, the tables are said to observe "Referential Integrity" - if not they are said to violate referential integrity rules. Primary Keys and Foreign Keys therefore permit tables to relate to each other in a clear, concise and unambiguous manner - but do not necessarily indicate the physical pathway used by the RDBMS to access the data.

***Keys** are used to maintain referential integrity*

***Indexes** are used to physically access the data.*

Indexes

Like keys, indexes come in 2 major varieties:

Primary - Unique (UPI) and Non-Unique (NUPI)
Secondary - Unique (USI) and Non-Unique (NUSI)

which are described at some length in "The Teradata Database - Introduction", Chapters 6 and 7.

Primary Indexes

Each and every table must have a column or group of columns designated as the Primary Index. The Primary Index may be unique or non-unique, and while NULL values are not permitted in PI columns by ANSI standards, the Teradata Database permits a single NULL value per table for a UPI, and multiple NULLs in NUPI columns.

On the basis that, "If you know where you left something, you will know where to find it", Teradata uses the primary index column not only to place the row on the disk, but also to find it again. Reversing this logic therefore, the primary index column(s) should be chosen, based on the data values most often supplied in the SQL to *access* the data. Primary keys and primary indexes then differ considerably in function:

> A Primary *key* is used to *identify* a row
> A Primary *index* is used to *find* a row.

Readers might well have noticed in *Figs. 2-2 and 2-3*, an apparent relationship between primary keys and primary indexes:

> Tables which have a single-column primary key, tend to have a UPI on the same column.
>
> Tables which have multiple column primary keys, tend to have a NUPI on one of the columns marked FK.

and this is indeed true - 90% of the time. Would that the choosing of the primary index were as simple as that -but a 90% success rate is simply not close enough to ensure top performance of the Teradata Database. On the contrary, the final choice of primary index columns is made only after an exhaustive analysis of each and every application which accesses the tables, and a thorough examination of its frequency and usage.

Secondary Indexes

While primary index columns are chosen on the basis of the *most frequently-used* access route to the tables, secondary indexes may be employed as an alternate access path for columns less frequently used.

Unique Secondary Index (USI)

A USI may be used to prevent the insert of duplicate values in a column or group of columns, and is widely used to enforce the primary key integrity of a table with a non-unique primary index (NUPI). At the same time, a USI provides a secondary access route to the data, only slightly less efficient than a UPI, and possibly more efficient than access by a NUPI which has multiple duplicate values.

Non-Unique Seconday Index (NUSI)

While the Teradata "*Optimizer*" (a software program responsible for evaluating multiple access alternatives and choosing the most efficient) will always use an available USI for access, it may choose to ignore a NUSI if it considers another plan to be more efficient. Each secondary index, unique or non-unique, requires the maintenance of a secondary index subtable - another table which references the primary data row, and has as its *primary index* the *secondary index value*.

The secondary index subtable must be maintained for each write transaction which affects the index value itself, or the location of the primary row to which it refers. As a result, secondary index subtable management becomes costly to the system, both in terms of disk space and CPU usage, and secondary indexes, particularly NUSIs, should be re-evaluated from time to time to ensure they are still being used.

Domains

In the previous chapter, we drew attention to the tendency of columns which participate in key relationships to be given identical names. This is because columns in different tables which are subject to logical comparison, refer to the same real-world person, place, thing or idea. The columns are therefore said to be in the *same domain.*

Domains help to bring all the columns in the tables under control. There are 48 columns in the "Classics" database, each of which must belong to one (and only one) of the 25 distinct domains listed in *Fig. 2-4*. Each domain has a unique name which becomes the basis of the column name.

For Example:

Each character is identified by a unique number- *Character_Number.*

Character_Number appears a total of four times in three tables:

Table	Column Name
CHR	Character_Number
CHR_CHR	Character_Number
	Related_to_Character_Number
STORY_CHR	Character_Number

Since two columns in the CHR_CHR table, each with the name, "Character_Number" would cause confusion, the domain name for at least one of them must be further qualified. Thus the primary key is composed of two columns drawn from the same domain:

Character_Number.
Related_to_Character_Number.

Domain Name	Column Name	Description	Data Type
Address Title	Add_Title	Mode of address	CHARACTER
Amount	(ends in) Amount	US$ amount	DECIMAL
Area Code	Area_Code	Area code	NUMERIC
Author Number	Author_Number	Author ID	NUMERIC
Book Name	Book_Name	Book title	CHARACTER
Book Number	Book_Number	Volume ID	NUMERIC
Book Type	Book_Type	Binding	CHARACTER
Character Description	CHR_Description	Describes character	CHARACTER
Character Number	Character_Number	Character ID	NUMERIC
Date	(ends in) Date	Calendar date	DATE
Description Number	Description_Number	Description ID	NUMERIC
Event	Event	Event in author's life	CHARACTER
Event Number	Event_Number	Event ID	NUMERIC
First Name	First_Name	First name	CHARACTER
Last Name	Last Name	Last name	CHARACTER
Phone Number	Phone Number	Phone number	NUMERIC
Publisher Name	Publisher Name	Publishing company	CHARACTER
Publisher Number	Publisher Number	Publisher ID	NUMERIC
Quantity	(ends in) Quantity	Quantity	NUMERIC
Relationship	Relationship	Character relationship	CHARACTER
Relationship Code	Relationship_Code	Relationship ID	CHARACTER
Story Name	Story_Name	Story title	CHARACTER
Story Number	Story_Number	Story ID	NUMERIC
Title Code	Title_Code	Address mode ID	CHARACTER
Year	(ends in) Year	Calendar year	NUMERIC

Figure 2-4

There are four "general" domains which appear in the "Classics" database:

Date.
Year.
Amount.
Quantity.

While it might not, at first glance, appear that Event_Year and Published_Year are in the same domain, it is certainly logical to compare the date a story was published with other events in the author's life.

Each column based on one of the "general" domains requires a "qualified" domain name:

> *Birth*_Date.
> *Died*_Date.
> *Page*_Quantity.
> *Price*_Amount, etc.

Efficient domain management can also serve to eradicate two more "plagues" of the data-processing world:

Synonyms	Words which sound different, but have similar meanings.
Homonyms	Words which sound alike, but have different meanings.

Synonyms

Unrecognized use of multiple names to describe the same thing can cause a great deal of confusion.

For Example:

> "Our corporate data tables are full of column names like:
>
> Employee_number.
> Manager_number.
> Supervisor_Number.
> Engineer_Number, etc.
>
> and since the same individuals seem to occur in different groups, this is causing no end of confusion."
>
> Once we recognize that all these people, whatever their specific function might be, are all *employees (*someone employed by the organization on a salaried basis), then it becomes clear that each

of these column names are synonyms for "Employee_Number". As a result the columns should be renamed using the domain name as the fundamental column name, but further qualified, as necessary to avoid ambiguity:

Employee_Number
Manager_*Employee_Number*
Supervisor_*Employee_Number*
Engineer_*Employee_Number*

In this way everyone in the organization can still use whatever term they wish, but the confusion no longer exists. While this solution might perhaps result in lengthy column names, SQL is generous in its 30 character limit.

Homonyms

Homonyms frequently result in somewhat more subtle and difficult-to-detect domain violations than synonyms:

If we ask the *Engineering Department* for a part identified by a unique *Part Number*, we will probably be handed a *drawing*. On the other hand, If we ask the Parts Department for the same numbered part, we would expect to receive an assembled *piece of machinery*. Thus a single name is used to describe two totally dissimilar objects and results in confusion and ambiguity.

Identifying columns in the same or different domains

Columns which can be logically *added, subtracted or compared* are said to be in the *same domain*, and the result will be in that domain:

Domain	Domain	Domain
(Books)	(Books)	(Books)
10 Books +	5 Books =	15 Books.

Columns which can be logically *multiplied or divided* by each other are said to be in *different domains* with the result in one or other of the domains:

Domain	Domain	Domain
(Books)	($ Amount)	($ Amount)
10 Books *	$15.00 =	$150.00

There is one known exception to this rule, where two items in the same domain can logically be multiplied by each other, in which event the result is in another domain:

Domain	Domain	Domain
(Length)	(Length)	(Area)
10 miles *	5 miles =	150 *square miles*

For example, the database of a major California bank has almost 400 tables, and in excess of 3000 columns. On the other hand, each of these 3000-or-so columns maps into fewer than 400 distinct domains. It is much easier to control 400 domains than 3000 columns.

Conclusions

While relational theory espouses a fairly large number of rules and guidelines, they are without exception, based on good common-sense principles. As a result, they can be mastered in a very short period of time. Once the underlying structure and logic of *anything in, or any part of* the known universe is well understood, it can be modeled in relational tables, and used to answer any reasonable question, within the scope of the model itself. This is what makes the Relational Database so powerful.

3 BTEQ

Even with the relational data on the Teradata *server,* on the one hand, and the ability to create host or *client*-based SQL on the other, we are still missing an essential link in the chain - how to communicate between the two. For this we need a Teradata utility known as "BTEQ" (pronounced "BeeTeek").

"BTEQ" is an acronym for "Basic Teradata SQL". BTEQ is designed to handle large-scale data maintenance transactions which accept input data from, and export data to, a host-resident file. BTEQ is also the primary tool used by system administrators and application developers to submit on-line interactive individual user queries with impressive performance in both areas.

As a user-interactive utility, BTEQ permits SQL to be input on-line from a terminal attached to any supported network or main-frame, in a simple and straight-forward manner, and return the response rows to the user as a formatted report. Quick to initialize and simple to use, interactive BTEQ is widely favored by Teradata SQL developers and administrators.

Accessing BTEQ

BTEQ is a host-based utility, and is fully supported on all platforms *(Fig. 3-1),* including:

Main Frames.
Local Area Networks.
NCR 3600 and WorldMark 5100 UNIX.

While a wide diversity of host (or *client*) platforms is supported by Teradata, the great majority of its larger users continue to rely heavily on IBM main frames and UNIX-based networks.

Access via a Main-Frame

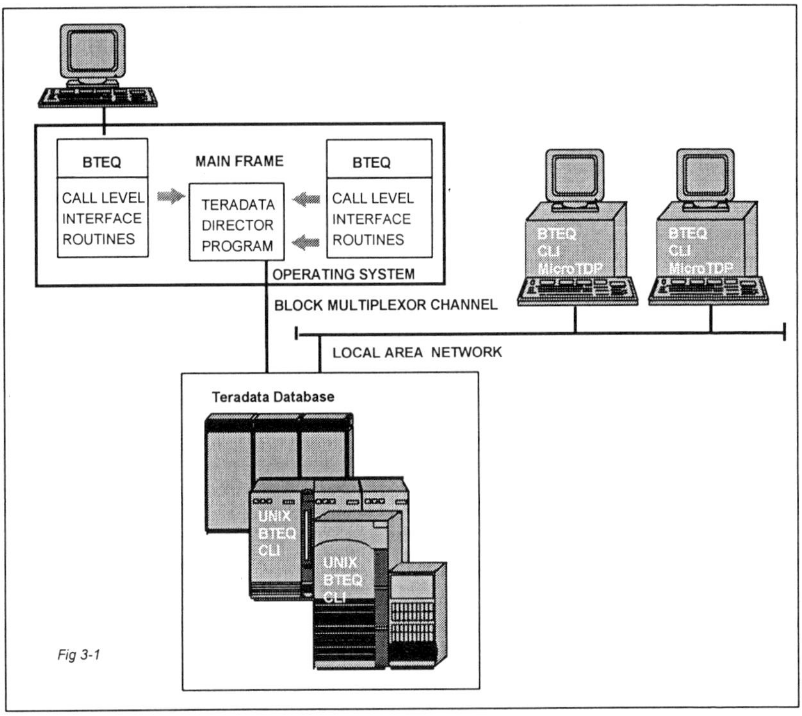

Fig 3-1

Traffic between the host (client) and the Teradata Database server is conducted as a series of "parcels" traveling back and forth across the channel or network. There are more than 50 different types of parcels which are built and managed by a series of high level callable sub-routines, collectively known as the Call Level Interface (CLI). In a main-frame host, the parcels from all the users accessing the Teradata Database from that host are passed to a single program called "Teradata Director Program" (TDP) which registers them, aggregates them into

32K channel blocks, and sends them to Teradata for processing. Response messages from Teradata destined for that host are similarly aggregated into 32K channel blocks, and it becomes the responsibility of TDP to ensure that each message is delivered to the correct user. The BTEQ user need not be aware of any of this "behind the scenes" complexity, but simply types the SQL, hits the "Enter" key and waits for the response.

Access via a Local Area Network (LAN)

In a Local Area Network environment, TDP resides in the PC or workstation and serves only the single user. Thus, greatly reduced in function, it is known as "micro TDP"

Access via NCR 3600 or WorldMark 5100 UNIX

In addition to main-frames, PCs and work-stations, BTEQ is also available from the UNIX-based AP (Application Processor) of the 3600, or the SMP (Symetic Multi-Processor) of the WorldMark 5100.

ANSI-or Teradata Mode

Users may elect to submit SQL in either ANSI-standard or Teradata mode. The system default is controlled by the Teradata System Administrator by setting the SessionMode flag in the DBSControl utility. Teradata recommends ANSI-standard mode for new systems, but Teradata mode for upgraded systems. Once the system default has been chosen, any individual session can be set as desired using the .following SET SESSION statements:

.SET SESSION TRANSACTION ANSI;	Changes mode from Teradata to ANSI
.SET SESSION TRANSACTION BTET;	Changes mode from ANSI to Teradata

It should be noted that these .SET commands do not take effect until the next .LOGON, and should therefore preceded the .LOGON statement.

Initialization and Logon (Interactive Mode)

BTEQ is initialized from the "Ready" or UNIX prompt *(Fig. 3-2):*

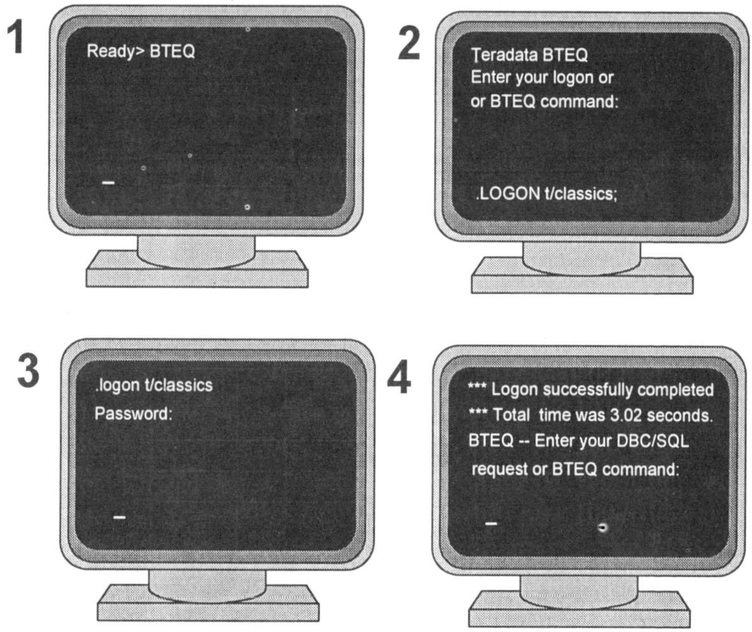

Figure 3-2

BTEQ <ENTER>
Teradata BTEQ. Enter your logon or BTEQ command:
.LOGON TDPId/Username ;
Password:
Password <ENTER> (Will not be visible on screen)
**** Logon successfully completed.*

**** Total elapsed time was 6.02 seconds.*
BTEQ – Enter your DBC/SQL request or BTEQ command:

BTEQ in Batch Mode:

In the UNIX environment, BTEQ is instructed to accept input from a file and/or output response to another file using the "redirect" characters:

BTEQ < *inputfile* > *outputfile*

If the "> *outputfile*" is omitted, the output is directed to the screen.

BTEQ access from an IBM main-frame requires Job Control Language (JCL) in the MVS environment, or File Definitions (FILEDEFs) for VM, and samples of these are provided as *(Fig.3-3).*

Notice that a typical BTEQ script contains both BTEQ commands and SQL. *BTEQ commands* such as *.logon* and *.quit, always* begin with a period *(.)* and *may* end with a semi-colon *(;)*. SQL commands *never* begin with a period and *must* end with a semi-colon.

MVS Job Control Language (JCL)

```
//JOBCARD   JOB
//BTEQ      EXEC PGM=ITBMAIN
//STEPLIB   DD   DSN=TERADATA.APPLOAD,DISP=SHR
//SYSPRINT  DD   SYSOUT=*
//DATAOUT   DD   DSN=USER.FILE.NAME,
                 DISP=(NEW,CATLG),
                 UNIT=DISK,SPACE=(TRK(10,10)),
                 DCB=(LRECL=80,RECFM=FB,BLKSIZE=4800)
//SYSIN     DD   DATA,DLM=##

.LOGON T/UserName, password;
SQL follows here
.QUIT;

##
//
```

VM File Definitions (FILEDEFs)

```
/* SAMPLE REXX EXEC FOR RUNNING BTEQ */
"FILEDEF SYSPRINT DISK Fn1 Ft1 Fm1 (LRECL 132 RECFM VA)
"FILEDEF DATAIN DISK Fn2 Ft2 Fm2
                     (LRECL 80 RECFM FB BLKSIZE 4800)
"FILEDEF SYSIN DISK Fn3 Ft3 Fm3"
"BTEQ NOTERM"
.LOGON T/UserName, password;
SQL follows here
.QUIT;
exit
```

Figure 3-3

BTEQ Output

BTEQ calculates the greater of the column name or maximum column value, and attempts to center the report on the page or screen, with characters aligned to the left, and numerics aligned to the right. If the report exceeds the maximum 80 characters for a screen or 132 for the default printer, the output is truncated on the right. BTEQ does not report an error.

As a default, output from a BTEQ job is sent to:

The screen (for an interactive session).
The SYSPRINT (for an IBM host).
The named output file for any other environment.

As can be seen in *Fig.3-4,* the default output contains:

Command acknowledgements.
Performance timings.
Response rows.

```
NCR CORPORATION   BTEQ 5.0.0 Thu Sep 12 08:38:16 1996
.logon Classics,
*** Logon successfully completed.
*** Total elapsed time was 2.43 seconds.
+---------+---------+---------+---------+---------+---
SELECT     Story_Number
          ,Story_Name
          FROM Story
          ORDER BY Story_Name;
*** Query completed. 16 rows found. 2 columns returned.
*** Total elapsed time was 2.42 seconds.
Story_Number  Story_Name
------------  ----------------------------------------
105  A Christmas Tree
101  A Christmas Carol
116  A Tale of Two Cities
113  David Copperfield
103  Doctor Marigold
108  Great Expectations
115  Hard Times
114  Martin Chuzzlewit
109  Our Mutual Friend
110  The Chimes
112  The Cricket on the Hearth
107  The Haunted Man
117  The Holly Tree
102  The Seven Poor Travellers
104  To Be Taken with a Grain of Salt
106  What Christmas Is As We Get Older
quit;
*** You are now logged off from the DBC.
*** Exiting BTEQ...
Ending BTEQ  Thu Sep 12 08:38:21 1996
```

Figure 3-4

BTEQ Error Reporting

BTEQ attempts to make its error messages "User-friendly". The mistype of an object name, "story_number" as "storr_number" for example, *(Fig. 3-5)* is reasonably easy to diagnose, and BTEQ delivers a helpful message. While the occurrence of erroneous syntax is relatively easy to recognize however, determination of the actual intent of the user, and the true nature of the error is not. Also in *Fig. 3-5,* the word "FROM" was typed as "FORM" - another perfectly valid English word. As a result, BTEQ cannot tell if "FORM" was a valid word used incorrectly, or some other kind of error entirely. The resulting error message might, for that reason appear obscure - but we invite the reader to look again. Notice how BTEQ provides a "$" symbol at the precise point in the SQL statement where the error was first detected. This tiny symbol is often much more helpful in diagnosing a problem than the error message itself.

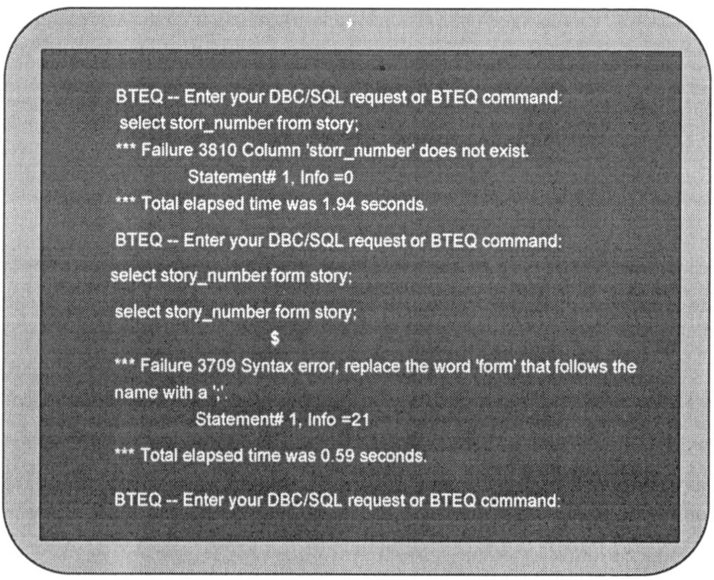

Figure 3-5

Setting up the "Classics Database"

The 3½ inch floppy diskette, which accompanies this book, contains only two files:

Classics.BTQ
Readme.DOC

The Classics.BTQ file is in ASCII format, and is the BTEQ script needed to create the version of the "Classics" database, used as a reference throughout this work.

Since the size, complexity and cost of the Teradata RDBMS render it unsuitable for installation in a PC environment, students wishing for first-hand Teradata experience, will need access to a DBC/1012, NCR 3550, NCR 3600 or WorldMark 5100 running the Teradata Database.

Once this has been arranged:

Copy the Classics.BTQ file and paste it to the appropriate host environment.

Modify the logon to reflect the correct TDPId, UserName and Password.

Be aware that the Teradata Database achieves many of its high performance characteristics by distributing the rows of each table evenly between multiple individual processors (AMPs) working in parallel. Each AMP on the system is required to maintain at least 512 bytes of "header" information for every table. A Teradata system with a large number of AMPs will therefore require more space to store a specific table than a Teradata system with fewer AMPs. The actual space required by the "Classics" database will consequently vary according to the number of AMPs in the system.

Execute BTEQ with Classics.BTQ as the input script, and it should complete within a short period (few minutes) of time.

Conclusions

Once all the various pieces are in place:

Main-frame, network or UNIX access to BTEQ.

A valid LOGON to the Teradata Database.

A good working understanding of the structure of the Relational Database.

A sample database.

it is time to go "solo". Go ahead, try logging on in interactive mode.

From the "Ready" prompt, type "BTEQ", and wait for the utility to prompt for a ".logon" command.

Remember that BTEQ commands *should* begin with a period, and *may* end with a semi-colon. SQL commands (like the SELECT statement) *must* end with a semi-colon (*or nothing will happen when you hit the "ENTER" key).*

Submit the SQL examples and exercises. You won't break the system.

When you have finished your exercises type, ".QUIT;"

That's all there is to it!

4 Getting Started

Unlike conventional computer languages which tend to deal with one record at a time, SQL deals with *sets* (or groups) of records.

Sets

From all the values existing in the known universe, we can select just that set which is used to identify books in the "Classics" database.

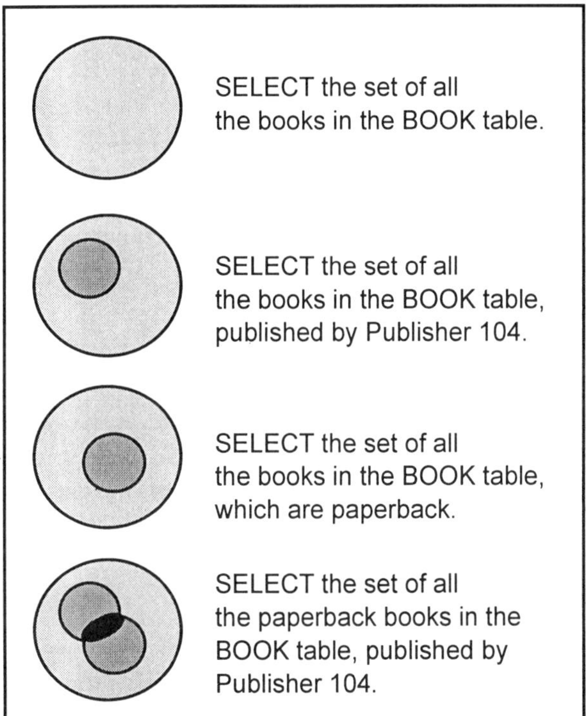

Figure 4-1

Of the set of values which identifies books, a certain sub-set are published by Publisher number 104 *(Fig. 4-1)*. Another subset of books are paperback.

Where all of these sets and subsets intersect, we have paperback books published by publisher 104. SQL statements are used to define the answer set to be returned.

SQL Functions

While SQL statements are powerful in function, they are few in number, and group into three major divisions:

Data Definition Language (DDL)

CREATE	Define a new user, database, table, view or macro
REPLACE	Replace an existing view or macro
DROP	Remove a user, database, table view or macro
ALTER	Change a table structure or protection level.

Data Manipulation Language (DML)

SELECT	Retrieve information from a table or tables
INSERT	Add a row to a table
UPDATE	Change the column values of a pre-existing row.
DELETE	Remove a row.

Data Control Language (DCL)

GRANT	Give a user some right or privilege.
REVOKE	Remove a privilege from a user.
GIVE	Transfer ownership of a user or database.

Relational Query Functions

Like the more fundamental arithmetic functions, such as add, subtract, multiply, divide etc, the RDBMS also has a number of functions it is required to perform, including:

SELECT	Return all or some rows from a table.
PROJECT	Return all or some columns from a row.
JOIN	Return related row data from multiple tables.
UNION	Return one set of rows end-on-end with another.
AGGREGATE	Calculate maximum, minimum, average values, etc.

All of the relational functions are performed by the *SELECT* SQL statement.

SELECT

Fig. 4-2 represents the Book table. An *unconstrained* SELECT of Book_Number from the Book table returns one response record for each row in the table.

```
SELECT Book_Number
       FROM Book
;
```

BOOK

Book Number	Book Name	Publisher Number	Published Date	Price Amount	Book Type
PK		FK			
UPI					
1002	Christmas Tales	104	95/04/30	6.99	P
1003	Great Expectations	103	94/0 1/20	5.95	P
1004	Our Mutual Friend	103	95/10/30	10.95	H
1001	A Christmas Carol	101	67/03/31	3.99	P
1005	The Christmas Books	104	71/06/09	4.95	P
1009	Martin Chuzzlewit	106	94/02/28	20.00	H
1006	The Christmas Books	104	85/05/02	6.95	P
1007	The Christmas Books	104	95/11/30	13.50	H
1008	David Copperfield	104	95/08/05	6.95	P
1010	Hard Times	106	95/04/10	6.95	P
1011	A Tale of Two Cities	104	85/11/10	5.95	P
1012	A Charles Dickens Christmas	103	76/06/15	14.99	H
1013	The Christmas Books	104	57/06/01		P
1014	The Christmas Books	104	46/02/01		P

Figure 4-2

```
Book_Number

      1008
      1010
      1012
      1003
      1002
      1004
      1011
      1009
      1005
      1013
      1007
      1009
      1005
      1013
      1007
```

```
1001
1006
1014
1000
```

The SQL is free form and not case sensitive, but by convention, the keywords, "SELECT" and "FROM" are uppercase, and each distinct component of the statement is written on a separate line. Each SQL statement must be terminated with a semi-colon ";" or an error will result.

The heading for the report is taken from the column name requested in the SELECT statement, and response rows are listed one beneath the other, in an apparently random order.

Selecting ALL the data

Using the SQL "wild card" symbol, the asterisk (*), we can select *all* the rows and *all* the columns of the BOOK table with very little effort:

```
SELECT *
        FROM Book
;
```

Book Number	Book Name	Publisher Number
1008	David Copperfield	104
1010	Hard Times	104
1006	The Christmas Books	104
1012	A Charles Dickens Christmas	103
1003	Great Expectations	103
1000	A Christmas Carol	?
1014	The Christmas Books	104
1002	Christmas Tales	104
1004	Our Mutual Friend	103
1011	A Tale of Two Cities	104
1009	Martin Chuzzlewit	106

```
1005        The Christmas Books              104
1013        The Christmas Books              104
1007        The Christmas Books              104
1001        A Christmas Carol                101
```

CONTINUATION

```
Published      Price        Book
Date           Amount       Type

95/08/05        6.95        P
95/04/10        6.95        P
85/05/02        6.95        P
76/06/15       14.99        H
94/01/20        5.95        P
?                  ?        ?
46/02/01           ?        P
95/04/30        6.99        P
95/10/30       10.95        H
85/11/10        5.95        P
94/02/28       20.00        H
71/06/05          00        P
57/06/01           ?        P
95/11/30       13.50        H
67/03/31        3.99        P
```

Once again, since the SELECT was unconstrained, the number of records returned is equal to the number of rows in the table. While response *rows* are still in an unpredictable order, the individual *fields* are returned in an order consistent with the table definition stored in the Data Dictionary/Directory (DD/D).

The wild-card SELECT may represent a useful shorthand, but imagine the effect, if the table has billions of rows, each of which must be received and processed by the host. In any event, this type of SELECT offers little control over the number and width of columns returned. If (as in the example above), the length of an output row exceeds 80 bytes for a screen, or 132 bytes for a printer, the output will be truncated.

WHERE

The "WHERE" clause is used to limit the number of rows returned to those of specific interest. In this example we are requesting a list of just those books published by publisher number 104:

```
SELECT Book_Number
      ,Book_Name
      ,Publisher_Number
    FROM Book
    WHERE Publisher_Number = 104
;
```

Book_Number	Book_Name	Publisher_Number
1005	The Christmas Books	104
1013	The Christmas Books	104
1002	Christmas Tales	104
1008	David Copperfield	104
1011	A Tale of Two Cities	104
1010	Hard Times	104
1014	The Christmas Books	104
1006	The Christmas Books	104
1007	The Christmas Books	104

ITEMS IN A LIST

SQL requires that individual *items within a list* are separated by *commas* (","). Thus "Book_Number, Book_Name and Publisher_Number" represents a 3-item list, and are separated by commas.

Key-word phrases are separated by *spaces*. Therefore there is no comma between "Publisher_Number" (the last item in the SELECT list) and the next key-word "FROM" - nor is there a comma between the "FROM" keyword phrase and the next keyword phrase beginning, "WHERE".

ORDER BY

It is extremely rare for any application to permit or tolerate data returned in a haphazard order. Almost all response data returned to the user will therefore need to be sorted alphabetically or numerically. This is easily accomplished in SQL using the "ORDER BY" clause:

```
SELECT Book_Number
      ,Book_Name
     FROM Book
     WHERE Publisher_Number = 104
     ORDER BY Book_Name
;
```

```
Book_Number              Book_Name

     1011                A Tale of Two Cities
     1002                Christmas Tales
     1008                David Copperfield
     1010                Hard Times
     1014                The Christmas Books
     1013                The Christmas Books
     1005                The Christmas Books
     1006                The Christmas Books
     1007                The Christmas Books
```

The output is now sorted in ascending alphabetical order by "Book_Name". Even so, since a number of books share the same title, "The Christmas Books", we might require them to be sorted by "Book_Number" (minor sort) within Book_Name (major sort):

```
SELECT Book_Number
      ,Book_Name
     FROM Book
     WHERE Publisher_Number = 104
     ORDER BY Book_Name, Book_Number
;
```

Book_Number	Book_Name
1011	A Tale of Two Cities
1002	Christmas Tales
1008	David Copperfield
1010	Hard Times
1005	The Christmas Books
1006	The Christmas Books
1007	The Christmas Books
1013	The Christmas Books
1014	The Christmas Books

"Book_Name" and "Book_Number" represent a list of items in the "ORDER BY" phrase and are separated by a comma.

DISTINCT

While duplicate rows may or may not be permitted in a table, there is no restriction whatever on duplicate output records. Hence if we were to make the following request we would expect to see five identical records for "The Christmas Books":

```
SELECT Book_Name
        ,Publisher_Number
    FROM Book
    WHERE Publisher_Number = 104
    ORDER BY Book_Name
    ;
```

On the other hand, we might try using the "DISTINCT" modifier to eliminate from the output, any duplication of the combination of ALL the items selected, ("Book_Number" AND "Publisher_Number").

```
SELECT DISTINCT Book_Name
                ,Publisher_Number
        FROM Book
        WHERE Publisher_Number = 104
        ;
```

```
Book_Name                    Publisher_Number

A Tale of Two Cities                      104
Christmas Tales                           104
David Copperfield                         104
Hard Times                                104
The Christmas Books                       104
```

Notice that the use of the "DISTINCT" option automatically results in output sorted (ascending) on the unique combination of fields.

Summary

The basic syntax for the SQL SELECT statement thus emerges:

SELECT	Column_Name(s)	*(separated by commas)*
FROM	Table_Name(s)	*(separated by commas)*
WHERE	Condition(s)	
ORDER BY	Column_Name(s)	*(separated by commas)*
;		

While SQL may be constructed in a free-form manner, we strongly suggest the following as a *minimum* convention for any SQL composed for a non-interactive environment:

SQL key-words should be in upper case.

Each individual field or expression selected should be on a new line.

Each individual key-word phrase should be on a new line.

Commas should used to *precede* each new item in a list (*rather than terminate* the previous item).

Hands-on Exercises

The following exercise questions are designed to provide the reader with an opportunity to further research the topics (or the SQL queries) covered in this chapter. Solutions are provided as Appendix A, however the reader should be aware that some results, such as unsorted records, may differ slightly from the answers provided.

1, Log on to BTEQ in interactive mode (*See Chapter 3)*.

2. Select all the columns and all the rows from the STORY table.

3. Select the Story_Name and the Published_Year from the STORY table for those stories published in 1859. Order the result by Story_Name.

4. Quit BTEQ.

5 Help, Show and Explain

In Chapter 2, we described how relational tables are used to model a business or some other kind of enterprise. If the tables are properly designed, there should be no reasonable question, within the scope of the model, which could not be answered using SQL. This is what makes the relational database so powerful. Getting the right answers however, depends on asking the right questions. Asking the right questions in turn, requires the analyst not only to have a good understanding of the data to be queried, but also a clear concept of the result to be achieved.

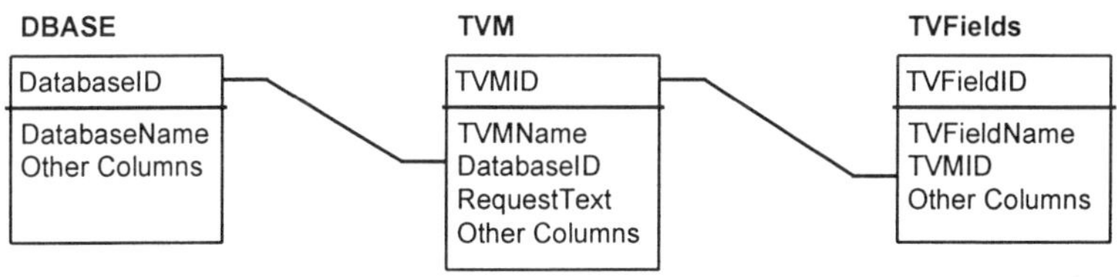

DD/D Table Name	Description
DBASE	Records information about all User and Database objects
TVM	Records information about Tables, Views and Macros
TVFields	Records information about each column within a Table or View

Figure 5-1

Information about objects and data structures in the Teradata Database is maintained in, and made available from, the Data Dictionary/Directory as a series of tables, views and macros in User "DBC" *(Fig. 5-1).*

The level of user access to the DD/D itself is controlled by the Teradata System Administrator, and varies depending on the level of security required at any specific site. Teradata SQL however provides a number of helpful commands which allows the user the information needed to create intelligent SQL queries without compromising site security.

The HELP, SHOW and EXPLAIN commands are Teradata enhancements to SQL, and are in consequence non ANSI - standard.

The ANSI Flagger program.

As part of the 1992 standards, ANSI requires that vendors provide users with a "Flagger" program to optionally identify SQL statements that:

- Do not conform to the standard, or
- Are supported in the standard, but behave differently.

SQL statements which are not flagged are consistent with the ANSI standard, and such statements become portable to another ANSI-compliant database vendor system.

Figure 5-2

In this book, SQL which will normally activate the NON-ANSI Flagger will be identified using the icon *(Fig.5-2).* If the icon is shown in the chapter heading, it indicates that the contents of the entire chapter are inconsistent with the ANSI standard. If it is shown in the main body of the text , it applies to that portion of the text alone.

HELP

Teradata SQL "HELP" requests below, are used to return information about objects listed in the Teradata Data Dictionary/Directory (DD/D) which the user either owns has been granted some right of access.

SQL Syntax	Result
HELP DATABASE databasename ;	All tables views and macros in the database.
HELP USER username ;	All tables views and macros in the user.
HELP TABLE tablename;	All columns, datatypes and comments in the table.
HELP VIEW viewname;	All columns, datatypes and comments in the view.
HELP MACRO macroname;	All input parameters and datatypes for the macro.
HELP COLUMN tablename.columnname;	Data characteristics of the column.
HELP INDEX tablename;	Primary and secondary indexes on a table.
HELP STATISTICS tablename;	The date and time when statistics were last collected.
HELP SESSION;	The date, time, User, account and host collation of the current session.

For Example:

HELP DATABASE CLASSICS;

(Lists the tables, views and macros in the "Classics" database)

Table/View/Macro name	Kind	Comment
AddTitle	T	Form of Address
Author	T	Author of Story
Book	T	Published Volume
Chr	T	?
Book_Sales_History	T	?
Book_Story	T	?
Chr_Chr	T	?
Chr_Description	T	?
Event	T	?
MainEvents	M	?
Publisher	T	?
Relationship	T	?
Story	T	?
Story_Chr	T	?
Story_Story	T	?
StoryView	V	?

Kind	**Description**
T	Table
V	View
M	Macro

HELP TABLE Story;

Lists the Columns, data types and Comments (if any) for the Story table. The data types likely to result are decoded below:

Column Name	Type	Comment
Story_Number	I2	Unique story ID
Story_Name	CV	Story name
Published_Year	I2	Year published
Chapter_Quantity	I2	Number of chapters
Page_Quantity	I2	Number of pages
Header_Code	CF	Chapter heading
Author_Number	I2	Author ID

Data Type	Description
CF	CHARACTER FIXED
CV	CHARACTER VARIABLE
D	DECIMAL
DA	DATE
I	INTEGER (4 Bytes)
I1	BYTEINT (1 Byte)
I2	SMALLINT (2 Bytes)

HELP VIEW StoryView;

(Lists the Columns, data types and Comments (if any) for the Storyview View)

Column Name	Type	Comment
SNbr	?	?
SName	CF	?
Yr	?	?
Chptr	?	?
Pge	?	?
Auth	?	?

FOLDLINE and SIDETITLES

The HELP commands discussed so far have returned only two or three columns of information which could easily be accommodated on an 80 column screen. There are however a number of HELP commands which return many more columns which, presented in linear fashion, would be guaranteed to exceed the capacity of any screen or line printer. For these HELP commands we need to instruct BTEQ to display the information in vertical fashion with the column titles to the left of the data by adding the following commands to the script:

.SET FOLDLINE ON;

.SET SIDETITLES ON;

In both cases, the word 'ON' is optional. Since BTEQ is designed to operate in both foreground and background environments, it is programmed to accept report formatting instructions without any acknowledgement or response which might be misinterpreted by the client program.

HELP COLUMN Book.Book_Number;

(Lists the column information for the Book_Number column of the Book table)

```
             Column Name     Book_Number
                    Type     I2
                Nullable     Y
                  Format     -(5)9
              Max Length     2
    Decimal Total Digits     ?
Decimal Fractional Digits    ?
               Range Low     ?
              Range High     ?
               UpperCase     N
             Table/View?     T
                Indexed?     Y
                 Unique?     Y
                Primary?     P
                   Title     ?
```

HELP COLUMN Book.Book_Name;

(Lists the column information for the Book_Name column of the Book table)

```
             Column Name     Book_Name
                    Type     CV
                Nullable     Y
```

```
                  Format      X(40)
              Max Length        40
    Decimal Total Digits         ?
Decimal Fractional Digits        ?
               Range Low         ?
              Range High         ?
               UpperCase      N
             Table/View?      T
                Indexed?      N
                 Unique?      ?
                Primary?      ?
                   Title      ?
```

HELP SESSION ;

(Lists the available information for the current logon or session):

```
User Name            CLASSICS
    Account Name           DBC
      Logon Date           97/01/31
      Logon Time           09:51:13
Current DataBase           CLASSICS
       Collation           ASCII
   Character Set           ASCII
Transaction Semantics      Teradata
```

SHOW

There are three varieties of the SHOW command, which are used to display the Data Definition Language statement most recently used to create or replace the named MACRO, TABLE. or VIEW.

SHOW MACRO macroname;
SHOW TABLE tablename;
SHOW VIEW viewname;

These commands are particularly helpful to an application developer who needs to create a faithful copy of an existing table, view or macro for test purposes.To use the "SHOW MACRO", "SHOWTABLE", or "SHOW VIEW" commands, the user must either be an owner, or have some right of access to the object being queried.

SHOW TABLE Book;

```
CREATE SET TABLE CLASSICS.book ,FALLBACK ,
     NO BEFORE JOURNAL,
     NO AFTER JOURNAL
     (
      Book_Number SMALLINT,
      Book_Name VARCHAR(40) NOT CASESPECIFIC,
      Publisher_Number SMALLINT,
      Published_Date DATE,
      Price_Amount DECIMAL(5,2),
      Book_Type CHAR(1) NOT CASESPECIFIC)
UNIQUE PRIMARY INDEX( Book_Number );
```

SET	**May not contain duplicate rows**
MULTISET	**May contain duplicate rows**

SHOW VIEW StoryView;

```
CREATE VIEW StoryView
 SNbr, SName, Yr, Chptr, Pge, Hcode,Auth) AS
 SELECT Story_number
       ,Story_Name
       ,Published_Year
       ,Chapter_Quantity
       ,Page_Quantity
       ,Header_Code
       ,Author_Number
    FROM Story;
```

SHOW MACRO MainEvents;

```
REPLACE Macro MainEvents AS (
SELECT Event_Year
      ,Event
 FROM Event
 ORDER BY Event_Number;
 );
```

The precise meaning and structure of the CREATE or REPLACE commands are examined more fully in Chapter 16.

SHOW CONTROL

In addition to the SQL "SHOW" commands which access the Teradata DD/D, there is another "SHOW" command which provides useful information about BTEQ's current input and output options and limits:

SHOW CONTROL;

```
Default Maximum Byte Count              = 32734
Default Multiple Maximum Byte Count = 2048
Current Response Byte Count             = 32734
Maximum number of sessions              = 200
Maximum number of the request size  = 32000
Maximum number of columns per SELECT= 100
Maximum number of WITH clauses          = 10
Maximum number of times in a REPEAT
                                  = 2147483647
Maximum number of script files          = 30
Maximum number of lines in a TITLE  = 3
Maximum number of lines per page        = 55
Maximum string length                   = 254
Maximum number of WIDTH in a report = 254
Minimum number of WIDTH in a report = 20
Maximum number of bytes saved for
SUPPRESS, PAGEBREAK, SKIPLINE,
UNDERLINE, or SKIPDOUBLE commands,
or for &n substitutions                 = 256
```

```
.EXPORT  RESET
 IMPORT  RECORD
 LOGON   0/Classics
 RUN
 [SET] ECHOREQ               = ON
 [SET] FOLDLINE              = ON 1-100.
 [SET] FOOTING               = NULL
 [SET] FORMAT                = OFF
 [SET] FORMCHAR              = DEFAULT
 [SET] HEADING               = NULL
 [SET] INDICDATA             = OFF
 [SET] NULL                  = ?
 [SET] OMIT                  = OFF ALL
 [SET] PAGEBREAK             = OFF ALL
 [SET] PAGELENGTH            = 55
 [SET] QUIET                 = OFF
 [SET] RECORDMODE            = OFF
 [SET] RETCANCEL             = OFF
 [SET] RETLIMIT              = No Limit
 [SET] RETRY                 = ON
 [SET] RTITLE                = NULL
 [SET] SEPARATOR             = two blanks
 [SET] SESSION CHARSET       = ASCII
 [SET] SESSIONS              = 1
 [SET] SIDETITLES            = ON
.[SET] SKIPDOUBLE            = OFF ALL
 [SET] SKIPLINE              = OFF ALL
 [SET] SUPPRESS              = OFF ALL
 [SET] TDP                   = t
 [SET] TITLEDASHES           = ON
 [SET] UNDERLINE             = OFF ALL
 [SET] WIDTH                 = 75
```

The "HELP" and "SHOW" commands, thus provide the SQL application developer with a comprehensive, efficient, and user-friendly access to much of the Teradata DD/D information needed to ask the right questions - a necessary precursor to getting the right answer.

EXPLAIN

By typing the word "EXPLAIN" on front of any SQL request, the user can cause Teradata not to fully execute the request, but instead to return information about:

The estimated cost of the query in terms of computer resources.

A *relative* time estimate.

The access method considered optimum by the Teradata Optimizer.

The output of the "EXPLAIN" provides all the information needed by a performance analyst in clear, concise and unambiguous English text. Since the output is computer-generated, the phrases used tend to be mathematical in their precision, exact in their meaning, and occasionally obscure to the unprepared. Once the intricacies and eccentricities of the language are mastered however, most analysts seem to agree that the Teradata "EXPLAIN" facility is beyond any, the most useful tool in the Teradata tool box.

The true benefits of the "EXPLAIN" are more obviously demonstrated when the Optimizer, which is responsible for choosing the most efficient way of executing the SQL request, is faced with multiple possibilities and considerations, all of which are crucial to the overall performance of the enterprise. It must determine:

The most efficient order in which to join multiple tables.

The most efficient type of join to use.

Whether or not to use secondary indexes.

The reliability of the best available statistics.

The example which follows is however a simple one:

EXPLAIN SELECT * FROM Story;

```
Explanation
--------------------------------------------------
1) First, we lock a distinct CLASSICS."psuedo
   table" for read on a
     RowHash to prevent global deadlock for
CLASSICS.Story.
2) Next, we do an all-AMPs RETRIEVE step from
   CLASSICS.Story by way of an all-rows scan
   with no residual conditions into Spool 1,
   which is built locally on the AMPs. The size
   of Spool 1 is estimated to be 24 rows.  The
   estimated time for this step is 0.09 seconds.
3) Finally, we send out an END TRANSACTION step
   to all AMPs involved in processing the
   request.The contents of Spool 1 are sent back
   to the user as the result of statement 1.
   The total estimated time is 0.09 seconds.
```

TRANSLATION:

We put a READ lock on the “Story” table to prevent any other users from writing to this object while we are reading from it.

Since there is no limiting “WHERE” clause (no residual conditions), each AMP puts all of its rows from the Story table into a (temporary) table called “Spool 1”. Each AMP has its own portion of Spool 1, and the total number of rows on *all* the AMPs is estimated to be 24 rows. This operation takes 0.09 seconds.The contents of Spool 1 then are sent back to the user. The total of all consecutive listed times is 0.09 seconds (less than 1/10th of a second).

The Estimates:

Number of rows:

This is a genuine estimate based on the best statistical information (demographics) available to Optimizer at this time.

Time Estimate:

There are generally a number of possible ways of executing a given query. The Teradata Optimizer identifies a number of the most promising possible methods, and calculates a relative time estimate for each based, for the most part, on values hard-coded in the RDBMS. No account is taken of system size nor of the anticipated workload on the system when the query is executed. As a result, while the estimated time output from one EXPLAIN may be reasonably compared with the estimated time of another, these values are unlikely to reflect the true elapsed time required for the operation.

Conclusions

Aided by the powerful "HELP", "SHOW" and "EXPLAIN" functions, the full potential of the relational database structure thus becomes available to the Teradata User. With the structure of the data well understood, the SQL developer is now in a strong position to frame the "right" questions - a necessary precursor to getting the "right" answers.

Hands On Exercises

List all the tables, views and macros in the "Classics" database.

Submit the "HELP" and "SHOW" commands for the Story table.

EXPLAIN query number 2 from the exercise following Chapter 4.

How close was the estimated number of rows returned?

6 Logical Expressions

In this section we shall consider a number of logical expressions including:

Logical Operators	AND, OR and NOT
Range Test Operators	BETWEEN AND
Partial String Operators	LIKE
SET Operators	IN and NOT IN

Logical Operators - AND, OR, NOT

Ask a friend whether he or she understands the meaning of the words, "AND" and "OR", and your friend will probably be puzzled or even amused, that you would bother to ask such a question. Nevertheless, imagine the following queries:

```
SELECT Last_Name
        ,First_Name
       FROM Chr
       WHERE Last_Name = 'Cratchit'
       AND Title_Code = 'MST'
       AND Title_Code = 'MIS' ;
```

At first glance, this query might be seen to be requesting a complete list of the male and female children (Master and Miss) of the "Cratchit" family, yet no rows are returned. To a computer programmer it is clear that no individual column for any row could have two distinct values at one and the same time. Hence there are no rows where "Title_Code" has *both* values of "MST" *AND* "MIS". Everyday speech tends to be much less precise than programming logic. To examine a record for EITHER Mr. Cratchit OR Mrs. Cratchit, (on the basis of everyday conversational English), I might submit the following SQL:

```
SELECT Title_Code
      , Last_Name
      , First_Name
    FROM Chr
    WHERE Last_Name = 'Cratchit'
    AND Title_Code = 'MR '
    OR Title_Code = 'MRS' ;
```

Title_Code	Last_Name	First_Name
Mrs	Cratchit	?
Mrs	Fezziwig	?
Mrs	Dilber	?
Mrs	Tetterby	Sophia
Mrs	Taunton	?
Mrs	Marigold	?
Mr	Cratchit	Bob
Mrs	Swidger	Millie

While the results are correct by computer standards, they are probably not what I was expecting, for not only are both Mr. and Mrs. Cratchit returned, but in addition, every other character with a Title_Code of "MRS".

Another interesting exercise might be to ask a group of computer programmers to state the opposite of the color, "black "?. If your group is typical, you should receive two distinct answers, "white" and "not black". By now it should be clear that the logical use of the terms "AND", "OR" and "NOT" can still trap the unwary.

AND	All specified conditions must be met
OR	Either condition must be met.
NOT	Negates the specified condition.

AND

The following query specifies two conditions, separated by "AND", both of which must be met:

```
SELECT Book_Number
       ,Book_Name
       ,Price_Amount
      FROM Book
      WHERE Publisher_Number = 104
      AND    Book_Type = 'P';
```

Book_Number	Book_Name	Price_Amount
1008	David Copperfield	6.95
1010	Hard Times	6.95
1006	The Christmas Books	6.95
1005	The Christmas Books	4.95
1011	A Tale of Two Cities	5.95
1002	Christmas Tales	6.99
1014	The Christmas Books	?
1013	The Christmas Books	?

Response rows represent paper back books published by publisher 104.

OR

On the other hand, I might need a list of books costing less than $12.00, as well as those published by publisher 104:

```
SELECT Publisher_Number
       ,Book_Name
       ,Price_Amount
      FROM Book
      WHERE Publisher_Number = 104
      OR Price_Amount < 12.00
;
```

Publisher_Number	Book_Name	Price_Amount
104	David Copperfield	6.95
104	Hard Times	6.95
104	The Christmas Books	6.95
103	Great Expectations	5.95
104	The Christmas Books	4.95
104	A Tale of Two Cities	5.95
101	A Christmas Carol	3.99
104	Christmas Tales	6.99
103	Our Mutual Friend	10.95
104	The Christmas Books	?
104	The Christmas Books	?
104	The Christmas Books	.00

MULTIPLE AND / OR

Even when the precise meaning of both "AND" and "OR" are individually well understood, the combination of these operators in a single query can still lead to confusion. It might be logically assumed from the example below, that the user was seeking a list of books published by Publisher 103 and 104, AND costing less than $5.00, or more than $15.00.

```
SELECT Publisher_Number
       ,Book_Name
       ,Price_Amount
     FROM Book
     WHERE Publisher_Number = 103
     OR Publisher_Number       = 104
     AND Price_Amount          < 5.00
     OR Price_Amount           > 15.00
     ;
```

A quick glance at the output indicates quite **different** results:

```
Publisher_Number  Book_Name                      Price_Amount

             106 MartinChuzzlewit                      20.00
             103 Great Expectations                     5.95
             104 The Christmas Books                     .00
             103 Our Mutual Friend                     10.95
             103 A Charles Dickens Christmas           14.99
```

To understand why, it must be recognized that the operator "AND" is given precedence over "OR", and the query as written requests rows where:

```
Publisher_Number = 103
OR     Publisher_Number = 104
AND    Price_Amount < $5.00
OR     Price_Amount > $15.00
```

Like arithmetic, the order of precedence can be changed using parentheses:

```
SELECT Publisher_Number
      ,Book_Name
      ,Price_Amount
      FROM Book
      WHERE (Publisher_Number = 103
      OR Publisher_Number = 104 )
      AND (Price_Amount < 5.00
      OR Price_Amount > 15.00)
      ;
```

This time only 1 row is found where the publisher is 103 or 104 on the one hand, and the price is less than $5 or greater than $15, on the other:

```
Publisher_Number  Book_Name                      Price_Amount

             104  The Christmas Books                    .00
```

NOT

The "NOT" operator returns the rows which do not meet the specified condition:

Both of the examples below deliver the same result - books *other than* those published by publisher 104:

```
SELECT Publisher_Number
      ,Book_Name
      ,Price_Amount
    FROM Book
    WHERE Publisher_Number NOT = 104 ;
```

OR

```
SELECT Publisher_Number
      ,Book_Name
      ,Price_Amount
    FROM Book
    WHERE NOT Publisher_Number  = 104 ;
```

```
Publisher_Number  Book_Name                      Price_Amount

             106  Martin Chuzzlewit                     20.00
             103  Great Expectations                     5.95
             103  Our Mutual Friend                     10.95
             101  A Christmas Carol                      3.99
             103  A Charles Dickens Christmas           14.99
```

Although the expression, "Where NOT Publisher = 104", might at first glance seem to be somewhat tortured English, this particular syntactical form of the "NOT" provides an incredibly simple solution to the occasionally overwhelming problem of determining the true *reciprocal* of a complex expression.

We might, for example, wish to capture all the rows from a table which qualify for a specific condition and process them in some way, before selecting the remainder of the rows which do not qualify. While it is a relatively simple matter to select the rows which qualify for the conditions:

```
WHERE (Publisher_Number = 103
OR Publisher_Number = 104)
AND (Price_Amount < 5.00
OR Price_Amount > 15.00);
```

identifying the remainder (where the Publisher_Number is *NEITHER* 103 *NOR* 104 *AND* the price amount is between $5 and $15) is more difficult. Nevertheless, by the simple expedient of inserting the word, "NOT" immediately following the keyword "WHERE", and enclosing the entire original select condition between an extra set of parentheses, we can achieve a completely accurate result with an absolute minimum of effort:

```
WHERE NOT ((Publisher_Number = 103
OR Publisher_Number = 104 )
AND (Price_Amount < 5.00
OR Price_Amount > 15.00));
```

Range Test Operators - BETWEEN AND

The "BETWEEN" operator is used to select rows which have a column or columns for which the value falls within a certain (inclusive) range. To select those books which fall within the price range of $7.00 or more but not greater than $15.00:

```
SELECT Publisher_Number
    ,Book_Name
    ,Price_Amount
FROM Book
WHERE Price_Amount
BETWEEN 7.00 AND 15.00
;
```

Publisher Number	Book Name	Price Amount
103	Our Mutual Friend	10.95
103	A Charles Dickens Christmas	14.99
104	The Christmas Books	13.50

The "BETWEEN" range test operator can also be used with alpha characters. In the example below we are searching for last names which are not less than "r" nor greater than the single character "s":

```
SELECT Last_Name
      ,First_Name
    FROM Chr
    WHERE Last_Name BETWEEN 'r' AND 's';
```

Last_Name	First_Name
Redlaw	?

There are two things of interest here:

"Scrooge" (which is greater than a single letter "s") is not returned.

Even though the search criteria was between lower-case "r" and lower-case "s", "Redlaw", which begins with an upper-case "R" was returned.

ANSI standards mandate that comparisons, by default are "CASESPECIFIC". In order to conform to this requirement, but still support pre-existing applications, Teradata introduced a column-level constraint of "NOT CASESPECIFIC" as an option for the "CREATE TABLE" statement. (*See Chapter 16*). The Last_Name column of the "Chr" table is therefore defined as "NON CASESPECIFIC", and this defines the comparison.

In order to render this query case-sensitive, we need to add the "CASESPECIFIC" modifier:

```
SELECT Last_Name
        ,First_Name
        FROM Chr
        WHERE Last_Name(CASESPECIFIC)
        BETWEEN 'r' AND 's'
        ;
```

This expression now behaves like the ANSI default, and since all last names in this table begin with an upper-case character, returns no rows.

The CASESPECIFIC modifier for the CREATE TABLE statement (Chapter 16) was introduced in Teradata Version 2 Release 2, and it is likely that tables created in earlier releases of the RDBMS have not yet been modified to reflect this change. As a result, comparisons with the character columns of such tables will now, by default, become CASESPECIFIC.

The UPPER Function

The UPPER function permits ANSI compliant case blind comparisons between character strings or expressions, by logically converting one or both the strings or expressions to uppercase.

For Example, the first letter of words such as "of" or "the" in titles is frequently relegated to lower case. As a result, a case-specific search of "A Tale Of Two Cities" would not locate "A Tale of Two Cities". This difficulty is avoided by making the comparison in upper case:

```
SELECT Book_Number
        ,Book_Name
        FROM Book
        WHERE UPPER(Book_Name) =
        'A TALE OF TWO CITIES'
        ;
```

```
Book_Number Book_Name

           1011 A Tale of Two Cities
```

Partial String Operator - LIKE

The "LIKE" command is, in a sense, a range test command of character data. It is used in the selection of rows based on the existence of a string or partial string value in a column.

The position of the string within the column value is specified based on the position of the percent character ("%"), which is used to denote zero, one or more other characters in the string. Thus, searching for 'Scrooge':

Expression	Meaning
LIKE 'sc%'	Begins with (non casespecific) 'sc'.
LIKE '%sc'	Ends with 'sc'
LIKE '%sc%'	'sc' occurs at the beginning, end or somewhere else within the string.
LIKE '__ro%'	Contains 'ro in the 3rd and 4th positions.
LIKE '%g_'	Contains 'g' in the next to last position.

Example:

This query looks for the occurrence of the characters "er", upper, lower or mixed case, anywhere in the Last_Name (The percentage sign ("%") indicates possible characters in that position'):

```
SELECT Last_Name
       , First_Name
       FROM Chr
       WHERE Last_Name LIKE '%ER%'
       ;
```

```
Last_Name          First_Name

Derrick            John
Swidger            Millie
Dilber             ?
Tetterby           Dolphus
etc.
```

A similar query, this time "CASESPECIFIC", produces no rows:

```
SELECT Last_Name
       , First_Name
       FROM Chr
       WHERE Last_Name (CASESPECIFIC)
       LIKE '%ER%';
```

LIKE with ANY, ALL or SOME

The qualifiers, "ANY", "ALL" or "SOME" provide us with the ability to perform partial string searches based on multiple values. "ANY" and "SOME" are synonyms, and become simply a matter of preference:

ALL	String must contain ALL values.
ANY or SOME	String must contain any or all values.

Example:

Find all those characters whose last_name contains the letters "er" and "sw". (The following query returns everyone in the "Swidger" family):

```
SELECT Last_Name
       , First_Name
   FROM Chr
   WHERE Last_Name LIKE ALL ('%ER%','%SW%');
```

The ESCAPE feature of LIKE

ANSI defines the specific characters, underscore (_) and percent (%) as wildcard characters in the LIKE expression, and this effectively precludes their use in the search pattern itself. A search which used the string "0.0%" or "Last_Name" as a pattern for the LIKE expression would fail with a syntax error.

ANSI does however allow the specification of a single alternative escape character in addition to the pattern string, using the following syntax:

WHERE *column* [NOT] LIKE *pattern* [ESCAPE *escapecharacter*]

Notwithstanding the 'escape' function, the underscore and percent wild-card characters do not change their meaning. However if a percent or an underscore is required as a literal in the search pattern, it must be preceded by the escape character.

For example, the following expressions will all result in a positive match and will return the value 'TRUE':

```
SELECT 'TRUE'
WHERE ' Total Sales 0.0%' LIKE '%0.0&%%'
ESCAPE '&';

SELECT 'TRUE'
WHERE 'Last_Name' LIKE '%Last$_%'
ESCAPE '$' ;

SELECT 'TRUE'
WHERE  'Last_Name' LIKE '__stX_%'
ESCAPE 'X';
```

In a left-to-right scan of the pattern string the following rules apply:

> Until an instance of the escape pattern occurs, the percent and underscore do not change their meaning.
>
> When a character which is defined as the escape character is encountered, immediately followed by another instance of the escape character, the two character sequence is treated as if it were a single character literal, and not an escape character.
>
> When an escape character is immediately followed by an underscore or a percent character, the sequence is treated as if it were a single underscore or percent character rather than a wild card.
>
> When an escape character is not immediately followed by an underscore, a percent, or another instance of itself, an error is reported.

The SET Operators - IN / NOT IN

The SET operators provide an efficient alternative to multiple "AND", or multiple "OR" statements. For example, the (corrected) query seen earlier:

```
SELECT Last_Name
        , First_Name
        FROM Chr
        WHERE Last_Name = 'Cratchit'
        AND (Title_Code = 'MR '
        OR Title_Code = 'MRS')
;
```

could just as easily have been written as:

```
SELECT Last_Name
      , First_Name
    FROM Chr
    WHERE Last_Name = 'Cratchit'
    AND Title_Code IN ('MR ','MRS');
```

Notice that the equality ("=") condition is replaced by the word 'IN' (since no single column can have multiple values at any one time), and the query returns rows which have *either* 'MR ' or 'MRS' in the Title_Code column.

Any SQL statement which includes an 'OR' condition forces the Teradata Optimizer to perform a full table scan of the data. The SET operators, on the other hand, provide the Optimizer with a possibly more efficient alternative. As a result, not only does the use of the "SET" operator result in a syntactically shorter query, but it might also result in a significant performance improvement.

To select all members of the Cratchit family, other than Mr & Mrs. Cratchit:

```
SELECT Last_Name
      , First_Name
    FROM Chr
    WHERE Last_Name = 'Cratchit'
    AND Title_Code NOT IN ('MR ','MRS');
```

or even:

```
SELECT Last_Name
      , First_Name
    FROM Chr
    WHERE Last_Name = 'Cratchit'
    AND NOT Title_Code IN ('MR ','MRS');
```

The ability to use an equality condition with a "SET" command is restored with the addition of the (synonymous) "ANY" or "SOME" operators to the syntax. "ALL" is not prohibited, but since a single column could not have multiple values at one and the same time, the expression becomes meaningless.

```
SELECT Last_Name
      , First_Name
    FROM Chr
    WHERE Last_Name = 'Cratchit'
    AND Title_Code = ANY ('MR ','MRS');
```

Hands-on Exercises:

From this point on, the amount of typing required for the hands-on exercises will begin to increase substantially. Readers are therefore strongly encouraged, if they are not already doing so, to type their SQL queries to a file and submit the file to BTEQ in "batch" mode (*See Chapter 3*).

Select the Story_Number and Story_Name for each Story where the Story_Name contains the word "Christmas" (not case specific). Order the report by Story_Name.

List the major events in the life of Charles Dickens from the Events table which occurred between the years 1824 and 1830 inclusive. Order the report by Event_Year. (You might find it helpful to "SHOW" the "Event" table for the column names).

7 Computations and Conversions

In this section we shall examine how SQL handles arithmetic functions including:

Data Types supported by the Teradata Database.

Arithmetic Functions and Operators.

Comparison Operators.

Computed Values.

Date Handling.

Data Conversions and Comparisons.

Data Types

Data types supported by the Teradata Database *(Fig. 7-1),* fall into four major categories:

Numeric.
Character.
Byte.
Graphic.

DATA TYPE	RANGE OF VALUES FROM	TO	DESCRIPTION	EXAMPLE
BYTEINT	-128	+127	1 byte whole number	Author_Number
SMALLINT	-32,768	+32,767	2 byte whole number	Area_Code
INTEGER	-2,147,438,648	+2,147,483,647	4 byte whole number	Character_Number
DECIMAL(m,n) NUMERIC(m,n)	Maximum 18 significant digits		Decimal number	Price_Amount
REAL	IEE Floating Point		A value in sign/ magnitude form. Exponent from *E-308 to E+307* *8-bytes*	
DOUBLE PRECISION	IEE Floating Point Same as FLOAT.			
FLOAT(n)	IEE Floating Point			
FLOAT	IEE Floating Point			
DATE	Special type of INTEGER		4 Bytes FORMAT YYMMDD	Birth_Date

	DESCRIPTION	LENGTH	EXAMPLE
CHAR(n)	Fixed length character	Maximum 32,000 bytes	Last_Name
VARCHAR(n)	Variable length character		First_Name
LONG VARCHAR	Variable length character		
BYTE	Fixed length binary		
VARBYTE	Variable length binary		
GRAPHIC	Fixed length 2-byte graphic		
VARGRAPHIC	Variable length 2-byte graphic		

Figure 7-1

In Version2, Release 2 of its RDBMS, Teradata has announced support of four new data types to comply with the ANSI standard:

NUMERIC.
FLOAT(n).
REAL.
DOUBLE PRECISION.

Of these, NUMERIC is synonymous with the DECIMAL data type. FLOAT(n) REAL and DOUBLE PRECISION are largely treated as synonyms of the pre-existing 8-byte IEEE FLOAT data type, except that FLOAT(n) will permit users to specify the degree of precision required

Any value based on the numeric or character data types may be freely converted to any other numeric or character data type. Data conversions to or from byte or graphic data types are not permitted.

Arithmetic Operators

The following SQL arithmetic operators are provided in the order of precedence. Notice that since parentheses are evaluated first, they can be effectively used to change the default protocol.

Operator	Meaning
( )	Parentheses - evaluated first.
**	Exponentiation.
*	Multiply.
/	Divide.
MOD	Modulo (integer remainder).
+	Add.
-	Subtract.

In addition to the arithmetic functions listed above, Teradata supports a number of computational functions:

Operator	Meaning
ABS(argument)	Absolute value.
EXP(argument)	Raises n to the power of the argument (n ** argument).
LOG(argument)	Base 10 logarithm.
LN(argument)	Natural logarithm.
SQRT(argument)	Square root.
NULLIFZERO(arg)	Returns NULL if argument is zero.
ZEROIFNULL(arg)	Returns zero if argument is NULL.

Most of the computational functions above are used primarily for scientific applications, and seldom in a normal commercial environment. The Teradata enhancements, "NULLIFZERO" and "ZEROIFNULL" are widely used over the entire spectrum, and will be covered at greater length in Chapters 9 and 10.

Computed Values

The example below calculates the cost of 12 copies of book number 1002, including 8% sales tax:

```
SELECT Book_Number
       ,Book_Name
       ,Price_Amount * 12 * 1.08
       FROM Book
       WHERE Book_Number = 1002;
```

```
Book_Number Book_Name         Price_Amount*12)*1 08)
       1002 Christmas Tales                  90.5904
```

In this example a decimal (Price_Amount) is multiplied by an integer (12), and the result is incremented by 8 percent. The result of the calculation is carried to 4 places of decimals. While the successful creation of a simple BTEQ report probably does not require the application developer to be aware of the precise format of the numeric response, other less user-friendly program interfaces might.

Arithmetic Data Conversions

The table below demonstrates that whenever a decimal value is involved in any arithmetic function, the result is an 18-digit decimal:

Multiplicand	Multiplier	Product
BYTEINT	DECIMAL(n,m)	DECIMAL(18,m)
SMALLINT	DECIMAL(n,m)	DECIMAL(18,m)
INTEGER	DECIMAL(n,m)	DECIMAL(18,m)
DECIMAL(n,m)	DECIMAL(n,m)	DECIMAL(18,2m)

Dividend	Divisor	Result
INTEGER	DECIMAL(m,n)	DECIMAL(18,n) (rounded)
DECIMAL(m,n)	DECIMAL(o,p)	DECIMAL(18,q)

where q is indeterminate, but the final result totals 18 digits.

DATE, TIME and USER

Teradata has implemented three important system variables in a manner somewhat inconsistent with ANSI standards:

Variable Name	Data Type	Description
DATE	DATE	Current date as INTEGER (Format YYYMMDD).
TIME	FLOAT	Current time as FLOAT (Format HH:MM:SS).
USER	CHARACTER	User ID of current logon.

Examples:

```
SELECT DATE;

DATE
97/07/31
```

```
SELECT TIME;

TIME
10:55:15
```

```
SELECT USER;

USER
CLASSICS
```

MODULO Operator

The MODULO (MOD) operator returns the remainder of an integer division. *For Example:*

The "Story" table has a primary key, "Story_Number", defined as an INTEGER value, which increments by one for each new story. This provides us with a useful means of building a test sample of a known percentage of rows.

For example, if our test calls for 20% of the rows, we might select those rows where the primary key value MOD 5 is equal to any value between 0 and 4. The result is a fully representative sample drawn from all parts of the table, including the anticipated exception data at either end:

```
SELECT Story_Number
       ,Story_Name
       FROM Story
       WHERE Story_Number MOD 5 = 1
       ;
```

```
Story_Number  Story_Name

         116  A Tale of Two Cities
         101  A Christmas Carol
         106  What Christmas Is As We Get Older
```

Dates

In anticipation of the approaching millennium, Teradata implemented its DATE data type as a 4-byte integer, constructed in the following manner:

(YEAR - 1900 * 10,000) + (MONTH * 100) + DAY.

Examples:

December 31st, **1999**, the date is stored internally as:

1999 - 1900 * 10,000	=	990000 +
12 * 100		1200 +
31		31
		991231

Dates for years prior to 1900 are stored as **negative** values:

December 31st, **1899** is stored internally as:

1899 - 1900 * 10,000	=	-10000 +
12 * 100		1200 +
31		31
		-11231

December 31st, **2099** will be stored internally as:

2099 - 1900 * 10,000	=	1000000 +
12 * 100		1200 +
31		31
		1001231

While this might initially prove disconcerting to the more conservative of readers, it should be remembered that:

Internal storage is unrelated to output format.
Integer arithmetic is both efficient and economical.
Century years are handled with ease.

Nevertheless date arithmetic (Teradata-style) is somewhat unusual.

If we assume today's date to be *April 30th, 1997*:

Description	**SQL expression:**	**Sample**
The date 30 days from today	DATE + 30;	970530
The date 30 days ago	DATE - 30	970331
A person's *approximate* age	(DATE - Birth_Date) / 365	39
The Current Year	DATE/10000	97
The Current Month and Day	DATE MOD 10000	0430
The Current Month	(DATE MOD 10000) / 100	04
The Current Day of the Month	DATE MOD 100	30

A date minus a date results in an integer value of the number of days between the two dates.

The EXTRACT Statement

The following functions are ANSI-compliant in terms of syntax, but the *expression* value must be a valid *Teradata* date or time:

EXTRACT (YEAR FROM *expression*)
EXTRACT (MONTH FROM *expression*)
EXTRACT (DAY FROM *expression*)
EXTRACT (HOUR FROM *expression*)
EXTRACT (MINUTE FROM *expression*)
EXTRACT (SECOND FROM *expression*)

Teradata enjoys a number of advantages from its innovative implementation of the "DATE" data type, and day-to-day calculations are handled efficiently and well. On the other hand, accurate month-to-month calculations become somewhat more complex.

For this reason, Teradata has added the ANSI-like function, "ADD_MONTHS" to address this issue.

ADD_MONTHS

Teradata's "ADD_MONTHS" function is not ANSI-standard, but is the bridge toward the ANSI Date Time capability planned for the next major software release. It provides the ability to calculate a future calendar date by adding a specified number of months. The syntax is in the form:

ADD_MONTHS(*expression, expression*)

where the first expression must have a valid date data type and the second an integer value.

Example:

SELECT ADD_MONTHS (DATE,3);

```
ADD_MONTHS(DATE,3)

1997-10-30
```

In adding months, if the target month has fewer days than the day value of the first argument, the last valid value for that YEAR and MONTH is returned:

For Example, assume that the column c1 is defined as a DATE data type, and has a value of 970131. To calculate the date 1 month in the future using the ADD_MONTHS function then becomes a simple matter:

SELECT ADD_MONTHS (c1,1);

```
ADD_MONTHS(c1,1)
      1997-02-28
```

DATA TYPE CONVERSIONS

The Teradata Database permits conversions between numeric and character data types by simply providing the desired data type name in parentheses immediately following the expression:

Examples:

SELECT 12345.70 (INTEGER);

```
12345.70 (INTEGER)
             12345        (truncated)
```

```
SELECT 12345.70 (DECIMAL(5,0));

12345.70 (DECIMAL(5,0))
                        12346 (rounded)

SELECT  Book_Number
          , Book_Name (char(6))
          , Price_Amount
        FROM Book
        WHERE Book_Number = 1011;

Book_Number Book_Name    Price_Amount

      1011  A Tale               5.95
```

The CAST Function

The ANSI syntax, supported by the Teradata Database, for data type conversion is:

CAST (*expression*) AS *datatype.*

The examples above converted to ANSI syntax:

```
SELECT CAST(12345.70  AS INTEGER);

CAST (12345.70 AS INTEGER)
                          12345      (truncated)

SELECT CAST(12345.70  AS DECIMAL(5,0));

CAST(12345.70 AS DECIMAL(5,0))
                                12346      (rounded)
```

```
SELECT Book_Number
    , CAST(Book_Name AS CHAR(6))
    , Price_Amount
  FROM Book
  WHERE Book_Number = 1011;
```

```
Book_Number CAST(Book_Name AS CHAR(6)) Price_Amount
       1011 A Tale                             5.95
```

DATA TYPE COMPARISONS

Teradata permits free and unspecified comparison between values of any two different data types (except byte and graphic) provided the data itself is valid for both data types being compared. *For Example:*

Assume Event_Year is defined as CHAR(4) with a value of '1824', and is being compared to a numeric value of 1824, the following SQL query will succeed:

```
SELECT Event
  FROM Event
  WHERE Event_Year =  1824
  AND Author_Number = 101;
```

```
Event

Works in blacking warehouse
Father imprisoned for debt
Attends Wellington House Academy
```

Provided 'Event_Year' contains numeric characters, Teradata converts the characters to numeric and makes the comparison directly. *ANSI syntax,* on the other hand, requires the use of the "CAST" function:

```
SELECT Event
        FROM Event
        WHERE CAST(Event_Year AS INTEGER)
                = 1824
        AND Author_Number = 101;
```

While both the Teradata and newly implemented ANSI syntax will continue to be supported side-by-side for some time to come, it is recommended that new applications adopt the more standard ANSI syntax over Teradata right from the start, and more mature applications adopt the new standards whenever possible and wherever reasonable.

Hands On Exercises

SELECT the current DATE, TIME and USER.

SELECT the calendar date 6 months from today.

Select approximately 10 percent of the rows from the "CHR" table. Limit the Last_Name to 10 characters and the First_Name to 7.

8 Titles, Formats and Names

Up to this point, we have concentrated our efforts in selecting the rows and columns needed to answer our business questions, but have given little thought to the aesthetics of its ultimate presentation. This section considers a number of ways to override the BTEQ defaults, and enhance not only the resultant report, but also clarify the SQL request.

The TITLE Function

Assigns a title to a column and overrides the default.

Can 'stack' up to 3 lines using '//' as a separator.

Is right justified for numeric data or left justified for character data.

Is enclosed in single quotes and may include spaces and/or special characters.

For Example:

```
SELECT Story_Number
                    (TITLE 'Story//Number')
        ,Story_Name
                    TITLE 'Book Name')
        ,Published_Year
                    (TITLE 'Year//First//Published')
        FROM Story;
```

```
Story    Book Name                           Year
Number                                       First
                                         Published
______   _________________________       _________

   105   A Christmas Tree                     1859
   101   A Christmas Carol                    1843
   117   The Holly Tree                       1849
   109   Our Mutual Friend                    1865
   115    Hard Times                          1854
  (Partial list)
```

The NAMED Function

Unlike the TITLE function which is purely an output formatting option, the NAMED function:

> Temporarily renames an expression within a single statement SQL request.
>
> Makes the SQL more readable.
>
> Is not enclosed in quotes, but is subject to the normal SQL naming convention *(see Chapter 2)*.
>
> Becomes the new default column heading, subordinate to "TITLE".

For Example:

```
SELECT Book_Name          (TITLE 'Book')
       ,Price_Amount      (NAMED Sale,
                          TITLE ' Sale//Price')
       ,Sale * 8/100      (NAMED Tax)
       ,Sale + Tax        (TITLE 'Total')
      FROM Book
      WHERE Book_Number  = 1010;
```

```
Book             Sale       Tax      Total
                 Price
____________     _______    ______   _______

Hard Times       6.95       0.56     7.51
```

The FORMAT Function

In addition to controlling the appearance of the report headings, we generally need to specify how the data itself is to be presented. Currency values, for example will often require dollar signs, commas and decimal points. Character values may need to be standardized in length, without subjecting the computer system to the expense of a full data conversion. Dates may need some presentation other than the default two digit year, month and day separated by slashes.

Teradata SQL supports a large number of format characters:

$	Fixed or floating dollar sign.
9	Decimal digit - not suppressed.
Z	Zero-suppressed decimal digit.
,	Comma - insert where specified.
.	Decimal point or period.
-	Dash - insert where specified.
/	Slash - insert where specified.
%	Percent - insert where specified.
X	Character - each 'X' represents one character.
B	Blank data - insert a space where specified.

Currency

For a fixed position dollar sign, a single ($) character occurs in the format pattern in the position required.

```
.SET FOLDLINE ON;
.SET SIDETITLES;

SELECT Book_Name
       , 1.99 * 498
              (NAMED Cost, FORMAT '$zz,zz9.99')
       , Price_Amount  * 498
              (NAMED Sale, FORMAT '$zz,zz9.99')
       , Sale * 8/100
              (NAMED Tax) (FORMAT '$zz,zz9.99')
       ,Sale + Tax
              (TITLE 'Total') (FORMAT '$zz,zz9.99')
       , Cost * 100/ Sale
              (TITLE 'Profit', FORMAT 'zz9.99%')
FROM Book
WHERE Book_Number = 1001;
```

```
Book_Name   A Christmas Carol
Cost                  $991.02
Sale                $1,987.02
Tax                   $158.96
Total               $2,145.98
Profit                 49.87%
```

The zero-suppress character (z) prevents leading zeros from printing.

The comma (,) is printed only if a significant digit appears on its left.

The numeric character (9), forces a numeric to print in that position even if it is zero.

The percent sign (%) is printed where indicated.

If multiple dollar signs are substituted for the zero-suppress character, the result will be a floating dollar sign to the immediate left of the left-most significant digit:

```
.SET FOLDLINE ON;
.SET SIDETITLES;

SELECT Book_Name
       , 1.99 * 498
            (NAMED Cost, FORMAT '$$$,$$9.99')
       , Price_Amount  * 498
            (NAMED Sale, FORMAT '$$$,$$9.99')
       , Sale * 8/100
            (NAMED Tax) (FORMAT '$$$,$$9.99')
       ,Sale + Tax
            (TITLE 'Total') (FORMAT '$$$,$$9.99')
       ,Cost * 100/ Sale
            (TITLE 'Profit', FORMAT 'zz9%')
     FROM Book
     WHERE Book_Number = 1001;
```

```
Book_Name   A Christmas Carol
Cost           $991.02
Sale         $1,987.02
Tax            $158.96
Total        $2,145.98
Profit       50%
```

When a floating dollar sign is specified, the format field must be defined at least one byte larger than the largest value it needs to accommodate, otherwise an overflow, shown as a string of asterisks, will result. Notice also that elimination of the decimal point in a format will cause the result to be rounded.

Other Format Examples:

FORMAT Pattern	Input Data	Result
'999999'	1234	001234
'999'	1234	* * *
'999-9999'	1234567	123-4567
'99-99-99'	123456	12-34-56

FORMAT Pattern	Input Data	Result
'999B999'	123456	123 456
'X'	John	J
'XXX'	Ms	Ms (+ space)
'X(8)'	April	April (+3 spaces)

DATE Formats

FORMAT Pattern	Input Data	Result
'YY/MM/DD'	970205	97/02/05
'MM/DD/YY'	970205	02/05/97
'DDBMMMBYYYY'	970205	05 Feb 1997
'mmmbddbyy'	970205	Feb 05 97
'MM-DD-YY'	970205	02-05-97
'DDDYY'	970205	03697 (Julian)
'YYDDD'	970205	97036 (Julian)

Example:

```
SELECT Last_Name
       ,First_Name          (FORMAT 'X', TITLE 'FI')
       ,Birth_Date          (FORMAT 'MMMBDD',
          TITLE 'Birth//Day', NAMED BirthDay)
       ,Birth_Date          (FORMAT 'YYYY',
                            TITLE 'Year//Born')
       ,Died_Date           (FORMAT 'YYYY',
                            TITLE 'Year//Died')
      FROM AUTHOR
      ORDER BY BirthDay ;
```

```
Last_Name   FI   Birth        Year   Year
                 Day          Born   Died
__________  __   _______      ____   ____

Austen      J    Dec 16       1775   1817
Dickens     C    Feb 07       1812   1870
```

The use of the FORMAT to limit the output of the First_Name to a single character is considerably more computer-efficient than forcing a data conversion to CHAR(1).

Any combination of DATE formats, character or numeric may be used in any sequence.

Despite the requested sort by Birthday, Jane Austen, whose birthday is in December, appears before Dickens, who was born in June. This is because a FORMAT pattern is invisible to the SQL itself and only affects the output. As a result the rows are (correctly) sorted by the column value or expression requested (the full Birth_Date).

To order this report just by the month and day of Birthday, we must sort, not by Birth_Date, but by the Birth´_Date MOD 10000. (See the previous Chapter).

```
SELECT Last_Name
       ,First_Name
                   (FORMAT 'X', TITLE 'FI')
       ,Birth_Date (FORMAT 'MMMBDD',
                   TITLE 'Birth//Day', NAMED BirthDay)
       ,Birth_Date
                   (FORMAT 'YYYY', TITLE 'Year//Born')
       ,Died_Date
                   (FORMAT 'YYYY', TITLE 'Year//Died')
     FROM AUTHOR
     ORDER BY BirthDay MOD 10000 ;
```

```
Last_Name    FI   Birth       Year  Year
__________   __   Day___      Born  Died

Dickens      C    Feb 07      1812  1870
Austen       J    Dec 16      1775  1817
```

Having thus acquired the skills to accurately define the information we need and present it in useful fashion, our next compelling need is to put that information to use in analyzing present trends and deriving future expectations. We need to calculate maximums, minimums and averages. We need to count our potential customers and determine the extent of the market for our products. We need the ability to calculate aggregates.

Hands On Exercise

A customer has ordered 50 copies of Book # 1008, at the regular price less 20% discount. State tax must be charged at 8 ½ percent. Prepare a statement with today's date as the order date in the following format. You will need to initialize BTEQ as:

```
.SET FOLDLINE ON;
.SET SIDETITLES;
```

Column	Format
Book Name	Fixed Character 20.
Order Date	MM/DD/YYYY.
Regular Price	Floating Dollar with commas, decimals and zero suppress.
Order Quantity	Zero suppress.
Discount Rate	Zero suppress and Percent sign.
Discount	Floating Dollar with commas, decimals and zero suppress.
Tax	Floating Dollar with commas, decimals and zero suppress.
Total Due	Floating Dollar with commas, decimals and zero suppress

9 Aggregates and Totals

While a substantial list of carefully organized detail information may be of significant interest to decision makers, it is seldom presented without some form of statistical summary information. These statistics may be a simple count or total, or even perhaps a sophisticated trend analysis. Either way, it is a rare report indeed which provides information on more than a single data record and does not attempt to calculate some form of:

COUNT	Total number of records.
SUM	Total of values.
AVERAGE (AVG)	Middle-of-the-road value.
MAXIMUM(MAX)	Highest value.
MINIMUM(MIN)	Lowest value.

These are known as "aggregates", and represent powerful functions of SQL. Aggregates provide single line answers and ignore NULLs (missing or unknown values - *see Chapter 10*).

With reference to the BOOK_SALES_HISTORY table (*Fig. 9-1*), the following request asks for:

The total number of sales.
The total number of books sold.
The largest number of books.
The smallest number of books.
The average number of books per sale transaction.

for all sales during the month of December ((Sales_Date MOD 10000) / 100 = 12):

BOOK_SALES_HISTORY
Description: Sales by Book

Book Number	Sales Date	Sales Quantity
PK,USI		
FK		
NUPI		
1001	961215	1
1009	961215	
1001	961220	2
1001	961210	1
1005	961010	5
1007	961220	3
1012	961205	4
1005	961215	1
1011	961215	1
1011	961105	1
1012	961215	3

Figure 9-1

```
SELECT COUNT(Sales_Quantity)        (TITLE 'COUNT')
      ,SUM (Sales_Quantity)         (TITLE 'SUM')
      ,MAX (Sales_Quantity)         (TITLE 'MAX')
      ,MIN (Sales_Quantity)         (TITLE 'MIN')
      ,AVG (Sales_Quantity)         (TITLE 'AVG')
FROM Book_Sales_History
WHERE (Sales_Date MOD 10000) / 100 = 12;
```

COUNT	SUM	MAX	MIN	AVG
8	14	4	1	2

Notice that while the COUNT or *total number of qualifying rows* is 8, aggregates produce a single row response.

To discover this information on a per book basis, one possibility might be to submit one SQL request for each book.

For Example:

```
SELECT COUNT(Sales_Quantity)        (TITLE 'COUNT')
        ,SUM (Sales_Quantity)       (TITLE 'SUM')
        ,MAX (Sales_Quantity)       (TITLE 'MAX')
        ,MIN (Sales_Quantity)       (TITLE 'MIN')
        ,AVG (Sales_Quantity)       (TITLE 'AVG')
       FROM Book_Sales_History
       WHERE (Sales_Date MOD 10000) / 100 = 12
       AND Book_Number = 1001;
```

COUNT	SUM	MAX	MIN	AVG
3	4	2	1	1

```
SELECT COUNT(Sales_Quantity)        (TITLE 'COUNT')
        ,SUM (Sales_Quantity)       (TITLE 'SUM')
        ,MAX (Sales_Quantity)       (TITLE 'MAX')
        ,MIN (Sales_Quantity)       (TITLE 'MIN')
        ,AVG (Sales_Quantity)       (TITLE 'AVG')
       FROM Book_Sales_History
       WHERE (Sales_Date MOD 10000) / 100 = 12
       AND Book_Number = 1012 ;
```

COUNT	SUM	MAX	MIN	AVG
2	5	4	1	2

Not only does this require the user to know what books were sold ahead of time, but building and submitting a sizable number of such requests would quickly prove tedious. What is clearly needed, is a syntax option which permits me to SELECT the required statistics FOR EACH book sold during the month of December.

Such a powerful option does indeed exist - the "*GROUP BY*".

GROUP BY

The following example requests the same statistics with *a single SQL statement* by selecting aggregates and non-aggregates in the same request. (It might help to think of "GROUP BY" as meaning "FOR EACH"):

```
SELECT Book_Number
       ,COUNT(Sales_Quantity)       (TITLE 'COUNT')
       ,SUM (Sales_Quantity)        (TITLE 'SUM')
       ,MAX (Sales_Quantity)        (TITLE 'MAX')
       ,MIN (Sales_Quantity)        (TITLE 'MIN')
       ,AVG (Sales_Quantity)        (TITLE 'AVG')
       FROM Book_Sales_History
       WHERE (Sales_Date MOD 10000) / 100 = 12
       GROUP BY 1;
```

Book_Number	COUNT	SUM	MAX	MIN	AVG
1012	2	5	4	1	2
1001	3	4	2	1	1
1007	1	3	3	3	3
1011	1	1	1	1	1
1005	1	1	1	1	1

Column names of aggregated values are always preceded by such expressions as, "AVG", "COUNT", "SUM", "MIN", "MAX" etc. and are enclosed in parentheses. While aggregates always deliver a single line response, non-aggregates may result in multiple rows. Hence, there is a potential conflict.

Mixed Aggregates and Non-Aggregates

Whenever there is a combination of aggregate and non-aggregate expressions in a single SELECT, and there is no "GROUP BY " clause, Teradata will terminate with the message:

> *ERROR: 3504 Selected non-aggregate values must be part of the associated group .*

In the example above, Book_Number is a non-aggregated column and a SELECT of books sold during the month of December would ordinarily yield 5 rows. Every other expression in the example is an aggregate. Aggregates always deliver a single line response. Since there is a *mixture* of aggregates and non-aggregates in the same SELECT, the 3504 error message is avoided by:

> The existence of the GROUP BY clause.
>
> The inclusion in the GROUP BY clause of *every* non-aggregate in the SELECT.

"GROUP BY" does not imply "ORDER BY". It is therefore quite rare for any SQL expression which includes a "GROUP BY" clause, not to also include an "ORDER BY":

```
SELECT Book_Number
        ,COUNT(Sales_Quantity)      (TITLE 'COUNT')
        ,SUM (Sales_Quantity)       (TITLE 'SUM')
        ,MAX (Sales_Quantity)       (TITLE 'MAX')
        ,MIN (Sales_Quantity)       (TITLE 'MIN')
        ,AVG (Sales_Quantity)       (TITLE 'AVG')
        FROM Book_Sales_History
        WHERE (Sales_Date MOD 10000) / 100 = 12
        GROUP BY 1;
```

Book_Number	COUNT	SUM	MAX	MIN	AVG
1001	3	4	2	1	1
1005	1	1	1	1	1
1007	1	3	3	3	3
1011	1	1	1	1	1
1012	2	5	4	1	2

GROUP BY, WHERE and ORDER BY

The "WHERE" clause eliminates some rows from the output *before* "GROUP BY" groups them, and "ORDER BY" orders them.

For Example, we are just interested in the "Christmas" books:

```
SELECT  Book_Number
        ,COUNT(Sales_Quantity)     (TITLE 'COUNT')
        ,SUM (Sales_Quantity)      (TITLE 'SUM')
        ,MAX (Sales_Quantity)      (TITLE 'MAX')
        ,MIN (Sales_Quantity)      (TITLE 'MIN')
        ,AVG (Sales_Quantity)      (TITLE 'AVG')
       FROM Book_Sales_History
      WHERE (Sales_Date MOD 10000) / 100 = 12
      AND Book_Number  IN
      (1001, 1002, 1005, 1006, 1007, 1012,1013, 1014)
      GROUP BY 1
      ORDER BY 1;
```

Book_Number	COUNT	SUM	MAX	MIN	AVG
1001	3	4	2	1	1
1005	1	1	1	1	1
1007	1	3	3	3	3
1012	2	5	4	1	2

GROUP BY on Multiple Columns

There is no specific limit to the number of columns which can be grouped, as long as the column name for each and every non-aggregate item in the SELECT appears in the GROUP BY clause. The following example groups the number of books sold by the months of November and December by book:

```
SELECT (Sales_Date MOD 10000) / 100 (NAMED Mth)
        ,Book_Number
        ,SUM(Sales_Quantity)
                (TITLE 'Sales Quantity')
       FROM Book_Sales_History
       WHERE Mth IN (11,12)
       GROUP BY  Mth, Book_Number
       ORDER BY Mth, Book_Number ;
```

Mth	Book_Number	Sales_Quantity
11	1001	5
11	1005	1
11	1011	1
12	1001	4
12	1005	1
12	1007	3
12	1011	1
12	1012	5

GROUP BY and HAVING

In the same way that the "WHERE" clause eliminates rows from the output, the "HAVING" clause serves to eliminate groups. The following example modifies the SELECT above to eliminate all Month/Book groups with fewer than two sales:

```
SELECT (Sales_Date MOD 10000) / 100   (NAMED Mth)
          ,Book_Number
          ,SUM(Sales_Quantity)
                              (TITLE 'Sales Quantity')
       FROM Book_Sales_History
       WHERE Mth IN (11,12)
       GROUP BY  Mth, Book_Number
       HAVING SUM(Sales_Quantity) GT 1
       ORDER BY Mth, Book_Number ;
```

```
Mth     Book_Number       Sales_Quantity

 11            1001                    5
 12            1001                    4
 12            1007                    3
 12            1012                    5
```

Using WITH … BY for Subtotals

WITH … BY is a Teradata enhancement to SQL which functions only with BTEQ. It differs from GROUP BY in that:

It creates subtotal lines without eliminating the detail.
It allows subtotal breaks on multiple columns.
ORDER BY is automatically performed on specified columns.

The following example requests a report of each book sale:

For the months of November and December.
With Sales_Date formatted with 3 letter month and 2 digit day.
Ordered by Sales_Date and Book_Number.
With subtotals for each month.

```
SELECT Sales_Date             (FORMAT 'MMMBDD')
        ,Book_Number
        ,Sales_Quantity        (TITLE 'Sales Quantity')
        FROM Book_Sales_History
        WHERE (Sales_Date MOD 10000) / 100 IN (11,12)
        WITH SUM(Sales_Quantity)
                               (TITLE 'Total')
        BY (Sales_Date MOD 10000) / 100
        ORDER BY 1,2;
```

```
Sales_Date    Book_Number      Sales Quantity

Nov 5             1011                      1
Nov 6             1001                      1
Nov 15            1001                      4
Nov 30            1005                      1
                                 ------------
                  Total                     7
Dec 05            1012                      4
Dec 10            1001                      1
Dec 15            1001                      1
Dec 15            1005                      1
Dec 15            1011                      1
Dec 15            1012                      1
Dec 20            1001                      2
Dec 20            1007                      3
                                -------------
                  Total                    14
```

Multiple Subtotals

Modify the above report to include the average sale quantity per month:

```
SELECT Sales_Date              (FORMAT 'MMMBDD')
       ,Book_Number
       ,Sales_Quantity          (TITLE 'Sales Quantity')
       FROM Book_Sales_History
       WHERE (Sales_Date MOD 10000) / 100 IN (11,12)
       WITH SUM(Sales_Quantity)
                                (TITLE 'Month Total')
       ,AVG(Sales_Quantity)  (TITLE 'Month Average')
       BY (Sales_Date MOD 10000) / 100
       ORDER BY 1,2;
```

```
Sales_Date   Book_Number    Sales_Quantity

Nov 5              1011                  1
Nov 6              1001                  1
Nov 15             1001                  4
Nov 30             1005                  1
                                --------------
               Month Total               7
               Month Average             2
Dec 05             1012                  4
Dec 10             1001                  1
Dec 15             1001                  1
Dec 15             1005                  1
Dec 15             1009                  ?
Dec 15             1011                  1
Dec 15             1012                  1
Dec 20             1001                  2
Dec 20             1007                  3
                                --------------
               Month Total              14
               Month Average             2
```

Multiple Subtotal Levels

In addition to multiple subtotal breaks, we can have multiple subtotal levels.

Let us modify the November/December sales report to include subtotals by book number and by month:

```
SELECT Sales_Date           (FORMAT 'MMMBDD')
       ,Book_Number
       ,Sales_Quantity      (TITLE 'Sales Quantity')
       FROM Book_Sales_History
       WHERE (Sales_Date MOD 10000) / 100 IN (11,12)
       WITH SUM(Sales_Quantity)
                            (TITLE 'Total By Book')
             BY Book_Number
       WITH SUM(Sales_Quantity)
                            (TITLE 'Total By Month')
             BY (Sales_Date MOD 10000) / 100
       ORDER BY 1;
```

```
Sales_Date    Book_Number       Sales_Quantity

Nov 6               1001                     1
Nov 15              1001                     4
                                  ------------
                    Total By Book            5
Nov 30              1005                     1
                                   -----------
                    Total By Book            1
Nov 5               1011                     1
                                  ------------
                    Total By Book            1
                                  ------------

                    Total By Month           7
Dec 10              1001                     1
Dec 15              1001                     1
Dec 20              1001                     2
                                  ------------
                    Total By Book            4
etc.
```

Using WITH - For Grand Totals

The "WITH" function (without "BY") creates a grand total for the report. Since there can logically be only one grand total, any SQL statement is limited to a single "WITH" command.

For Example, assume we need to create a report which summarizes book sales for November and December and provides a grand total and an average total for the combined months:

```
SELECT (Sales_Date MOD 10000) / 100
                              (NAMED MTH, TITLE 'MONTH')
      ,SUM (Sales_Quantity)        (TITLE 'SALES')
     FROM Book_Sales_History
     WHERE MTH IN (11,12)
     WITH SUM(Sales_Quantity)    (TITLE 'TOTAL')
     GROUP BY 1
     ORDER BY 1;
```

```
MONTH        SALES

   11            7
   12           14
               ----
   TOTAL        21
```

Using WITH ... BY and WITH for Subtotals and Grand Totals

Example - The Book sales report for November and December with subtotals by month and a grand total:

```
SELECT Sales_Date              (FORMAT 'MMMBDD')
       ,Book_Number
       ,Sales_Quantity         (TITLE 'Sales Quantity')
       FROM Book_Sales_History
       WHERE (Sales_Date MOD 10000) / 100 IN (11,12)
       WITH SUM(Sales_Quantity)
                               (TITLE 'Total')
             BY (Sales_Date MOD 10000) / 100
       WITH SUM(Sales_Quantity)
                               (TITLE 'Grand Total')
       ,AVG(Sales_Quantity)    (TITLE 'Average Sale')
       ORDER BY 1,2;
```

```
Sales_Date    Book_Number        Sales_Quantity

Nov 5                1011                     1
Nov 6                1001                     1
Nov 15               1001                     4
Nov 30               1005                     1
                                  -------------
                     Total                    7
Dec 05               1012                     4
Dec 10               1001                     1
Dec 15               1001                     1
Dec 15               1005                     1
Dec 15               1011                     1
Dec 15               1012                     1
Dec 20               1001                     2
Dec 20               1007                     3
                                 --------------
                     Total                   14
                                  -------------
                     Grand Total             21
                     Average Sale             2
```

Summary

WITH and WITH ... BY are Teradata enhancements, not found in standard SQL.

WITH BY:

Creates subtotals for detail lists.
Can specify multiple columns and multiple break points.
Implies ORDER BY (ascending).
WITH ... BY columns become the MAJOR sort keys.
Additional ORDER BY clauses specify MINOR sorts.
No specific limit to the number of WITH ... BYs in a single SQL statement.

WITH:

Creates a final or grand total.
Can specify multiple columns.

Even with powerful, high-level, statistic-gathering devices like aggregates, GROUP BY, WITH and WITH BY in our tool box, we might discover a need to micro-manage the results. If customer information is solicited, but no merchandise changes hands, should this be considered as a transaction and allowed to participate in the calculation of revenue generated by the AVERAGE sale?

Clearly there is a need for some degree of fine-tuning to ensure that the occasional happenstance does not become a permanently imbedded consideration in the development of future plans. We cannot, of course, meddle with the rules of arithmetic - that would not be honest. What we can do, however, is exercise a larger measure of control over what is, or is not, to be considered in the calculation of averages, and to achieve this, we need to fully understand the impact of NULLs in the data, which is the subject of Chapter 10.

Hands On Exercises

1. Build a report which lists the Story_Number and the total number of characters per story from the Story_Chr table. Order the report by Story_Number.

2. Modify the report above to list each Character_Number by Story_Number and provide a subtotal of the number of characters per story, as well as a final grand total.

   The report should be ordered by Character_Number within Story_Number, and both subtotals and the grand total should have appropriate titles.

10 NULL

Dr. Edgar Codd, generally recognized as the father of the relational database, was once asked, if he could go back and do it all over again, what he would change. His reply was instantaneous, "If I had known of all the trouble "NULL" would cause, I would never have insisted on it". William Shakespeare, on the other hand, took a different approach when he named his play, "Much Ado About Nothing". Either way, once we recognize the existence of the "NULL" state, we can safely dispense with many of the "kluges" which complicated the data processing of the past. No longer, for example, need we use spaces (which are valid characters) to indicate the absence of character data, nor need we use zeros or high-values etc. to indicate a missing numeric value. "NULL" tells it as it is.

NULL IS:

An SQL keyword.

A state of missing or unknown data.

Compressible to occupy zero space in the Teradata Database.

NULL IS NOT:

A data type, nor a characteristic of a data type.

Identified as spaces, zeros or any other type of data representation.

Arithmetic and Comparison Operations on NULL

Since NULL is not a value, but indicative of a missing value, no arithmetic function involving NULL can yield a meaningful result:

Any Value + NULL = NULL.
Any Value - NULL = NULL.
Any Value * NULL = NULL.
Any Value / NULL = NULL.

Similarly, if we compare any value (including another NULL) to NULL, the result must be FALSE or UNKNOWN.

Any Value > NULL = FALSE or UNKNOWN
Any Value < NULL = FALSE or UNKNOWN
Any Value <> NULL = FALSE or UNKNOWN
Any Value >= NULL = FALSE or UNKNOWN
Any Value <= NULL = FALSE or UNKNOWN
Any Value = NULL = FALSE or UNKNOWN

NULL > NULL = FALSE or UNKNOWN
NULL < NULL = FALSE or UNKNOWN
NULL <> NULL = FALSE or UNKNOWN
NULL >= NULL = FALSE or UNKNOWN
NULL <= NULL = FALSE or UNKNOWN
NULL = NULL = FALSE or UNKNOWN

For sorting purposes however NULLs are considered identical, sort equally, and occur prior to negative numeric values and blank characters. Additionally, as we discussed in the previous chapter, NULLs do not invalidate aggregate expressions, but are simply ignored in the calculation.

NULL in the SELECT

Since any comparison to NULL must be FALSE, we can only test the existence or non existence of NULL - where some value IS or IS NOT NULL.

Example:

```
SELECT Title_Code
       , Last_Name
       , First_Name
       FROM Chr
       WHERE First_Name IS NULL;
```

Testing for the **non-existence** of a First name:

Title_Code	Last_Name	First_Name
Mr	Fezziwig	?
Mr	Topper	?
Mr	Mim	?
Mr	Longford	?
etc.		

Note that BTEQ's *default output* for NULL is a *question mark*. It should be emphasized that this value "?" is *not* stored in the Teradata Database.

Testing for the **existence** of a First Name:

```
SELECT Title_Code
       , Last_Name
       , First_Name
       FROM Chr
       WHERE First_Name IS NOT NULL;
```

Title_Code	Last_Name	First_Name
Mr.	Denham	Edmund
Mr	Derrick	John
Mrs	Swidger	Millie
Mis	Cratchit	Belinda
etc.		

CASE

The CASE expression is used in an SQL statement in place of a value when there are multiple possible values required, depending on specified conditions. CASE allows the user to define either a predicate (condition) to be evaluated, or a value expression to be matched. If the predicate is "true" or the match occurs, the specified value is set. If the predicate is not "true" or the match does not occur, the alternative value (specified in the "ELSE" condition) is set. If no "ELSE" condition is specified, the result becomes "NULL".

There are two types of CASE expression:

The Valued CASE:

CASE expression1 WHEN expression2 THEN result1
[WHEN expression3 THEN result2 . . .]
[ELSE result_n]
END

The Searched CASE:

CASE WHEN SearchCondition1 THEN result1
[WHEN SearchCondition2 THEN result2 . . .]
[ELSE result_n]
END

The Valued CASE expression:

```
SELECT Book_Number          (TITLE 'Number')
       ,Book_Name,          (CHAR(17)) (TITLE 'Title')
       ,Price_Amount        (TITLE 'Price')
       ,CASE Book_Type
             WHEN 'H' THEN 'Hard Cover'
             WHEN 'P' THEN 'Paper Back'
             ELSE NULL
             END (TITLE 'Book Type')
       FROM Book
       WHERE Publisher_Number = 103;
```

This query uses the single-character value of the Book_Type column to specify the kind of binding as hard cover, paperback or nothing at all:

```
Number Title                Price Book Type

1003   Great Expectations    5.95 Paper Back
1004   Our Mutual Friend    10.95 Hard Cover
1012   A Charles Dickens    14.99 Hard Cover
```

The Searched CASE expression

The following SELECT produces identical output to the example above:

```
SELECT Book_Number          (TITLE 'Number')
        ,Book_Name          (CHAR(17)) (TITLE 'Title')
        ,Price_Amount       (TITLE 'Price')
        ,CASE WHEN Book_Type = 'H'
                            THEN 'Hard Cover'
             WHEN Book_Type =  'P'
                            THEN 'Paper Back'
             ELSE NULL END (TITLE 'Book Type')
       FROM Book
       WHERE Publisher = 103;
```

CASE expressions may be used in place of any value expressions. The "WHEN" clauses in a "CASE" statement are processed sequentially. When the first "true" condition is located, the process ends. If no condition is found to be "true", the "else" expression becomes the default response. If no "else" expression is provided, "NULL" is returned.

The following example calculates the percentage of Books 1001 and 1012 sold during the month of December, 1996. In using the CASE statement to calculate multiple simultaneous aggregates in a single step, we neatly avoid the complexities involved in attempting to build a single report from the results of multiple SQL statements.

```
SELECT COUNT(
        CASE WHEN Book_Number = 1001
                THEN COUNT(Sales_Quantity)  * 100
                ELSE 0
                END) / COUNT(Sales_Quantity)
                (FORMAT 'zz9%', TITLE '1001 PerCent')
        ,COUNT (
        CASE WHEN Book_Number = 1012
                THEN COUNT(Sales_Quantity)  * 100
                ELSE 0
                END) / COUNT(Sales_Quantity)
                (FORMAT 'zz9%', TITLE '1012 PerCent')
        FROM Book_Sales_History
        WHERE (Sales_Date MOD 10000) / 100 = 12
        AND Sales_Date /10000 = 96;
```

1001 Percent	1012 Percent
13%	26%

NULLIF

The expression:

```
NULLIF (expression1, expression2)
```

is a specific short form of "CASE" expression and is equivalent to:

```
CASE WHEN expression1 = expression2
        THEN NULL
        ELSE expression1
END
```

Example (using Fig. 10-1):

```
SELECT Customer_Number
                (TITLE 'Customer//Number')
        , NULLIF
                (Consigned_Amount, Received_Amount)
                (TITLE 'Amount')
        FROM Consignments_Receivable
;
```

If the Consigned_Amount is equal to the Received_Amount, the result is NULL. If the Consigned_Amount is not equal to the Received_Amount the result is the Consigned_Amount.

Consignments Receivable

Customer Number	Consigned Amount	Received Amount
PK, UPI		
101	500	500
102	600	NULL
103	50	25
104	100	200
105	NULL	300
106	NULL	NULL

Figure 10-1

```
Customer     Amount
Number       ______

   1              ?
 102            600
 103             50
 104            100
 105              ?
 106              ?
```

COALESCE

1. The expression:

```
COALESCE (expression1, expression2)
```

is equivalent to:

```
CASE WHEN expression1 IS NOT NULL
        THEN expression1
        ELSE expression2
END
```

PHONE

(Temporary table)

Last_Name	First_Name	Office_Phone	Home_Phone
Scrooge	Ebenezer	327 5000	329 1100
Cratchit	Bob	327 5002	329 1701
Wilkins	Dick		524 1106
Doubledick	Richard		422 5578
Marshall	Mary	383 2211	383 2211
Marigold	Doctor	665 1102	
Swidger	George	223 1122	

Figure 10-2

For Example, in reference to *Fig. 10-2*, the statement:

```
SELECT Last_Name
        ,First_Name
        CASE WHEN Office_Phone IS NOT NULL
        THEN Office_Phone
        ELSE Home_Phone END (FORMAT '999-9999')
        FROM   Phone;
```

is equivalent to:

```
SELECT Last_Name
       ,First_Name
       ,COALESCE (Office_Phone , Home_Phone)
                      (FORMAT '999-9999')
       FROM  Phone;
```

and will return the Home_Phone only if the Office_Phone is NULL.

```
Last_Name          First_Name  CASE <expression>

Scrooge            Ebenezer          327-5000
Cratchit           Bob               327-5002
Wilkins            Dick              524-1106
Doubledick         Richard           422-5578
Marshall           Mary              383-2211
Marigold           Doctor            665-1102
Swidger            George            223-1122
```

2. COALESCE may have multiple expressions associated with it:

```
COALESCE (expression1, expression2,. . . expression_n)
```

In this event, the statement becomes equivalent to:

```
CASE WHEN expression1 IS NOT NULL
       THEN expression1
       ELSE
       COALESCE(expression2, . . . expression -n)
       END
```

In other words, try each operation in sequence. If the result is "NULL" then continue the COALESCE operation with each of the remaining values until a value is found which is not NULL. If no non-NULL value is encountered, then "NULL" is returned. *COALESCE then, returns the first NOT NULL value in the expression list.* The "CASE", "NULLIF" and "COALESCE" expressions therefore provide a simple but powerful conditional capability to SQL - which wisely used, can eliminate a great deal of complexity in application design.

NULLIFZERO and ZEROIFNULL

NULLIFZERO and ZEROIFNULL are two important Teradata enhancements which provide the User with the ability to:

> Specify what values are of interest in computing an average.
> Avoid dividing by zero when possible values are unknown.

The next example treats any zero price in the Price_Amount column as if it were NULL. Since NULL is ignored in aggregate calculations, any such value would be disregarded in computing an average:

```
SELECT Book_Number
       ,Book_Name
       ,NULLIFZERO(Price_Amount)
            (TITLE 'NIZ Price')
   FROM Book
   WHERE Publisher_Number = 104
   WITH COUNT(NULLIFZERO(Price_Amount))
            (TITLE 'NIZ Count'),
   AVG(NULLIFZERO(Price_Amount))
            (TITLE 'NIZ Avg Price' ,FORMAT 'zz9.99')
   ORDER BY 1;
```

```
Book_Number Book_Name                NIZ Price

       1002 Christmas Tales             6.99
       1005 The Christmas Books         ?
       1006 The Christmas Books         6.95
       1007 The Christmas Books         3.50
       1008 David Copperfield           6.95
       1010 Hard Times                  6.95
       1011 A Tale of Two Cities        5.95
       1013 The Christmas Books            ?
       1014  The Christmas Books       ____?
            NIZ Count                      6
            NIZ Avg Price               7.88
```

Using ZEROIFNULL, on the other hand, treats any NULL in the Price_Amount column as if it were zero. Zeros do participate in averages. As a result the average book price is now calculated by dividing the total price by 9 (instances of Price_Amount), instead of 6:

```
SELECT Book_Number
      ,Book_Name
      ,ZEROIFNULL(Price_Amount)
                              (TITLE 'NIZ Price')
      FROM Book
      WHERE Publisher_Number = 104
      WITH COUNT(ZEROIFNULL(Price_Amount))
                              (TITLE 'ZIN Count')
      ,AVG(ZEROIFNULL(Price_Amount))
              (TITLE 'ZIN Avg Price' ,FORMAT 'zz9.99')
      ORDER BY 1;
```

```
Book_Number Book_Name                  NIZ Price

       1002 Christmas Tales                 6.99
       1005 The Christmas Books                0
       1006 The Christmas Books             6.95
       1007 The Christmas Books            13.50
       1008 David Copperfield               6.95
       1010 Hard Times                      6.95
       1011 A Tale of Two Cities            5.95
       1013 The Christmas Books                0
       1014 The Christmas Books             ___0
            ZIN Count                          9
            ZIN Avg Price                   5.25
```

NULLIFZERO for DIVISION

If we wish to find the average number of pages per chapter for each story, we might submit the following SQL:

```
SELECT Story_Number
       , Story_Name
       , Chapter_Quantity)    (TITLE 'Chapters')
       , Page_Quantity        (TITLE 'Pages')
       , Page_Quantity / Chapter_Quantity
                              (TITLE 'Average')
       FROM Story ORDER BY 1;
```

Since at least one story, "What Christmas Is as We get Older" has zero chapters, an error is returned for attempting to divide by zero. Using NULLIFZERO however, delivers a result of NULL, but effectively avoids the error:

```
SELECT Story_Name             (CHAR(20),TITLE 'Name')
       ,Chapter_Quantity      (TITLE 'Chapters')
       ,Page_Quantity         (TITLE 'Pages')
       ,Page_Quantity /
            NULLIFZERO( Chapter_Quantity)
                              (TITLE 'Average')
       FROM Story
       ORDER BY 1;
```

```
Name                  Chapters   Pages  Average

A Christmas Carol            5      63       12
A Christmas Tree             1      15       15
A Tale of two Cities        45     404        8
David Copperfield           64     950       14
Doctor Marigold              2       5        2
Great Expectations          59     526        8
Hard Times                  37     298        8
What Christmas Is As         0       4        ?
            etc.
```

Though we have examined some of the implications of NULL in this chapter, we have not, by any means, exhausted its possibilities. We have yet to discuss, for example, the effects of NULL on such topics as table joins, string expressions, inserts, updates, deletes and much, much more.

Considering its diminutive dimensions, NULL seems to exert a degree of influence on the universe at large, out of all proportion to its size.

Hands On Exercises

1. Prepare SQL statements which access the Chr table and calculate a total count of:

   Last names which are missing (NULL)

   First names which are missing (NULL)

   Characters with both First and Last Names.

2. Use the "CASE" statement to query the Book_Sales_History table to determine the percent of total sales represented by sales of book 1001.

11 String Functions

No matter how often we may be told that the way data is output should have no bearing on how it is stored internally in the database, this good advice is all too often disregarded. An insurance company stored its insurance policy numbers as a string of 10 numeric characters because, they said, they were always printing it that way on reports. Of course, with today's technology they could just as easily have stored the complete number as a 4-byte INTEGER, and saved 6 megabytes of space for each million records in that one table alone.

SQL's rich data conversion and string manipulation functions not only permit us to take advantage of all possible economies in the storage of data, but provide us with the confidence that no matter how we must output the data, the tools are readily at hand. These include:

CONCATENATION.
TRIM.
CHARACTERS.
SUBSTRING.
INDEX.

CONCATENATION

The concatenation function, expressed as the two vertical bars on the standard keyboard:

string1 || string2

has the effect of joining string1, end on end, with string 2.

For Example, since First_Name is defined as VARCHAR(10), and therefore has no trailing blanks, the following request results in a single field composed of First_Name and Last_Name separated by a single blank:

```
SELECT First_Name || ' ' || Last_Name
       FROM Chr
       WHERE Character_Number = 1017;
```

```
First_Name || ' ' || Last_Name
Robin Crusoe
```

CONCATENATION may also be used on BYTE and GRAPHIC data types, although these may not be mixed in the same concatenation.

TRIM

The TRIM function is used to strip leading or trailing blanks or nulls from fixed or variable, character or byte strings, as well as trailing double-byte zeros from graphic strings.

TRIM takes a single argument *(See Fig 11-1),* which *must* identify the column or expression to be trimmed, and *may* specify the combination of leading and/or trailing blanks or nulls to be stripped.

In the absence of the "TRAILING FROM" , "LEADING FROM" or "BOTH FROM" modifiers, TRIM functions differently in Teradata mode, than in ANSI mode:

```
         (expression                 )
TRIM  {  (BOTH FROM expression       )  }
         (LEADING FROM expression)
         (TRAILING FROM expression)
```

Option	Mode	Trims
expression	Teradata	Trailing blanks or NULLs
	ANSI	Leading and trailing blanks or NULLs
TRAILING FROM	BOTH	Leading and trailing blanks or NULLs
BOTH FROM	BOTH	Leading blanks or NULLs
LEADING FROM	BOTH	Trailing blanks or NULLs

Figure 11-1

In Teradata mode, TRIM(expression) strips trailing blanks or NULLs only.

In ANSI mode, both leading and trailing blanks or NULLs are stripped.

Use of the "TRAILING FROM" , "LEADING FROM" or "BOTH FROM" modifiers avoids any possible confusion.

Fig. 11-2 describes the results of the TRIM function with different types of argument.

If the argument is :	The Result is
NULL	NULL.
Numeric	The value is converted to a character string.
CHAR or VARCHAR	VARCHAR, blank trimmed with a possible zero length
BYTE or VARBYTE	VARBYTE, binary zero trimmed, with possible zero length
GRAPHIC or VARGRAPHIC	VARGRAPHIC, binary zero trimmed, with possible zero length

Figure 11-2

Returning to the concatenation example above, since Last_Name is defined as CHAR(12) and may have trailing spaces, the concatenation of first name to last name is not quite as successful:

```
SELECT Last_Name || ', ' || First_Name
        FROM Chr
        WHERE Character_Number = 1017;
```

```
Last_Name || ', ' || First_Name
Crusoe         , Robin
```

The TRIM function can be used to avoid the trailing spaces on the last name:

```
SELECT TRIM( TRAILING FROM Last_Name) || ', ' ||
        First_Name (TITLE 'Name')
        FROM Chr
        WHERE Character_Number = 1017;
```

```
Name
Crusoe, Robin
```

CHARACTERS

The CHARACTERS function counts the actual number of characters in a VARCHAR column:

```
SELECT First_Name
        , CHARACTERS(First_Name)
                        (TITLE 'Characters')
        FROM Chr
        WHERE Character_Number = 1017;
```

```
First_Name          Characters
Robin                        5
```

Since Last_Name is defined as fixed-length CHAR(12), the expression:

CHARACTERS(Last_Name)

would count the trailing blanks as characters, and would result in a value of 12.

SUBSTR and SUBSTRING

The Teradata Database has traditionally supported substrings with the syntax:

SUBSTR(expression, StartingPosition, OptionalLength)

which used to error if the StartingPosition expression or value was:

Less than 1.
Greater than the length of the string counting from 1.

OR if the OptionalLength expression or value was:

Greater than the length of the string less the StartingPosition + 1
OR Negative.

In V2R2, the Teradata SUBSTR function has been modified to have the same semantics as the ANSI SUBSTRING function and will now return a valid character string result where it used to return an error.

For Example, in Teradata V2R2:

SUBSTR('ABC',-3)	returns	'ABC'
SUBSTR('ABC',7)	returns	zero length string
SUBSTR('ABC',-3,6)	returns	'AB'

The ANSI standard SUBSTRING syntax (below) will never error unless the OptionalLength is specified and is negative:

SUBSTRING(expression, FROM StartingPosition, OptionalLength)

NOTE that in both SUBSTR and SUBSTRING, a starting position of zero will not result in an error, but will return a zero length string.

The following examples of SUBSTR and SUBSTRING deliver the same result:

```
SELECT  Last_Name
          ,SUBSTR(First_Name,1,1) (TITLE 'FI')
         FROM Chr
         WHERE Character_Number = 1017;

SELECT Last_Name
         ,SUBSTRING(First_Name,FROM 1,1) (TITLE 'FI')
         FROM Chr
         WHERE Character_Number = 1017;
```

```
Last_Name     FI

Crusoe        R
```

SUBSTR or SUBSTRING on Numerics

Numeric values may be directly converted to characters within the Teradata Database.

BYTEINT	defaults to 4 Bytes
SMALLINT	defaults to 6 BYTES
INTEGER	defaults to 11 BYTES

Teradata does not however realign the output data, and the character field which results from such a conversion begins with the sign as the left-most character, and the numeric characters aligned to the right. For example:

For Example:

BYTEINT	34 becomes '+034'.
SMALLINT	1234 becomes '+01234'.
INTEGER	1234 becomes '+0000001234'.

Phone_Number is defined as an INTEGER. Converted to a string, it would appear as in *Fig. 11-3:*

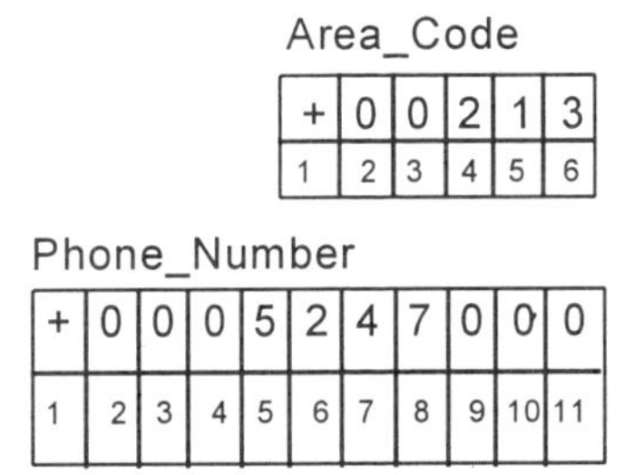

Figure 11-3

We can use the SUBSTR function to create a formatted Area_Code and Phone_Number, with the Area_Code in parentheses, followed by a single space and the telephone number formatted with a hyphen:

```
SELECT Publisher_Name, '(' ||
        SUBSTR(Area_Code,2,3) || ' )' ||
        SUBSTR(Phone_Number,5,3) || '-' ||
        SUBSTR(Phone_Number,8,4) (Title 'PHONE')
       FROM Publisher
       ORDER BY 1;
```

```
Publisher_Name              PHONE
Every Man's Library         (415) 665-1000
MacMillan Publishing        (212) 335-5100
Oxford University Press     (213) 524-7000
Penguin Books               (213) 625-0040
The Modern Library          (312) 661-2244
Washington Square Press     (212) 223-2000
```

NOTE that:

Parentheses are not supported as format characters.
FORMAT cannot be used within a concatenated expression.

INDEX

The INDEX function returns the starting position (relative to 1) of a substring within a string. *For Example:*

Imagine that we have been given a list of names in the format:

Last_Name, First_Name
(separated by a comma and a space) with the column name of 'Name'
(*See Fig. 11-4*)

Name

C	r	a	t	c	h	i	t	,		B	o	b
C	r	u	s	o	e	,		R	o	b	i	n
1	2	3	4	5	6	7	8	9	10	11	12	13

Figure 11-4

We need to resolve the Name column into first and last names. We could use INDEX to search for the instance of the comma + space and add 1 to calculate the starting position of the first name. We could then use SUBSTR with no length parameter to resolve the full first name. At the same time, we know that the starting position for the last name is 1, and we can use INDEX to determine the final character of the last name in the position prior to the comma:

```
SELECT SUBSTR(Name, INDEX(Name,', ') + 2)
                              (TITLE 'First Name')
       ,SUBSTR(Name,1,INDEX(Name,', ') -1)
                              (TITLE 'Last_Name')
      FROM TableName;
```

```
First Name          Last Name

Bob                 Cratchit
Robin               Crusoe
```

With a firm command of its string manipulation and data formatting capabilities, we should now feel confident of SQL's ability to handle almost any kind of output we might be asked to provide.

Hands On Exercise

Provide a list of story names from the Story table starting with the second word of the title, and ending with the first word. Title the output field, "Story Names'.

Example:

```
Story Name

Christmas Carol A
Haunted MAN The
Holly Tree The
```

12 Subqueries and Joins

"It will never work", he said, "There are too many tables. What we should do is put all the data in one big table, and then we wouldn't have to do all those joins." I looked at him in some amazement. Here was someone whose experience and technical skills in developing relational database management systems I had long held in high esteem. Nevertheless he had clearly failed to recognize that it was precisely the multiplicity of tables which gives the relational database its tremendous power. More tables provide the opportunity for the more creative and flexible queries needed to turn raw data into useful intelligence. SQL provides two methods of integrating data from multiple tables into a single answer set:

Subqueries.
Joins.

Subqueries

An SQL subquery is often referred to as an imbedded SELECT. Subqueries provide an extension to the SET operators described in Chapter 6. *For Example,* if the character IDs are known, it is a simple matter to SELECT the names of all "The Seven Poor Travellers", story number 102:

```
SELECT  Title_Code (TITLE 'Title')
         ,Last_Name
         ,First_Name
        FROM Chr
        WHERE Character_Number IN
                (1017,1019,1020,1021,1022,1023,1024)
        ORDER BY Last_Name;
```

```
Title         Last_Name          First_Name

?             Crusoe             Robin
Mr            Doubledick         Richard
Mis           Marshall           Mary
Cap           Taunton            ?
Mrs           Taunton            ?
Mr            ?                  Ben
Mr            Watts ESQ          Richard
```

On the other hand, if the story number is known but the character numbers are not, we could use a subquery to SELECT the relevant character numbers from the Story_Chr table, and *logically* populate the 'IN' clause.

```
SELECT  Title_Code (TITLE 'Title')
        ,Last_Name
        ,First_Name
      FROM Chr
      WHERE Character_Number IN  (
            SELECT Character_Number
                  FROM Story_Chr
                  WHERE Story_Number = 102)
      ORDER BY Last_Name;
```

The imbedded SELECT:

```
(SELECT Character_Number
      FROM Story_Chr
      WHERE Story_Number = 102)
```

results in the values, 1017 and 1019 through 1024, which when *logically* substituted in the SQL for the imbedded SELECT, render the second example, in effect, identical to the first:

```
SELECT  Title_Code (TITLE 'Title')
        ,Last_Name
        ,First_Name
       FROM Chr
       WHERE Character_Number IN
              (1017,1019,1020,1021,1022,1023,1024)
ORDER BY Last_Name;
```

As with the regular "SET" commands, subqueries are always the subject of an "IN" or "NOT IN" clause, unless the qualifiers, "ANY", "ALL" or "SOME" are used. Thus the above request could equally have been submitted as:

```
SELECT  Title_Code (TITLE 'Title')
        ,Last_Name
        ,First_Name
       FROM Chr
       WHERE Character_Number = ANY
              (SELECT Character_Number
                     FROM Story_Chr
                     WHERE Story_Number = 102)
       ORDER BY Last_Name;
```

"= ANY" and " = SOME" are of course synonymous, and return all eight characters from story 102.

"= ALL" returns no rows, since a single character number cannot equal the character numbers of all seven characters in the story.

Subqueries:

May be used to qualify SELECT, UPDATE or DELETE statements.

Are always enclosed in parentheses.

Are the subject of an IN or NOT IN clause.

Support LIKE or NOT LIKE quantifiers.

Support qualifiers ANY, ALL or SOME.

May be used in the WHERE clause or the HAVING clause.

Can specify multiple match columns.

A maximum of 16 tables or view can be specified in any SQL query. (This might be one table 16 times (self join), 16 tables once, or anything in between)

Defining and Using ALIAS Names

An ALIAS is:

A temporary name for a table or view.

Defined in the FROM clause.

An optional feature to clarify complex SQL.

Required in a SELF JOIN operation.

An alias name exists only for the life of the SQL statement in which it is defined. Once an alias name is defined however, any reference to the object for which the alias was defined, must use the alias name, or ambiguity might result. Alias names are generally required for correlated subqueries and, as we shall see on pages 299 and 305, must always be used for self-joins.

Correlated Subqueries

A subquery is "correlated" when it references columns of the outer query from the inner subquery. It differs from the regular subquery in that the correlated subquery is required to be re-evaluated for each row considered in the outer query.

As an example, if we are asked to list the most expensive books for each Book_Type, we must use a subquery to determine the maximum price amount for the Book_Type of each row referenced by the main query.

The subquery is considered correlated, since it must be re-evaluated for each row considered by the outer query. At the same time, a comparison must be made between the Book_Type column of the inner query and the Book_Type column *of the same table* in the outer query. As a result the Book table is being logically joined to itself. This is therefore a self-join, and the use of ALIAS names becomes mandatory.

```
SELECT Book_Number
       , Book_Name
       , Price_Amount
       , Book_Type
FROM Book Book1
       WHERE Price_Amount =
       (SELECT MAX(Price_Amount)
       FROM Book Book2
       WHERE Book1.Book_Type=
                 Book2.Book_Type);
```

Book_Number	Book_Name	Price_Amount	Book_Type
1002	Christmas Tales	6.99	P
1009	Martin Chuzzlewit	20.00	H

The EXISTS Function

The EXIST condition is a logical expression used to test the existence or non-existence of specified rows in a subquery. *For Example*, are there any publishers in the Publisher table who do not have books in the Book table?

```
SELECT Publisher_Number
       , Publisher_Name
       FROM Publisher
       WHERE NOT EXISTS
              (SELECT * FROM Book
              WHERE Book.Publisher_Number =
              Publisher.Publisher_Number );
```

Publisher_Number	Publisher_Name
102	MacMillan Publishing
105	The Modern Library

For each row from the Publisher table, if the result of the NOT EXISTS subquery is "TRUE" (the Publisher_Number does not exist in the Book table), the row from the Publisher table is returned. To reverse the sense of this query, and SELECT the publishers who do have books listed in the Book table, the word 'NOT' is removed:

```
SELECT Publisher_Number
       , Publisher_Name
       FROM Publisher
       WHERE EXISTS
              (SELECT * FROM Book
              WHERE Book.Publisher_Number =
              Publisher.Publisher_Number );
```

```
Publisher_Number   Publisher_Name
                                 
             101   Washington Square Pr
             106   Every Man's Library
             104   Penguin Books
             103   Oxford University Pr
```

In the previous examples, the inner table (Book) is accessed by the subquery for no other reason than to qualify the rows from the outer table (Publisher). In other words, *although multiple tables may have participated in the SQL query, only one of them contributed to the result.* This is a feature of the subquery, and becomes the primary difference between a subquery and a join.

JOINS

A JOIN is a technique for combining columns from multiple tables into a single answer set. The most common type of join is the INNER join, which compares column values of rows from different tables for equality. If the join columns are determined to be equal, all the columns of both rows may be logically returned in a single answer set. For an INNER join condition to be logically "true", the columns being compared must be based upon the same domain.

DOMAINS

Fig. 12-1, which was previously seen in Chapter 2, charts the "Classics" as an Entity relationship diagram with special emphasis on the common domains.

> Columns which are in the same domain refer to the same real-world person, place, thing or idea .

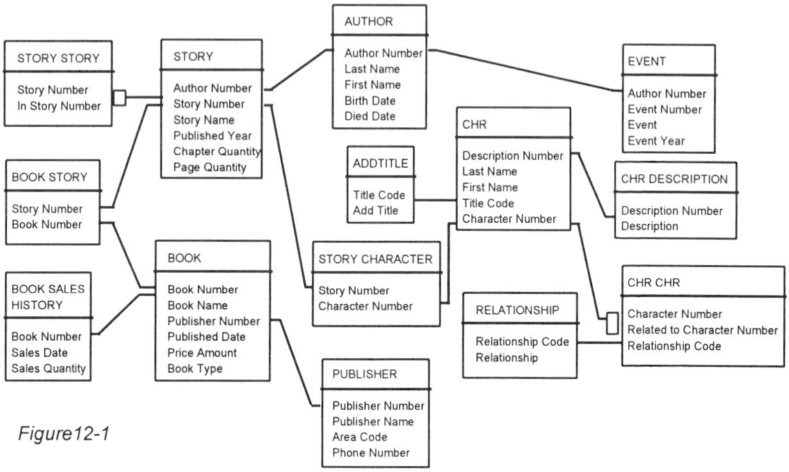

Figure12-1

If it makes logical sense to add, subtract or compare two values, they must be in the same domain.

If it makes logical sense to multiply or divide two values, they are generally in different domains. (The one exception is length multiplied by length, giving area).

If columns are in the same domain, their names should be based on a common domain name. For example, all columns which have a name of, or based on, Character_Number are in the Character Number domain and represent a unique ID for a character in a story. Joins should *always* be based on a comparison of columns which share a common domain.

The example on the opposing page SELECTs the Last_Name and First Name from the Chr table and matches them with the Description from the Chr_Description table based on an equality of the Description_Number columns in each table.

```
SELECT Last_Name
        , First_Name
        , Char_Description (TITLE'Description')
        FROM Chr, Chr_Description
        WHERE Chr.Description_Number =
                Chr_Description.Description_Number
        ORDER BY 1,2;
```

Note that the columns, Last_Name, and First_Name appear only in the Chr table, and not in the Chr_Description table. As a result, there is no possibility of ambiguity or confusion (on the part of the operating system), and these names do not need to be qualified with the table name. Similarly the column name Char_Description appears only in the Chr_Description table, is not ambiguous, and therefore does not need to be further qualified. The column Description_Number, however appears in both tables, and must be qualified each time it is used or an error will be returned.

```
Last_Name   First_Name   Description

?           Ben          Waiter
?           Joe          Receiver of stolen goods
Crusoe      Robin        Parrot
Denham      Edmund       Student
Doubledick  Richard      Enlists in the army
Fezziwig    ?            Jovial old merchant
Fezziwig    ?            A worthy match for
etc.
```

For a join of two tables, at least one join condition (where a column of one table equals a column of the other) is necessary.

The next example joins the Book, Story and Book_Story tables together to produce a report which matches the Story_Name from the Story table with the Book_Name from the Book table in which it appears, if the Book_Name includes the word "Christmas".

Since we are joining three tables, we must have at least two equality join conditions which touch all of the tables involved in the join:

> WHERE the Book_Number from the Book table equals the Book_Number from the story table AND
>
> The Story_Number from the Story table equals the Story_Number from the Book_Story table.

The remainder of the WHERE clause which compares Book_Name to "Christmas" is not a join condition, but merely serves to qualify the rows to be returned:

```
SELECT Book.Book_Name
      ,Story.Story_Name
      FROM Book, Story ,Book_Story
      WHERE Book.Book_Number =
               Book_Story.Book_Number
      AND Story.Story_Number =
      Book_Story.Story_Number
      AND Book.Book_Name LIKE '%Christmas%';
```

```
Book_Name              Story_Name

The Christmas Books    Christmas Carol
The Christmas Books    The Chimes
Christmas Tales        The Cricket on the Hearth
A Christmas Carol      A Christmas Carol
The Christmas Books    The Chimes
The Christmas Tales    The Seven Poor Travellers
The Christmas Books    A Christmas Carol
The Christmas Books    A Christmas Carol
The Christmas Books    The Seven Poor Travellers
```

The qualification of Book_Name and Story_Name is not necessary, but is often preferred as a local site standard.

Self Joins

The following example builds a report of Mr. Scrooge and each of his employees. To achieve this it is necessary to:

> Access the Chr table to determine the Character_Number for Mr.Scrooge,
>
> Apply that number to the Chr_Chr table to determine the Character_Numbers of the employees, and
>
> Revisit the Chr table to determine the Last_Names of the employees.

Thus we are required to join the Chr table to itself.

```
SELECT Mgr.Last_Name          (TITLE 'Manager')
        ,Emp.Last_Name        (TITLE 'Last Name')
        ,Emp.First_Name       (TITLE 'First_Name')
       FROM Chr Emp, Chr Mgr, Chr_Chr Rel
       WHERE Emp.Character_Number =
                  Rel.Character_Number
       AND Mgr.Character_Number =
       Rel.Related_to_Character_Number
       AND Rel.Relationship_Code = 'EMP'
       AND Mgr.Last_Name = 'Scrooge';
```

Manager	Last_Name	First_Name
Scrooge	Cratchit	Bob
Scrooge	Dilber	?

In a SELF-JOIN, a single table is logically duplicated by the RDBMS and each image must then be individually referenced by an ALIAS name. In the example above we are using the alias names EMP and

MGR to differentiate between each logical image of the Chr table. This permits us to address both images as if they were separate and distinct tables, even though they have identical column names. Since the column names in the EMP and MGR tables are common to both, they are considered ambiguous, and must always be qualified with the ALIAS name. In this way there is no further barrier to prevent a logical comparison of EMP.Character_Number to MGR.Character_Number.

ALIAS names must always be used in a SELF JOIN.

Cartesian Product Joins

The only limit to the number of tables which can be involved in a join, is the rule which specifies that no more than 16 tables (16 tables once, one table 16 times, or anything in between) can be referenced in a single SQL statement. If "n" tables are being joined, there must be at least "n-1" join conditions which make an equality comparison between domain-compatible columns in different tables. The "n-1" join conditions must include each and every table involved in the join. If by error or design, the following conditions are not met the result is known as a "Cartesian Product Join":

> There are too few join conditions.
>
> Join conditions are not based on equality.
>
> The join conditions do not include all the tables involved in the join.
>
> ALIAS names are missing or incorrectly used.

While there are some real-world uses for the Cartesian product join, they are relatively rare. More often Cartesian joins occur as a result of error.

For Example, consider the previous example, minus the join conditions:

```
SELECT Book_Name
        ,Story_Name
        FROM Book, Story ,Book_Story
        WHERE Book_Name LIKE '%Christmas%';
```

The Book table has 7 rows which include the word "Christmas". The Story table has 16 rows, and the Book_Story table has 17. All three tables will be joined since they are referenced in the "FROM" clause, but there are no limiting join clauses. As a result all *seven* qualifying rows from the Book table will be joined with *each* row from the Story table, and each of those will be joined with *every* row of the Book_Story table. This will result in a total of *2048* rows being returned - none of which provide useful information.

The next example has the correct number of join conditions, but the ALIAS names are inconsistent. As a result the RDBMS will be joining 4 tables, s, b, sb and Book, but with only two join conditions. Again, the result is a Cartesian product, which returns *135* rows:

```
SELECT Book.Book_Name (Char(20))
        , s.Story_Name      (Char(20))
        FROM Book b, Story s ,Book_Story sb
        WHERE b.Book_Number = sb.Book_Number
        AND  s.Story_Number = sb.Story_number
        AND b.Book_Name LIKE '%Christmas%';
```

Subquery Vs Join

A subquery is used to qualify rows, but does not contribute to the output of a query. A join, on the other hand, could be used to qualify rows and may contribute to the output. Any SQL statement which can be composed as a subquery, therefore could also be designed as a join.

For Example, the following SQL query, which accesses the Story_Chr table to identify characters in story 101 from the Chr table, can be written as a subquery or a join.

Subquery:

```
SELECT Title_Code (TITLE 'Title')
       , Last_Name
       , First_Name
       FROM Chr
       WHERE Character_Number IN
       (SELECT Character_Number
       FROM Story_Chr
       WHERE Story_Number = 101);
```

Join:

```
SELECT Title_Code (TITLE 'Title')
       , Last_Name
       , First_Name
       FROM Chr, Story_Chr
       WHERE Chr.Character_Number =
         Story_Chr.Character_Number
       AND Story_Number = 101;
```

The result in both cases is identical:

Title	Last_Name	First_Name
?	?	Fred
Mst	Cratchit	Tim
Mr	Fezziwig	?
Mr	Topper	?
Mis	Cratchit	Belinda
Mis	Scrooge	Fan
Mr	Marley	Jacob
Mr	Cratchit	Bob
Mrs	Dilber	?
Mrs	Fezziwig	?
?	?	Joe
Mis	Cratchit	Martha
Mst	Cratchit	Peter
Mis	?	Belle
Mr	Scrooge	Ebenezer

SUBQUERY:

```
EXPLAIN SELECT  Title_Code
              , Last_Name
              , First_Name
    FROM Chr
    WHERE Character_Number IN (
          SELECT Character_Number FROM Story_Chr
           WHERE Story_Number = 101);
```

Explanation

---

1) First, we lock a distinct CLASSICS."pseudo table" for read on a RowHash to prevent global deadlock for CLASSICS.Story_Chr.
2) Next, we lock a distinct CLASSICS."pseudo table" for read on a RowHash to prevent global deadlock for CLASSICS.Chr.
3) We lock CLASSICS.Story_Chr for read, and we lock CLASSICS.Chr for read.
4) We do an all-AMPs RETRIEVE step from CLASSICS.Chr by way of an all-rows scan with no residual conditions into Spool 2, which is redistributed by hash code to all AMPs. Then we do a SORT to order Spool 2 by row hash. The size of Spool 2 is estimated to be 40 rows. The estimated time for this step is 0.08 seconds.
5) We do an all-AMPs JOIN step from Spool 2 (Last Use) by way of an all-rows scan, which is joined to CLASSICS.Story_Chr with a condition of ("CLASSICS.Story_Chr.Story_Number = 101"). Spool 2 and CLASSICS.Story_Chr are joined using an inclusion merge join, with a join condition of ("Spool_2.Character_number = CLASSICS.Story_Chr.Character_Number"). The result goes into Spool 1, which is built locally on the AMPs. The size of Spool 1 is estimated to be 8 rows. The estimated time for this step is 0.20 seconds.
6) Finally, we send out an END TRANSACTION step to all AMPs involved in processing the request.

-> The contents of Spool 1 are sent back to the user as the result of statement 1. The total estimated time is 0 hours and 0.28 seconds

Figure 12-2

JOIN:

```
EXPLAIN SELECT  Title_Code
               , Last_Name
               , First_Name
  FROM Chr, Story_Chr
  WHERE Chr.Character_Number =
  Story_Chr.Character_Number
  AND Story_Number = 101;
```

Explanation

---

1) First, we lock a distinct CLASSICS."pseudo table" for read on a RowHash to prevent global deadlock for CLASSICS.Chr.
2) Next, we lock CLASSICS.Chr for read
3) We do a single-AMP RETRIEVE step from CLASSICS.Story_Chr by way of the primary index "CLASSICS.Story_Chr.Story_number = 101" with no residual conditions into Spool 2, which is redistributed by hash code to all AMPs. Then we do a SORT to order Spool 2 by row hash. The size of Spool 2 is estimated to be 8 rows. The estimated time for this step is 0.14 seconds.
4) We do an all-AMPs JOIN step from Spool 2 (Last Use) by way of a RowHash match scan, which is joined to CLASSICS.Chr. Spool 2 and CLASSICS.Chr are joined using a merge join, with a join condition of ("CLASSICS.Chr.Character_number = Spool_2.Character_Number"). The result goes into Spool 1, which is built locally on the AMPs. The size of Spool 1 is estimated to be 8 rows. The estimated time for this step is 0.15 seconds.
5) Finally, we send out an END TRANSACTION step to all AMPs involved in processing the request.
The contents of Spool 1 are sent back to the user as the result of statement 1. The total estimated time is 0 hours and 0.29 seconds.

Figure 12-3

The EXPLAIN

To decide which of the two methods is optimum, we use the EXPLAIN. If we compare the EXPLAIN of the subquery (*Fig.12-2*) with that of the join (*Fig. 12-3)*, we can easily demonstrate that, for this particular query, the Teradata Optimizer favors the subquery over the join by a tiny margin.

Conclusion

While we have taken a fairly good look at subqueries and joins, we have yet to consider the mischief which can be caused by that relational poltergeist known as "NULL". For that, we must continue the study by examining the SET operators and OUTER JOINs in the next chapter.

Hands On Exercises

1. Use EXISTS to SELECT the total Sales_Quantity of Book 1001 from the Book_Sales_History for the month of December- *only if we sold any.*

2. SELECT the Last_Name and First_Name of all Characters from story number 103. first as a subquery and then as a join.

3. Use EXPLAIN to evaluate the results of Exercise 2 (above) and determine which is the more efficient.

4. Using the EXPLAIN, determine how many rows are returned as a result of the following SELECT:

```
SELECT Story_Name
       , Last_Name
       FROM Chr, Story_Chr, Story
       WHERE Chr.Character_Number =
              Story_Chr.Character_Number
       AND Story.Story_Number =
       Story_Chr.Story_Number;
```

5. Finally, delete the WHERE clauses. This will result in a full Cartesian product join. Determine how many rows will now be returned.

13 Outer Joins, Set Operators and Derived Tables

In the previous chapter we discussed joins based on an equality condition between tables having columns which share a common domain, known as INNER joins. In Chapter 10, we demonstrated that two NULLs are never equal. As a result, rows where one of the join columns is NULL are excluded from the output, unless some special provision is made in the WHERE clause. OUTER joins return rows, even though one or both of the columns on which the join is based are NULL. *Fig. 13-1* shows the syntax.

```
SELECT    cname [ ,cname [ , . . . ]
                                    [INNER]
FROM      tname [  aname ]        { LEFT  [OUTER] }
                                  { RIGHT [OUTER] }
                                  { FULL  [OUTER] }
                                    CROSS
JOIN      tname [  aname ]

ON        condition
```

Figure 13-1

TYPE OF JOIN	DESCRIPTION
LEFT OUTER JOIN	References the first (leftmost) table listed in the join.
RIGHT OUTER JOIN	References the second (rightmost) table listed in the join.
FULL OUTER JOIN	Both tables involved in the join.
CROSS	Cartesian Join

Consider an INNER join (WHERE the Publisher_Number in the Book table is compared for equality to the Publisher_Number in the Publisher table):

```
SELECT DISTINCT
                Publisher.Publisher_Number (TITLE 'Nbr')
               , Publisher_Name
               , Book_Name                (FORMAT 'X(20)')
               FROM Book, Publisher
               WHERE Book.Publisher_Number =
                   Publisher.Publisher_Number
               ORDER BY Publisher.Publisher_Number;
```

```
Nbr  Publisher_Name             Book_Name

101  Washington Square Press    A Christmas Carol
103  Oxford University Press    Great Expectations
103  Oxford University Press    Our Mutual Friend
103  Oxford University Press    A Charles Dickens
104  Penguin Books              Christmas Tales
104  Penguin Books              The Christmas Books
104  Penguin Books              David Copperfield'
104  Penguin Books              A Tale of Two Cities
104  Penguin Books              Hard Times
106  Every Man's Library        Martin Chuzzlewit
```

The Book table has no Publisher_Number listed for Book_Number 1000, and there are no books listed for Publisher_Numbers 102 and 105. As a result Book 1000 and Publisher_Numbers 105 are not included in the report. To include Book_Number 1000 ('A Christmas Carol') , but not Publisher_Numbers 102 and 105:

```
SELECT DISTINCT p.Publisher_Number (TITLE 'Nbr')
        ,p.Publisher_Name
        ,b.Book_Name          (FORMAT 'X(20)')
    FROM Book b LEFT OUTER JOIN Publisher p
    ON b.Publisher_Number =
        p.Publisher_Number
    ORDER BY p.Publisher_Number;
```

```
Nbr  Publisher_Name              Book_Name

  ?  ?                           A Christmas Carol
101  Washington Square Press     A Christmas Carol
103  Oxford University Press     Great Expectations
103  Oxford University Press     Our Mutual Friend
103  Oxford University Press     A Charles Dickens
104  Penguin Books               Christmas Tales
104  Penguin Books               The Christmas Books
104  Penguin Books               David Copperfield'
104  Penguin Books               A Tale of Two Cities
104  Penguin Books               Hard Times
106  Every Man's Library         Martin Chuzzlewit
```

To include Publishers 102 and 105, but not Book_Number 1000;

```
SELECT DISTINCT p.Publisher_Number (TITLE 'Nbr')
        , p.Publisher_Name
        , b.Book_Name          FORMAT 'X(20)')
    FROM Book b
    RIGHT OUTER JOIN Publisher p
    ON b.Publisher_Number =
        p.Publisher_Number
    ORDER BY p.Publisher_Number;
```

Nbr	Publisher_Name	Book_Name
101	Washington Square Press	A Christmas Carol
102	**MacMillan Publishing**	**?**
103	Oxford University Press	Great Expectations
103	Oxford University Press	Our Mutual Friend
103	Oxford University Press	A Charles Dickens
104	Penguin Books	Christmas Tales
104	Penguin Books	The Christmas Books
104	Penguin Books	David Copperfield'
104	Penguin Books	A Tale of Two Cities
104	Penguin Books	Hard Times
105	**The Modern Library**	**?**
106	Every Man's Library	Martin Chuzzlewit

To include Books with no publishers and publishers without books:

```
SELECT DISTINCT p.Publisher_Number   (TITLE 'Nbr')
              , p.Publisher_Name
              , b.Book_Name      FORMAT 'X(20)')
      FROM Book b FULL OUTER JOIN
Publisher p ON b.Publisher_Number =  p.Publisher_Number
      ORDER BY p.Publisher_Number ;
```

Nbr	Publisher_Name	Book_Name
?	?	**A Christmas Carol**
101	Washington Square Press	A Christmas Carol
102	**MacMillan Publishing**	**?**
103	Oxford University Press	Great Expectations
103	Oxford University Press	Our Mutual Friend
103	Oxford University Press	A Charles Dickens
104	Penguin Books	Christmas Tales
104	Penguin Books	The Christmas Books
104	Penguin Books	David Copperfield'
104	Penguin Books	A Tale of Two Cities
104	Penguin Books	Hard Times
105	**The Modern Library**	**?**
106	Every Man's Library	Martin Chuzzlewit

SET Operators

All the subqueries and joins we have examined so far have generated a single answer set. Occasionally however, we might require an end-on-end list from multiple tables (UNION), the results of one select excluding the duplicate results in a second set (MINUS), or a comparison of two answer sets which returns only those rows common to both (INTERSECT). UNION, MINUS and INTERSECT are known as SET operators.

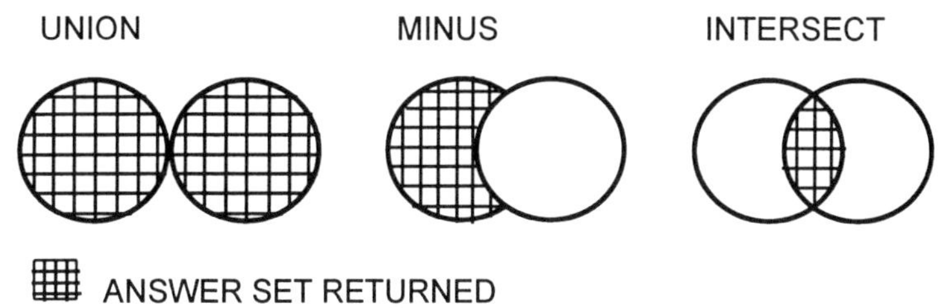

Figure 13-2

In Fig. 13-2, the shaded portions of the circles represent the responses to UNION, MINUS and INTERSECT queries. A UNION returns the complete results of two or more compatible SELECT operations end-on-end. A MINUS returns the results on one SELECT, less the rows from the second SELECT which are duplicate to rows in the first SELECT. The INTERSECT also makes two SELECTs, but returns only those rows which are common to both.

SET Operators - Rules for Usage

Only the final SELECT clause is terminated with a semi-colon.

All SELECT clauses must have the same number of expressions.

Corresponding expressions must have compatible domains.

The first SELECT determines output length, format and title.

The last SELECT contains the (numeric) ORDER BY statement.

Each SELECT must have a "FROM tablename" clause.

GROUP BY applies to an individual SELECT and not to the answer set as a whole.

Duplicate rows in the output are eliminated unless the "ALL" option is used.

SET Operators are evaluated in the following order of precedence, but may be overridden using parentheses:

INTERSECT.
UNION.
MINUS.

The UNION Operator

Suppose we wish to create a list of Mr. Fezziwig (Character_Number 1010), and all the characters related to him. This operation involves two distinct SELECTs - one for Mr. Fezziwig himself, and another for the related characters. The UNION operator permits us to combine both (or multiple) SELECT operations in a single seamless request.

The UNION operator eliminates duplicates from the output unless " UNION ALL" is used instead of "UNION".

```
SELECT Last_Name
        ,First_Name
        ,' ' (Char(20),TITLE 'Relationship')
        FROM Chr
        WHERE Character_Number = 1010
UNION
SELECT Last_Name
         ,First_Name
         ,Relationship
        FROM Chr, Chr_Chr, Relationship
         WHERE Chr.Character_Number =
        Chr_Chr.Character_Number
        AND Chr_Chr.Relationship_Code =
        Relationship.Relationship_Code AND
        Chr_Chr.Related_to_Character_Number = 1010
        ORDER BY 1,2;
```

Last_Name	First_Name	Relationship
Fezziwig	?	
Fezziwig	?	Wife
Scrooge	Ebenezer	Employee
Wilkins	Dick	Employee

MINUS

The MINUS operator eliminates the results of the second SELECT from the first SELECT. *For Example,* in order to SELECT all the characters in Story 101 except the Cratchits, we can first SELECT all the characters and use the MINUS operator to eliminate anyone with the last_Name of "Cratchit":

```
SELECT Last_Name
        ,First_Name
        FROM Chr, Story_Chr
        WHERE Chr.Character_Number =
        Story_Chr.Character_Number
        AND Story_Number = 101
```

```
MINUS
SELECT Last_Name
       ,First_Name
       FROM Chr
       WHERE Last_Name = 'Cratchit'
       ORDER BY 1,2;
```

Last_Name	First_Name
?	Belle
?	Fred
?	Joe
Dilber	?
Fezziwig	?
Marley	Jacob
Scrooge	Ebenezer
Scrooge	Fan
Topper	?

INTERSECT

Returns just those rows which are common to both sets. *For example*, to eliminate all the characters from story 101 except the Cratchit family, we might first SELECT everyone and INTERSECT the Cratchits:

```
SELECT Last_Name
       ,First_Name
       FROM Chr, Story_Chr
       WHERE Chr.Character_Number =
       Story_Chr.Character_Number
       AND Story_Number = 101
INTERSECT
SELECT Last_Name
       ,First_Name
       FROM Chr
       WHERE Last_Name = 'Cratchit'
       ORDER BY 1,2;
```

```
Last_Name       First_Name

Cratchit        ?
Cratchit        Belinda
Cratchit        Bob
Cratchit        Martha
Cratchit        Peter
Cratchit        Tim
```

Derived Tables

Derived tables are used to provide interim storage for the results of imbedded subqueries, which may be accessed directly from an outer query, or joined with another table with a single pass of the data.. In this way, derived tables largely eliminate the need for user-created temporary tables.

The following example derives a list of all books which cost more than the average price. It achieves this by selecting the average price in a subquery and inserting that value into a column named “Avgprice” in a derived table called “TEMP”. Control then passes to the outer SELECT which joins Book table to the TEMP table as a Cartesian join. (Since there is only one row in TEMP, this is not a problem.)

```
SELECT Book_Name
      ,Price_Amount
      , Avgprice
      FROM (SELECT AVG(Price_Amount)
            FROM Book) TEMP (Avgprice) ,Book
            WHERE Price_Amount > Avgprice
      ORDER BY 2 DESC;
```

```
Book_Name                  Price_Amount   Avgprice

Martin Chuzzlewit                 20.00       7.47
A Charles Dickens Ch              14.99       7.47
Our Mutual Friend                 10.95       7.47
```

Derived Tables:

Must have a unique name.

Must name columns if the derived table is created by an expression.

The number of columns in the derived table definition must be equal to the number of fields in the SELECT list.

Conclusion

With subqueries, correlated subqueries, inner joins, outer joins and derived tables at its disposal, SQL is thought to be able to handle any type of join. The limitation of 16 table references per SQL query is generous, and presents more of a challenge for the database vendor to handle, than for the application developer to code.

Hands On Exercises

1 (a) Create a report by first selecting all Book_Numbers, Book_Names and Publisher_Numbers from the Book table, and then use the MINUS operator to eliminate "Penguin Books" from the report.

1 (b) Perform the same request as a subquery.

From a subquery, SELECT the Book_Number and the total of the Sales_Quantity column from the Book_Sales History table, and store them in a derived table call "TEMP" as "Book_Number" and "SumSales". From the outer query, SELECT the average of SumSales. (In this way you are taking an aggregate of an aggregate)

14 Insert, Update and Delete

After the glamour and excitement of the SELECT statement, the Data Manipulation Language statements, Insert, Update and Delete seem colorless and drab by comparison. Were it not for these three DML statements however, there could be no data to SELECT.

The **INSERT** statement adds one or more rows to a table.

The **UPDATE** changes column values in one or more rows of a table.

The **DELETE** removes one or more rows from a table.

The INSERT, UPDATE and DELETE examples which follow will reference the Author and Chr tables as shown in *Fig. 14-1*.

INSERT

There are three syntactic forms of the INSERT statement:

The **Positional** form.

The **Non-Positional** form.

The **INSERT SELECT**.

AUTHOR
Description: Writer of Stories

Author Number	Last Name	First Name	Birth Date	Died Date
PK				
UPI				
101	Dickens	Charles	Feb 07 1812	Jun 09 1870

CHR
Description: Fictional character in story

Character Number	Last Name	First Name	Title Code	Description Number
PK			FK	FK
UPI	NUSI			
1002	Marley	Jacob	Mr	102
1003	Scrooge	Fan	Mis	

Figure 14-1

The Positional Form:

The positional form of the INSERT requires the user to supply a value for each column of the table in the precise order of the original CREATE TABLE statement. NULLs are represented either by the keyword, "NULL" or by adjacent commas.

The following statements insert new rows into the Chr table:

```
INSERT Chr VALUES  (1001, 'Scrooge','Ebenezer','Mr ',101);

INSERT Chr VALUES  (1003, 'Scrooge','Fan','Mis',NULL);
```

The word, "VALUES" in the syntax is optional.
Column values are separated by commas.
Alpha values are enclosed by single quotes.
The inserted values are enclosed within parenthesis.

The use of the positional forms avoids the necessity of providing the column names in the INSERT statement. As a result, this form is generally considerably shorter than the Non-Positional form.

The Non-Positional Form

The Non-Positional form of the INSERT does not require the user to be aware of the order of the columns in the original CREATE TABLE statement. Because this type of insert requires specification of the column names, only those names for which a non-NULL value is supplied need be listed, and NULLs may be effectively ignored:

For Example, in the INSERT below no value is provided for the last column in the Chr table - Description_Number. As a result, (provided the Description_Number column is nullable), we may effectively ignore it:

```
INSERT Chr (First_Name, Last_Name, Character_Number,
Title_Code) VALUES  ('Fan','Scrooge',1003,'Mis');
```

The INSERT SELECT

While both the Positional and Non-Positional forms of the INSERT are each used to add no more than a single row to a table, the INSERT SELECT is generally used to SELECT one or more rows from one table and INSERT them into another. The INSERT SELECT is the only form of the INSERT which adds multiple rows to a table in a single statement.

The following INSERT SELECT statement copies a complete set of rows from the Chr table to Chr2:

```
INSERT INTO Chr2
SELECT * FROM Chr;
```

OR, if only certain columns are required:

```
INSERT INTO Chr2
(Character_Number2, Last_Name2, First_Name2)
SELECT Character_Number, Last_Name, First_Name
        FROM Chr ;
```

Despite its appearance, the SELECT part of the INSERT SELECT contributes to the output, and for that reason is *not a subquery.* Since it is not a subquery, the inner SELECT does not need to be enclosed in parentheses.

The UPDATE

The UPDATE statement is used to change the column values in rows identified by a WHERE clause. If the WHERE clause is missing, ***ALL*** the rows are changed. *For Example:* we wish to add another author, Jane Austen to the Author table, but cannot remember the dates of her birth or death. The INSERT treats these values (for the time being) as NULL:

```
INSERT Author (102,'Austen','Jane',,);
```

Later, we decide to UPDATE the row to add the missing information:

```
UPDATE  Author
SET Birth_Date = 'Dec 16 1775'
    ,Died_Date = 'Jul 18 1817'
WHERE Author_Number = 102;
```

(The Birth_Date and Died_Date columns of the Author table are used to store dates prior to 1900, as negative values. To facilitate input of these values, these columns were given a default format of 'MMMBDDBYYYY' in the CREATE TABLE statement. In view of the possible ambiguity of the 2-digit year '00' between 1900 and 2000, it is strongly recommend that all future date input or change be formatted in this way- with a four digit year.)

Had we (in error) omitted the WHERE clause:

```
UPDATE  Author
        SET Birth_Date = 'Dec 16 1775'
          , Died_Date = 'Jul 18 1817';
```

the row of ***every*** author would have been changed to reflect a birth in 1775, and a death in 1817.

UPDATE in a Subquery

As an example, assume that Penguin Books have decided to reduce the retail price of all their hard cover books by 10%:

```
UPDATE Book
        Set Price_Amount = Price_Amount * .9
        WHERE Publisher_Number IN
        (SELECT Publisher_Number
                FROM Publisher
                WHERE Publisher_Name
                LIKE '%Penguin Books%')
                AND Book_Type = 'H';
```

UPDATE in a JOIN

An identical result to the example above could be achieved by coding the request as a join:

```
UPDATE Book
Set Price_Amount = Price_Amount * .9
WHERE Book.Publisher_Number =
          Publisher.Publisher_Number
AND Publisher_Name LIKE '%Penguin Books%'
AND Book_Type = 'H';
```

Once again the *optimal* method is determined using the EXPLAIN facility.

The DELETE

The DELETE statement is used to remove one or more rows from a table, but despite this, it shares much of its functionality with the UPDATE:

Rows to be deleted are identified by a WHERE clause.

If the WHERE clause is missing, the default is **ALL.**

DELETES can be constructed as a subquery or a join.

Figure 14-2 provides examples of the SQL DELETE statement:

`DELETE FROM Publisher;`	Removes all rows from the Publisher table.
`DELETE FROM Publisher WHERE Publisher_Number = 105;`	Removes only Publisher 105
`DELETE FROM Publisher WHERE Publisher_Number NOT IN (SELECT Publisher_Number FROM Book);`	Deletes publishers from the Publisher table who do not have books listed in the Book table
`DELETE FROM Book WHERE Book.Publisher_Number = Publisher.Publisher_Number AND Publisher_Name = 'The Modern Library';`	Deletes any books from the Book table published by 'The Modern Library'

Figure 14-2

Conclusions

While INSERTs, UPDATEs and DELETEs are, in themselves, relatively simple operations, they often represent a single step in a more complex multiple statement transaction. An INSERT, for example, will probably be followed by a SELECT of the new row, as confirmation of a successful operation. It is important to ensure that if the INSERT does not succeed, the confirming SELECT also fails. Transaction boundaries must be defined in such a way that if one part of the transaction fails, the whole transaction fails. Equally if any part is allowed to succeed, the entire transaction succeeds.

While few people doubt the value of well maintained transaction integrity, its implementation is generally left to the ingenuity of the programmer, rather than the SQL itself. Teradata addresses this important issue with the macro - the subject of the next chapter.

Hands On Exercises

1. Insert a row into the author table for Author_Number 103 and leave all other columns NULL. Use the non-positional form of the INSERT.

2. Update the row you have just inserted with the following data:

Last_Name:	Bronte
First_Name:	Charlotte
Birth_Date:	Apr 21 1816
Died_Date:	Mar 31 1855

3. Use the positional form of the INSERT to add another row into the Author table:

Author Number:	104
Last_Name:	Bronte
First_Name:	Emily
Birth_Date:	Jul 30 1818
Died_Date:	Dec 19 1848

4. SELECT both rows to confirm the succesful INSERT/UPDATE.

5. With a single statement, DELETE the rows for Author_Number 103 and 104. (Remember the default for DELETE is ALL).

15 Macros

Of all Teradata's contributions to SQL, the macro is probably the most significant and innovative. Macros can:

Eliminate the risk of accidental damage to the data.

Used to limit the scope of the change to that pre-approved by the system administrator.

Improve performance of the SQL through pre-parsing and pre-syntax checking techniques.

Provide almost cost-free *data, transaction and referential integrity* checking.

Although referential integrity has since been incorporated into standard SQL, data integrity and transaction integrity are still largely left to the user and to the SQL delivery application.

Standard SQL provides no effective linkage between one SQL statement and another. Teradata macros, on the other hand, can represent complete, coordinated, multiple statement SQL transactions, fueled by a single input record. Each macro requires a name, unique within the database and consistent with the SQL naming conventions described in Chapter 2. Macros are fully parsed, resolved and syntax-checked when created, and are stored in the Teradata Data Dictionary/Directory (DD/D).

The macro is executed with a simple two-word command. Since the SQL has already been determined to be syntactically accurate, the workload of the SQL Parser is greatly reduced and the application reaps the benefit of improved performance. Equally, in order to execute the SQL statements within a macro, the user simply requires the EXECUTE MACRO privilege. In this way a user's access to the data can be strictly limited to the execution of the macro and nothing else. Macros therefore provide the system administrator with the ability to fine-tune and control user access to the data.

There are five SQL commands concerned with macro maintenance and use:

CREATE MACRO	Defines a macro and stores it in the DD/D.
REPLACE MACRO	Replaces an existing object with that name, and stores a new macro definition in the DD/D.
EXECUTE *macroname*	Executes the statements within the macro.
DROP MACRO	Removes a macro definition from the DD/D
SHOW MACRO	Retrieves a macro definition from the DD/D.

CREATE MACRO

To create a macro, the user requires the CREATE MACRO privilege. If an object of the same name already exists in the database, the CREATE MACRO statement will fail. In this way the user is, to some degree, insulated against unintentional delete of a previously created object.

Macros can be created with or without input parameters. The example below shows the CREATE MACRO in perhaps its simplest form:

```
CREATE MACRO ListPub104 AS (
        SELECT  Book_Number (TITLE 'NUMBER')
                ,Book_Name   (TITLE 'TITLE')
              FROM Book
              WHERE Publisher_Number = 104
              ORDER BY Book_Name;
        );
```

Each SQL statement within a macro is terminated with a semi-colon in the usual manner. The statement or group of statements is enclosed within parentheses and imbedded between the CREATE MACRO statement and its terminating semi-colon.

REPLACE MACRO

To replace a macro, the user must have both CREATE and DROP MACRO privileges. If an object of the same name already exists in the database, the REPLACE MACRO statement will replace it. If the object does not already exist, the REPLACE MACRO statement will create it. Either way, provided it is syntactically correct and passes all security tests etc., the REPLACE macro statement should never fail. Since REPLACE MACRO is potentially destructive to pre-existing objects however, it requires a higher level of privilege than CREATE MACRO.

```
REPLACE  MACRO ListPub104 AS (
         SELECT Book_Number (TITLE 'NUMBER')
               ,Book_Name    (TITLE 'TITLE')
            FROM Book
            WHERE Publisher_Number = 104
            ORDER BY Book_Name;
      );
```

EXECUTE *Macroname*

To execute the SELECT contained in the ListPub104 macro requires the keyword "EXECUTE" or "EXEC" followed by the macro name and a trailing semi-colon:

```
EXEC ListPub104;
```

NUMBER	TITLE
1011	A Tale of Two Cities
1002	Christmas Tales
1008	David Copperfield
1010	Hard Times
1013	The Christmas Books
1006	The Christmas Books
1005	The Christmas Books
1014	The Christmas Books
1007	The Christmas Books

DROP MACRO

When the macro is no longer needed, it can be removed from the DD/D by any user with DROP MACRO privilege

```
DROP MACRO ListPub104;
```

Parameterized Macros

The ListPub104 macro is limited in scope, since it specifies a literal value for Publisher_Number. The following example is more generally useful, in that it permits the user to specify any Publisher number as an execution-time parameter:

```
REPLACE  MACRO ListPub (PubNo SMALLINT)
        AS  (
           SELECT :PubNo
                       (TITLE 'PUBLISHER//NUMBER')
                   ,Book_Number
                       (TITLE 'BOOK//NUMBER')
                   ,Book_Name (TITLE 'BOOK//TITLE')
               FROM Book
               WHERE Publisher_Number = :PubNo
               ORDER BY Book_Name;
        );
```

Each input parameter must have a unique name (which can be identical to the related column name). This unique name, prefixed with a colon, may then be referenced anywhere in the body of the macro, and becomes an execution-time variable. If the macro is then executed with the statement:

```
EXEC ListPub (103);
```

the value 103 is substituted for :ListPub, and is seen by the Teradata Parser as:

```
SELECT   103              (TITLE 'PUBLISHER//NUMBER')
        , Book_Number        (TITLE 'BOOK//NUMBER')
        , Book_Name             (TITLE 'BOOK//TITLE')
       FROM Book
       WHERE Publisher_Number = 103
       ORDER BY Book_Name;
```

```
PUBLISHER   BOOK     BOOK
   NUMBER   NUMBER   TITLE

      103   1012     A Charles Dickens Christmas
      103   1003     Great Expectations
      103   1004     Our Mutual Friend
```

Transaction Integrity

Most SQL transactions which add, change or remove rows from a table or tables are required to reconfirm to the user that:

The transaction successfully completed.
The data submitted was correct.

An INSERT transaction would normally involve at least two SQL statements:

An INSERT to add the row.
A SELECT to reconfirm the validity of the data.

Its execution however, needs to be controlled to ensure that the SELECT operation occurs *only* if the INSERT is successful.

All the SQL statements in a macro are treated by the RDBMS as a single transaction, and the user is guaranteed that if any of the statements succeed, they will all succeed. Equally if any of the statements fail, they will all fail. This principle remains true even if one macro executes another. In this event all the SQL statements from the first to the last, including any imbedded "EXEC macroname" statements, are treated as a single transaction and will succeed as a group, or fail as a group, but will never partially succeed or partially fail.

For Example, a parameterized macro is needed to insert a new row into the Book_Sales_History table and reconfirm the values to the user:

```
REPLACE MACRO NewSale (
        BookNum SMALLINT
       , SDate DATE
       , Qty SMALLINT )
       AS (
       SELECT :BookNum      (TITLE 'Book')
              ,:SDATE       (TITLE 'Date'
              ,'FORMAT 'MMMBDDBYYYY')
             ,:Qty          (TITLE 'Nbr Sold');

       INSERT INTO Book_Sales_History
             (Book_Number
             ,Sales_Date
             ,Sales_Quantity)
             VALUES
             (:BookNum
             , :SDate
             , :Qty);
       );
```

This macro has two SQL statements, the SELECT of the literal input values, (which requires no disk access to the database, and is therefore extremely efficient), and the INSERT itself. Since we are guaranteed by Teradata that both statements will succeed, or both statements will fail as a unit, we are secure in the knowledge that the literal values SELECTED will not be returned unless the INSERT is successful.

Syntax Options

Like the INSERT operations described in the previous chapter, the "EXECUTE *macroname*" statement has a positional and a non-positional form.

The Positional Form

```
EXEC NewSale (1001,970110,6);
```

In the example above, the user needs to be aware that the NewSale macro has exactly three parameters, and that they are ordered as "BookNum, SDate and Qty". Moreover, any NULLs in the input must be indicated by the keyword "NULL", or marked positionally by 2 adjacent commas.

The Non-Positional Form

The non-positional form, on the other hand, matches the input values to the macro parameters in an order specified in the EXEC statement, and permits NULL values to be ignored:

```
EXEC Newsale
        (Qty =6
        , SDate = 970110
        , BookNum = 1001);
```

Using MACROS to Preserve Data, Transaction and Referential Integrity

Unlike other SQL statements, macros have the ability to "ROLLBACK" (or force a failure) after a failed test of data values or column existence.

For Example:

```
REPLACE MACRO NewChr
                (CharNo INTEGER
                , LName CHAR(15)
                , FName CHAR(12)
                , StoryNo SMALLINT
                , TCode CHAR(3))
        AS (
        ROLLBACK 'Invalid Story Number'
                WHERE :StoryNo < 99
                OR :StoryNo > 999;
```

```
ROLLBACK 'Invalid Character Number'
        WHERE :CharNo < 999
        OR :CharNo > 9999;
SELECT
        'CHARACTER ' || :Lname || ' SUCCESSFULLY
        INSERTED' (TITLE '');
ROLLBACK 'Invalid Story'
        WHERE :StoryNo NOT IN
        (SELECT Story_Number
        FROM Story
        WHERE Story_Number = :StoryNo);
ROLLBACK 'Invalid Title Code'
        WHERE :TCode NOT IN
        (SELECT Title_Code
        FROM AddTitle
        WHERE Title_Code = :TCode);


INSERT INTO Chr
        (Character_Number
        , Last_Name
        , First_Name
        , Title_Code)
    VALUES (
        :CharNo
        , :Lname
        , :Fname
        , :TCode);
INSERT INTO Story_Chr
        (Story_Number
        , Character_Number)
    VALUES
        (:StoryNo
        , :CharNo);
);
```

The following analysis of the NewChr macro will be clearer for those who have already read the introductory work, "The Teradata Database", where it is explained that:

Each table has a column or columns defined as the "primary index" based upon those columns most often used to access the data.

A SELECT operation against a table using a unique primary index never costs more than a single disk read operation.

Single disk read operations in the Teradata Database generally happen in parallel.

With those principles in mind, we can now examine the relative cost of executing the NewChr macro in terms of the number of expensive disk read operations needed to complete the task:

The macro has five input parameters, CharNo, Lname, Fname, StoryNo and TCode.

If the input value for StoryNo is not between 100 and 999 the macro will terminate immediately with a message "Invalid Story Number". ***This is a data integrity test and requires no access to disk.***

If the input value for CharNo is not between 1000 and 9999 the macro will end immediately with a message "Invalid Character Number" - ***another memory-only based data integrity test - no disk access required.***

The SELECT request constructs a confirmation message directly from the input data. This will not be returned unless the entire macro completes successfully. Transaction integrity is maintained ***without need for disk access.***

If the input value for StoryNo is not a valid Story_Number from the Story table, the macro will end immediately with a message "Invalid Story Number". Story_Number is the unique primary index of the Story table and so this *referential integrity* test costs no more than ***a single disk read operation***.

If the input value for TCode is not a valid Title_Code from the Add_Title table, the macro will roll back with a message "Invalid Title_Code". This is also a single disk read *referential integrity* request, and will almost certainly happen in parallel with the disk read in step 4.

Execution of the entire macro to this point, including all the data validation, the referential integrity and the user confirmation has thus consumed the total elapsed time required for *a single disk read* operation. If the macro is required to roll back at this point for any reason, it will happen with remarkably little cost. Only when all the tests have been fully satisfied, is the actual productive work of the macro committed.

While there is admittedly no free lunch, the Teradata macro certainly renders the cost affordable.

Hands On Exercises

This exercise largely duplicates the Hands On Exercises from the previous chapter.

1. Ensure that all the Bronte sisters have been deleted from the Author table.

2. Create a parameterized macro called "NewAuthor" to re-insert the Bronte sisters into the Author table with a reconfirmation message to the user in the format:

   Insert of Charlotte Bronte successful.

3. Execute the NewAuthor macro using the positional form to insert a row into the Author Table for:

Author Number	104,
Last_Name	Bronte
First_Name	Emily
Born:	Jul 30 1818
Died:	Dec 19 1848

4. Execute the NewAuthor macro again, this time using the non-positional form to insert the following information into the Author table:

   Author Number = 103,
   Last name = “Bronte”, First name = “Charlotte”.

16 Databases, Tables and Views

The primary resource of the Teradata Database is space - the total amount of disk space available on the hardware platform for permanent and temporary storage of data.

In *Fig. 16-1*, the large rectangle represents the total amount of disk space available to the Teradata Database. Initially, all this space is owned by a user called "DBC" (DataBase Computer). User DBC is also known as the Data Dictionary/Directory (DD/D), and uses part of its space to house all the tables, views and macros needed by Teradata to operate the RDBMS. To most users of the system, a single collection of tables, views and macros is known as a DATABASE. DBC is a database. DBC is however rather more than simply a logical boundary between one part of the universe and another, since DBC has a password it can therefore log on to the Teradata Database and issue instructions in SQL. In addition to being a DATABASE therefore, DBC is also known as a USER - and the most powerful one at that! A USER might then be somewhat loosely defined as a uniquely named *database with a password.*

When the Teradata system is delivered from the factory, DBC will already have sub-let part of its space to a number of other users/databases also needed by the RDBMS.

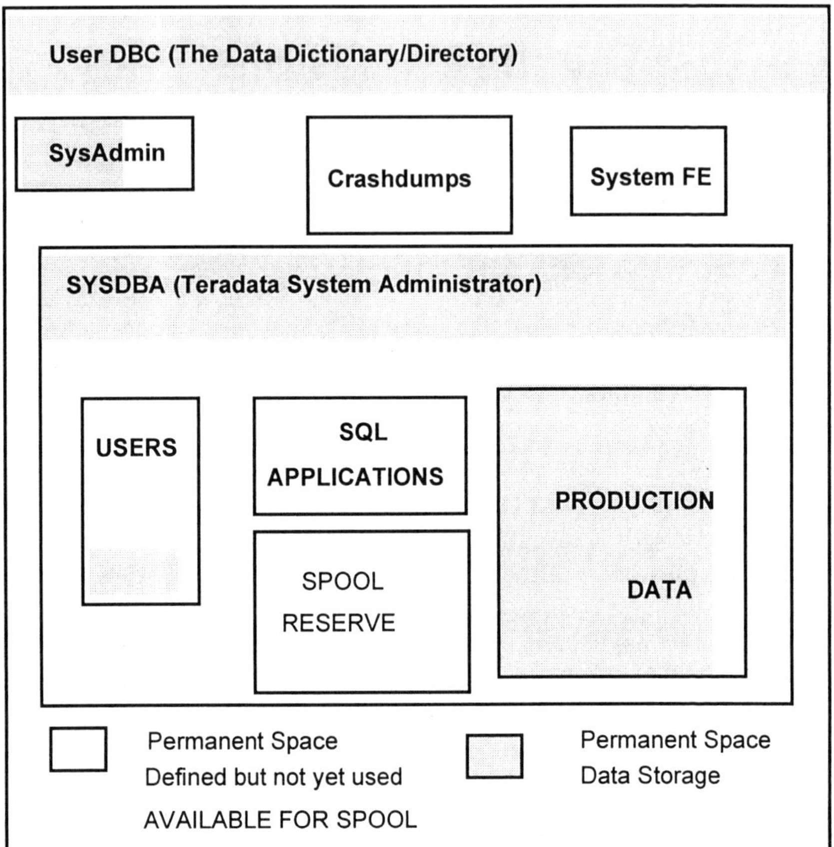

Figure 16-1

Object Name	Database/User	Main Purpose
SysAdmin	User	Houses utility Restart Logs
CrashDumps	Database	Diagnostic information capture
System FE	User	Diagnostic tables and macros needed by the Field Engineer

Upon receipt of a new system the Teradata System Administrator (TSA) will need to log on to Teradata as "DBC", calculate how much space is needed by DBC and the other system-required objects, and assign the rest of the space to a subordinate user (suggested name "SYSDBA"). SYSDBA then becomes the control point from which the TSA can ensure that each user of the system is provided with the disk resources needed for each application or task.

In dividing up the space between the users and applications (PERMANENT SPACE), and in allowing sufficient temporary space (SPOOL) for the interim results of their queries, the TSA should be aware that the Teradata Database is unusual in that it does not require the allocation of *contiguous* disk space for each user or database. A user or a database might therefore be alternatively defined as "a *statement* of space maintained in the DD/D", since the physical disk space itself is allocated only as needed when rows are actually inserted into tables. In the meantime, space defined for users, but not presently being used for physical storage of data, can be made available to the system or any other user, as temporary SPOOL. In this way, Teradata users are able to get double-mileage from temporarily unused disk space.

Users and Databases

The syntax for the CREATE USER and CREATE DATABASE statements are shown in Figures 16-2 and 16-3. (Items between square brackets [. . .] are optional):

The various features and options of the CREATE DATABASE and CREATE USER statements are primarily of interest to the TSA.

```
CREATE USER username
[ FROM ownerdb ] AS
PERM[ ANENT] = n [ BYTES ] [ , ]
PASSWORD = name
[ [ , ] option [ . . . [ , ] option ] ] [ ; ]
Any of the following options may be listed in any order:
SPOOL = n [BYTES]
STARTUP = ' string; [ . . . string ; ] '
            [ ' accountID '
ACCOUNT =   [ ( ' accountID ' [ . . . , ' accountID ' ] ) ]
DEFAULT DATABASE = dbname
[ NO ] FALLBACK   [ PROTECTION ]
[ NO   ]  [ AFTER  ]
[ DUAL ]  [ BEFORE ]  JOURNAL
DEFAULT JOURNAL TABLE = [ dbname. ] tname
              [ ASCII    HOST         ]
COLLATION =   [ EBCDIC   MULTINATIONAL ]
```

Figure 16-2

```
[ CREATE DATABASE ]
[ CD              ]  dbname
[ FROM ownerdb ] AS
PERM[ ANENT] = n [ BYTES ] [ , ]
[ [ , ] option [ . . . [ , ] option ] ] [ ; ]
Any of the following options may be listed in any order:
SPOOL = n [BYTES]
STARTUP = ' string; [ . . . string ; ] '
ACCOUNT =   ' accountID '
[ NO ] FALLBACK   [ PROTECTION ]
[ NO   ]  [ AFTER  ]
[ DUAL ]  [ BEFORE ]  JOURNAL
DEFAULT JOURNAL TABLE = [ dbname. ] tname
```

Figure 16-3

PERMANENT SPACE	Limit of disk space for permanent storage of data in tables.
PASSWORD	Mandatory if creating a user.
SPOOL	Limit of permitted temporary disk space.
STARTUP	Customized user logon procedure
ACCOUNT	Resource usage tracking IDs.
DEFAULT DATABASE	Allows a user to access another database as a default.
FALLBACK	Duplicate data maintenance
COLLATION	Permits USER to set preferred data representation for specific hosts.
JOURNAL/DEFAULT JOURNAL	Permanent journal options for Archive and Recovery purposes.

(**BEFORE IMAGE** journals allow a user to recover damaged tables by ROLLING the data back to an earlier point in time. **AFTER IMAGE** journals allow the user to ROLL FORWARD to a later point in time.)

Examples of Database/User DDL commands:

```
CREATE USER Classics AS
        PERM = 50000000,
        PASSWORD = Class;
```

Creates User Class

```
CREATE DATABASE Dickens AS
        PERM = 10000000;
```

Creates Database Dickens

```
MODIFY USER Classics AS
        PASSWORD = MySecret;
```

Changes password

```
DELETE DATABASE Dickens;
```

Drops tables, views and macros from Database Dickens

```
DROP DATABASE Dickens;
```

Removes Database definition from DD/D

Tables

When planning to cross the country, a highly detailed city map can often be more of a hindrance than a help. Too much information at one time can easily obscure the objective. This is true of the CREATE TABLE statement, which with the addition of referential integrity and other table level data constraints, has evolved from something reasonably comprehensible into the kind of monster guaranteed to delight the average dragon slayer. Compared to the complex requirements of other vendors however, which require the user to define table spaces etc., the Teradata syntax becomes a model of simplicity.

The King of Hearts understood the problem well, when he advised Alice, "Begin at the beginning and go on till you come to the end; then stop". Taking his advice, therefore let us begin with a somewhat simplified syntax (*Fig. 16-4)* which initially ignores referential integrity issues.

```
          SET
CREATE [           ] TABLE tname [ , option [ . . . , option ] ]
          MULTISET
(cname datadesc [ . . . , cname datadesc ] )
          DATABASE dbname
[ IN {                   } ]
          tname
[ [UNIQUE ] PRIMARY INDEX ( cname  [ . . . , cname ] ) ]
[ [UNIQUE ] INDEX ( cname [ . . . , cname ] )
[. . . , [ UNIQUE ] INDEX ( cname [ . . . , cname ] ) ] ]
Any of the following options may be listed in any order
   FALLBACK
[             ]
   NO FALLBACK
    NO      BEFORE                    NO       BEFORE
[[       ][        ] JOURNAL [ , ] [      ][        ] JOURNAL]
   DUAL     AFTER                     DUAL     AFTER
[ WITH JOURNAL TABLE = [ dbame .] tname ]
[ FREESPACE integer [ PERCENT ]
                      BYTES
[ DATABLOCKSIZE     { KBYTES     }]
                      KILOBYTES
    MINIMUM
[ {          } DATABLOCKSIZE ]
    MAXIMUM

{ . . . } MANDATORY SYNTAX
[ . . . ] OPTIONAL SYNTAX
```

CREATE USER/DATABASE Parameters

SET or MULTISET

While many database aficionados believe that allowing duplicate rows in tables is a violation of basic relational principles, ANSI standards nevertheless permit them. A table for which duplicate rows are to be supported is defined as a "MULTISET". Otherwise the table will have a default definition of "SET", and any attempt to insert a duplicate row will generate an error.

FALLBACK or NO FALLBACK -

Specifies the protection type of the table.

BEFORE and AFTER JOURNALS

Permanent Journal options in the CREATE TABLE statement allow the user to override the default Archive/Recovery options for the database or user.

FREESPACE and DATABLOCKSIZE

This option tells the RDBMS the preferred data block size for this table and specifies the amount of free space which should ideally be maintained in each data block. Smaller data blocks and substantial free space might favor transaction type processing while decision support might benefit from larger blocks and less free space.

COLUMN NAMES (cname) and DESCRIPTIONS (datadesc)

Each column in a table must have a unique name, discussed in Chapter 2, and a supported data type from the list in Chapter 7. This may be followed by one or more of the column attributes listed in *Fig 16-5*.

A column name, its data type and any attributes are separated by spaces. Column names are separated from each other using commas, and the column names as a whole are enclosed in parentheses.

OPTION	DESCRIPTION	EXAMPLE
BETWEEN	Value range check	BETWEEN n1 AND n2
CASESPECIFIC	Character compare Upper case <> lower case	CASESPECIFIC
NOT CASESPECIFIC	Character compare Upper case = lower case	NON CASESPECIFIC
CHECK	Value constraint	CHECK (DayCol IN (1,3,5))
COMPRESS	Use zero space to store NULL for fixed lengthcharacter column Use zero space to store specific fixed lengthcharacter value Use zero space to store NULL or column default value	COMPRESS COMPRESS 'Engineer' COMPRESS WITH DEFAULT
CONSTRAINT	Names a value constraint	CONSTRAINT ConstraintName CHECK col1 IS NOT NULL
DEFAULT	Default value if none supplied	DEFAULT 'Engineer'
FORMAT	Set default input/output format	FORMAT 'MM/DD/YYYY'
NOT NULL	Column must have a value	NOT NULL
TITLE	Set default title for column	TITLE 'Manager'
UNIQUE	No duplicate values	UNIQUE
UPPERCASE	Convert characters to upper case	UPPERCASE

Figure 16-5

IN DATABASE

From the perspective of Teradata, this is "dummy" syntax. While the RDBMS will recognize it for reasons of compatibility with other vendors, and will not error if the option is included in the syntax, any table location specified in this option will be ignored.

INDEXES

Primary and Secondary indexes for the table (see Chapter 2) are defined after the closing parenthesis of the column names and descriptions. Indexes defined in the CREATE TABLE statement default to secondary unless identified as "PRIMARY" and to non-unique unless specified as "UNIQUE". If no primary index nor primary key is specified, the RDBMS will automatically assign the first unique column as the unique primary index.

The following example might be used to define the Book Table:

```
CREATE SET TABLE CLASSICS.Book ,FALLBACK (
        Book_Number          SMALLINT NOT NULL
       ,Book_Name            VARCHAR(20)
                             NOT CASESPECIFIC
       ,Publisher_Number     SMALLINT
       ,Published_Date       DATE
       ,Price_Amount         DECIMAL(5,2)
       ,Book_Type            CHAR UPPERCASE
             CHECK (Book_Type IN ('P','H','F'))
UNIQUE PRIMARY INDEX (Book_Number)
INDEX                       (Book_Name)
;
```

<u>**Analysis**</u>

Table Name	Book
Duplicate rows ?	NO (defined as "SET" with Unique Primary Index)
Protection Level	FALLBACK
Permanent Journals	None
Unique Primary Index	Book_Number
Non-Unique Secondary Index	Book_Name (case non-specific compare)
Other	Book_Type must be a single upper case character "P", 'H" or "F".

Referential Integrity

From Chapter 2, each table must have a column or group of columns identified as the "primary key". This primary key must be:

Unique.
Never NULL.
Not subject to frequent change.

Tables may also have single or multiple columns designated as "foreign keys". Any value in a column or columns identified as a foreign key must either be a valid value in the primary key of the same or another table, or it may be NULL. (Teradata extends this by allowing foreign keys to reference any unique column or combination of columns in the same or another table).

As a result the CREATE TABLE syntax has been expanded to support optional, automatic referential integrity checks for every insert, update and delete operation.

Primary Keys and Primary Indexes

If the table has a single column primary key it may be identified in the CREATE table statement as a column constraint. Note that any column or columns identified as a primary key must also be constrained as "NOT NULL". If the identified primary key is also intended to be the unique primary index, it may be allowed to default.

Example 1 (PK defined at column level):

```
CREATE SET TABLE CLASSICS.Author , FALLBACK
        (Author_number      BYTEINT NOT NULL
                            PRIMARY KEY
        ,Last_Name          CHAR(20)
                            NOT CASESPECIFIC
```

```
        ,First_Name           VARCHAR(10)
                              NOT CASESPECIFIC
        ,Birth_Date           DATE
                              FORMAT 'mmmbddbyyyy'
        ,Died_Date            DATE
                              FORMAT 'mmmbddbyyyy');
```

Author_Number is both the primary key and a unique primary index.

Example 2 (PK defined at table level):

```
CREATE SET TABLE CLASSICS.Book_Story
                    ,FALLBACK
        (Book_Number          SMALLINT NOT NULL
        ,Story_Number         SMALLINT NOT NULL
        ,PRIMARY KEY
                (Book_Number, Story_Number));
```

The combination of Book_Number and Story_Number is both the primary key and unique primary index.

Example 3 (Both PK and primary index defined):

```
CREATE SET TABLE CLASSICS.Book_Story
                    ,FALLBACK
        (Book_Number          SMALLINT NOT NULL
        ,Story_Number         SMALLINT NOT NULL
        ,PRIMARY KEY
                    (Book_Number, Story_Number))
        PRIMARY INDEX (Story_Number);
```

Story_Number becomes a non-unique primary index, and the combination of Book_Number and Story_Number is mapped to a unique secondary index.

Foreign Keys

While Teradata does not require that the parent table containing the PK, UPI, USI or other UNIQUE column(s) be created prior to the definition of a foreign key which references it, INSERT or UPDATE operations which attempt to insert a value into the FK column will fail if the parent table does not exist. Foreign keys are defined at table level. *For Example:*

```
CREATE SET TABLE CLASSICS.Story ,FALLBACK
        (Story_Number          SMALLINT
                               NOT NULL PRIMARY KEY
        ,Story_Name            VARCHAR(32)
                               NOT NULL UNIQUE
                               NOT CASESPECIFIC
        ,Published_Year        SMALLINT
        ,Chapter_Quantity      SMALLINT DEFAULT 0
        ,Page_Quantity         SMALLINT
        ,Author_Number         BYTEINT
        ,FOREIGN KEY           (Author_Number)
        REFERENCES  Author (Author_Number));
```

In this way no row can be inserted into the story table which has an invalid value for Author-Number.

CONSTRAINT

The CONSTRAINT option which can be defined at column or table level, is used to assign a name to a data constraint. *For Example*:

```
CREATE SET TABLE CLASSICS.Story , FALLBACK
     (Story_Number     SMALLINT
                       NOT NULL PRIMARY KEY
     ,Story_Name       VARCHAR(32)
                       NOT NULL CONSTRAINT
                       Unique1 UNIQUE
     ,Published_Year   SMALLINT
```

```
,Chapter_Quantity SMALLINT DEFAULT 0
,Page_Quantity    SMALLINT
,Author_Number    BYTEINT
,FOREIGN KEY      (Author_Number)
 REFERENCES       Author(Author_Number),
,CONSTRAINT REF1
CHECK (Chapter_Quantity <= Page_Quantity));
```

The column-level CONSTRAINT (Unique1) enforces the uniqueness of Story_Name. Any column with a UNIQUE constraint must also be NOT NULL.

The table-level constraint on Chapter_Quantity ensures that no story has more chapters than pages.

COMMENTS

Good application development discipline demands that any database object whose life span is expected to extend beyond the temporary, should be properly commented.

Comments can be placed on tables, views, macros and columns using the "COMMENT ON" statement and stored in the DD/D until retrieved with a "HELP TABLE" command. *For example:*

```
COMMENT ON Classics.Story IS
                    'Individual work of fiction';
COMMENT ON Classics.Story.Story_Number IS
                    'Unique Story ID';
COMMENT ON Classics.Story.Story_Name AS
                    'Unique name of Story';
COMMENT ON Classics.Story.Published_Year IS
                    'Year originally published';
```

ALTER TABLE

The ALTER TABLE command is used to:

Add or drop columns from an empty or populated table:

```
ALTER TABLE Chr
        ADD Sex_Code CHAR(1)
       ,ADD Class_Code BYTEINT;
```

Change the attribute options on existing columns:

```
ALTER TABLE Book_Sales_History
       ADD Sales_Date FORMAT 'mmmbddbyyyy';
```

Change the protection level of a table:

```
ALTER TABLE Relationship, NO FALLBACK;
```

Combine various changes in same statement:

```
ALTER TABLE Chr, NO FALLBACK
        DROP Class_Code
       ,ADD Sex_Code CHAR(1);
```

Secondary Indexes

Secondary Indexes may be dynamically created and dropped with a single statement:

CREATE INDEX (Last_Name) ON Chr;
Builds a non-unique secondary index subtable

CREATE UNIQUE INDEX (Story_Name) ON Story;
Builds a unique secondary index subtable

```
DROP INDEX(Last_Name) ON Chr;
```
Removes secondary index subtable.

(In Chapter 5 we discussed how to list all the indexes on a table with the "HELP TABLE tablename;" statement.)

VIEWS

Most Teradata System Administrators recommend creating at least one view for every base table in the production database, because views:

Provide an additional level of security.

Help control read and update privileges.

Reduce the need for maintenance programming and administration.

Are not affected if rows are added to a table.

Are not affected if a non-referenced column is dropped from a table.

Simplify end-user SQL.

A VIEW is:

A Virtual table.

A definition stored in the Data Dictionary/Directory.

Used to access data from one or more tables. Data is not duplicated or shared.

CREATING / REPLACING VIEWS

As with the macro (Chapter 15), if an object with the identical name to the VIEW being created does not already exist in the database, a "CREATE VIEW" will create it. If such an object does already exist, the "CREATE VIEW" statement will fail.

Similarly, if an object with the identical name to the VIEW being created already exists in the database, a "REPLACE VIEW" will replace it. If the object does not already exist, "REPLACE VIEW" statement will create it.

For example, to create a view which accesses all the rows and all the columns of the Book table:

```
REPLACE VIEW BookView
        AS SELECT    Book_Number
                    ,Book_Name
                    ,Publisher_Number
                    ,Published_Date
                    ,Price_Amount
                    ,Book_Type
                    FROM Book;
```

From the user's perspective, "BooKView" appears to be a normal table, from which data may be *SELECTED*:

```
SELECT * FROM BookView
          ORDER BY Book_Number ;
```

or *UPDATED*:

```
UPDATE BookView SET Price_Amount =
         Price_Amount * 1.1
        WHERE Publisher_Number = 104;
```

A VIEW may access data from multiple tables using a *JOIN* operation:

```
CREATE VIEW StoryChrView AS
    SELECT  Story.Story_Number
            ,Story_Name
            ,Last_Name
            ,First_Name
            FROM Story, Chr, Story_Chr
            WHERE Story_Chr.Character_Number =
                  Chr.Character_Number
            AND Story.Story_Number =
                  Story_Chr.Story_Number;
```

By SELECTING from the view, the JOIN becomes transparent to the user:

```
SELECT * FROM StoryChrView
      WHERE Story_Number =104
      ORDER BY Last_Name;
```

REPLACE VIEW may also be used to change an existing VIEW and add, change or delete column attributes:

```
REPLACE VIEW BookView
  AS SELECT Book_Number
      TITLE 'Reference//Number', FORMAT '999')
      ,Book_Name            (TITLE 'Book//Title')
      ,Publisher_Number
                  (TITLE 'Publisher//Number')
      ,Published_Date
                  (FORMAT 'mmmbddbyyyy',
                  TITLE 'Date of //Publication')
      ,Price_Amount * .40
                  (TITLE 'Cost//Amount', FORMAT
                  '$,$$9.99', NAMED DiscountPrice)
   FROM Book;
```

Views may also SELECT aggregate information:

```
REPLACE VIEW BookSlsView AS
        SELECT Book_Number             (NAMED BNbr)
               ,(Sales_Date MOD 10000) / 100
                                       (NAMED Smon)
               ,SUM(Sales_Quantity)  (NAMED SumSls)
        FROM Book_Sales_History
        GROUP BY 1,2;
```

```
SELECT BNbr
        ,SumSls
        FROM BookSlsView
        WHERE Smon = 12
        ORDER BY 1;
```

BNbr	SumSls
1001	4
1005	1
1007	3
1011	1
1012	5

And perform joins on them:

```
SELECT BNbr
        ,Book_Name (FORMAT 'X(20)')
        ,Smon
        ,SumSls
   FROM Book, BookSlsView
   WHERE BNbr = Book.Book_Number;
```

BNbr	Book_Name	Smon	SumSls
1006	The Christmas Books	10	1
1005	The Christmas Books	11	1
1007	The Christmas Books	12	3
1005	The Christmas Books	12	1
1009	Martin Chuzzlewit	10	2
1005	The Christmas Books	10	5
1012	A Charles Dickens	10	1
1001	A Christmas Carol	11	5
1012A	Charles Dickens	12	5
1001	A Christmas Carol	12	4
1001	A Christmas Carol	9	1
1008	David Copperfield	10	1
1011	A Tale of Two Cities	12	1
1011	A Tale of Two Cities	11	1

Additional notes on VIEWS

To create a view, the user must have the "CREATE VIEW" privilege.

To replace a view, the user must have both "CREATE VIEW" and "DROP VIEW" privileges.

An index cannot be created on a view.

A view cannot contain an ORDER BY clause.

Derived and aggregated columns must have a NAMED clause.

Views can be used to update and delete, provided they do not contain:

Data from multiple tables (JOIN).
The same column more than once.

Derived columns.
A DISTINCT clause.
A GROUP BY clause.

Conclusion

While user and database objects, tables and views, are relatively easy to create using SQL, the information they deliver is generally crucial to the success of the business and must be secured from unauthorized prying eyes. Any discussion with regard to their creation and maintenance would be incomplete unless the equally important questions of access and security are also discussed. The group of SQL statements which deal with ownership and access to databases, tables, view and macros is known as Data Control Language (DCL) and is the subject of the next chapter.

Hands On Exercises

Create a User from the Classics database with your last name, perm space of one million bytes and a password of your initials.

Create a table in that user called "MyFriends", with the following columns:

FNbr	SMALLINT NOT NULL
Last_Name	CHAR(15)
First_Name	CHAR(10)
AddressLine1	CHAR(30)
AddressLine2	CHAR(30)
City	CHAR(20)
State_Code	CHAR(2)
Zip	INTEGER

The Primary Key is FNbr.
The Non-Unique Primary Index is Last_Name.

Compress AddressLine 1 to zero space if NULL.
Create a Non-unique secondary index on City and State_Code.
Comparisons should be non case-specific except for State_Code, which should be upper case.

Populate the table with a few rows.

Create a view called FriendsView which accesses all the columns and all the rows of the table with titles and formats.

SELECT all columns and all rows from the VIEW.

Experiment, have fun, and finally, logon as Classics and submit the following SQL:

```
DELETE DATABASE MyName;
```

The DELETE statement will drop all tables views and macros in the MyName user, but will leave the user definition, which we will use in the Chapter 17, in place in the DD/D.

Modify user MyName to set permanent space (PERM) to zero bytes.

17 Ownership and Access Rights

Although the Teradata Database is designed to operate on strict relational principles for access to data, it still tolerates an element of hierarchy with regard to ownership.

In the Teradata Database the ultimate seat of power, and the ownership of all things rests with User DBC (the Data Dictionary/Directory). It is from DBC that all other users and databases in the system are created.

Fig. 17-1 depicts a typical Teradata hierarchy. When a new Teradata system arrives from the factory, User DBC and 3 descendants will be already in place:

SysAdmin
CrashDumps
System FE.

These objects are required by the Teradata RDBMS, and care should be taken to ensure these objects are not compromised in any way.

The first task of the Teradata System Administrator (TSA) will be to create a user beneath DBC from which he or she can exercise the day-to-day control needed to ensure that every user of the system has access to all the computer resources needed to do the work - but no more. A suggested name for this user is "SYSDBA". SYSDBA then becomes the source of all other user / database objects in the system.

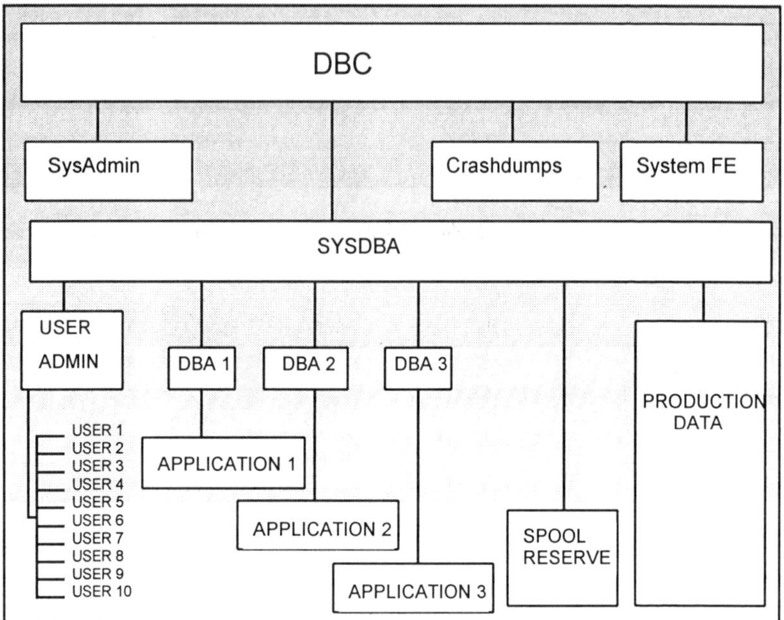

Figure 17-1

Hierarchical Terms

Since DBC is the object from which all other objects are created, it is known as an OWNER or PARENT of all other objects on the system. All other objects on the system are DESCENDENTS or CHILDREN of DBC. From any other object's perspective, any object in a direct lineage higher in the hierarchy is an OWNER or PARENT (synonyms), while any object in direct line below is a DESCENDENT or CHILD (synonyms).

In *Fig. 17-1* for example, User Admin has two parents , SYSDBA and DBC. It also has ten children, User 1 through User 10. Database Administrator 1 (DBA1) also has the same two parents, but only one child, Application 1.

A user or database object therefore can have any number of owners or parents, or any number of descendants or children. Even so, ownership or parenthood is not for ever, and can be changed using an SQL "GIVE" statement. The following statement transfers ownership of Application1 from DBA1 to DBA2:

```
GIVE Application1 TO DBA2;
```

As a result, DBA1 is now childless, while DBA2 has two.

The DD/D view DBC.Children can be used to display a non-sequenced list of the parents or children of any user or database:

```
SELECT Parent FROM DBC.Children
       WHERE Child = USER;

SELECT Child FROM DBC.Children
       WHERE Parent = USER;
```

While the type of hierarchical diagram shown in *Fig. 17-1* is useful to document object ownership, it says little for access. Access to objects in the Teradata Database by any user is not entirely governed by position in the hierarchy, but by whether or not a row validating that action, exists in the DBC.AccessRights table.

Any user who has the appropriate access right row in the DBC.AccessRights table may exercise that privilege to create a new user or database from another user or database's space. *For Example*, DBA2 has been given CREATE USER privilege on USERADMIN by SYSDBA, and acquires another employee. DBA2 might submit the following statement to add User11 as a Logon to the system from USERADMIN's allocation of disk space.

```
CREATE USER User11 FROM UserAdmin
       AS PERM = 0, PASSWORD = User11;
```

*In this way, DBA2 becomes the **CREATOR** of User11, but is neither its parent nor its owner.*

Summary

Any user or database in the Teradata system may have multiple owners or parents, or multiple descendants or children, but can have only one creator. While ownership of a user or database can be transferred from one database/user to another using the "GIVE" statement, the creator never changes. It remains defined for the entire life of the object as the user who submitted the SQL statement which created the object.

Access Rights

All SQL activity in the Teradata Database is governed by access rights or privileges. An access right or privilege is the right of a user, or group of users, to perform a specific type of SQL operation.

The following access rights grant all rights on a specific object:

GRANT DATABASE	All rights for all objects in the database.
GRANT USER	Same as GRANT DATABASE.
GRANT TABLE	All rights on all tables in the database/ user.
GRANT VIEW	All rights for all views in the database/ user.
GRANT MACRO	All rights for all macros in the database/ user.

Access rights can also be authorized for a specific activity on a named object:

CREATE	Create an object from a specific source.
DROP	Remove an object.

SELECT	Read data from an object.
INSERT	Add rows.
UPDATE	Change column values. *(Also available at column level.)*
DELETE	Remove rows.
EXECUTE	Execute a macro.
INDEX	Create a secondary index. *(Table level only.)*
REFERENCES	Define a column as a foreign key. *(Also available at column level)*
CHECKPOINT	Place a logical book-mark in a permanent journal.
DUMP	Archive data.
RESTORE	Recover data from an archive.

The named objects may be one of the following:

DATABASE/USER	All tables, views, columns and macros in the database/user.
TABLE	A named table.
VIEW	A named view.
MACRO	A named macro.
COLUMN	A named column or columns. *(Applicable only to UPDATE and REFERENCES)*

A complete list of the Access Rights held by any user can be generated by the following SELECT from the DBC.AllRights view:

```
SELECT DatabaseName        (FORMAT 'X(10)')
       ,Tablename          (FORMAT 'X(10)')
       ,AccessRight
       ,AllnessFlag
      FROM DBC.AllRights
      WHERE Username = USER;
```

If a privilege is granted at the database or user level (and therefore applies to all tables, views and macros in the database), only a *single* row is stored in DBC.AccessRights and the "AllnessFlag" column is set to a value of "Y" to indicate the privilege applies to all objects. Privileges granted at table, view, macro or column level are represented by a separate row for each privilege, and the "AllnessFlag" is not set. This becomes important when attempts are made to revoke the privilege for one object in the database and yet leave privileges for the remainder intact.

Access Rights Mechanisms

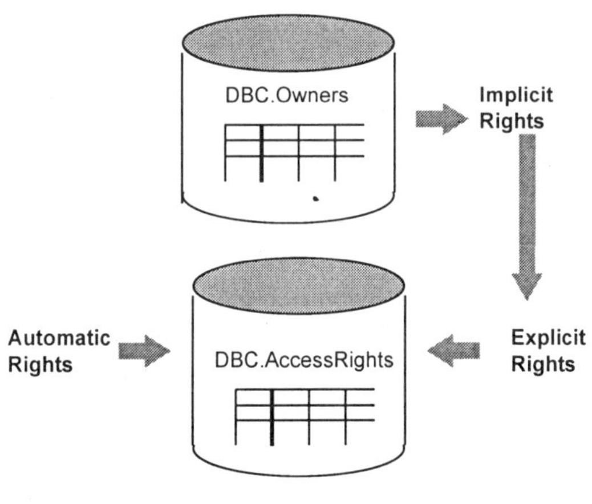

Figure 17-2

Rows are inserted into the DBC.AccessRights table in three distinct ways *(See Fig. 17-2)*:

Implicitly.
Automatically
Explicitly.

Every user has the implicit and irrevocable right to grant himself or herself any and all rights over any object owned by that user. This *implicit right* is the *only* access right not documented in the DBC.AccessRights table.

In order to exercise rights over an owned object, the owner must first submit an SQL GRANT statement which inserts the necessary rows into DBC.AccessRights.

As part of the creation process, rows for all privileges on a created object are immediately inserted into the DBC.AccessRights table on behalf of the creator. The creator can then immediately exercise the rights to access the created object. The creator's rights are not irrevocable however, and may be REVOKED by an owner or by any other user with the right to do so. If the creator is also an owner, the privileges can still be removed from DBC.AccessRights, but this does not affect the owner's irrevocable right to restore those rights any time in the future.

Continuing the creation process, the created user also has rows for all the access rights on itself, with the exceptions of:

CREATE DATABASE/USER
DROP DATABASE/USER.

Rows representing all the privileges except CREATE/DROP DATABASE/USER are automatically inserted into DBC.AccessRights. Again, the created user's rights are not irrevocable, and can be revoked by any owner or other user with the required level of privilege.

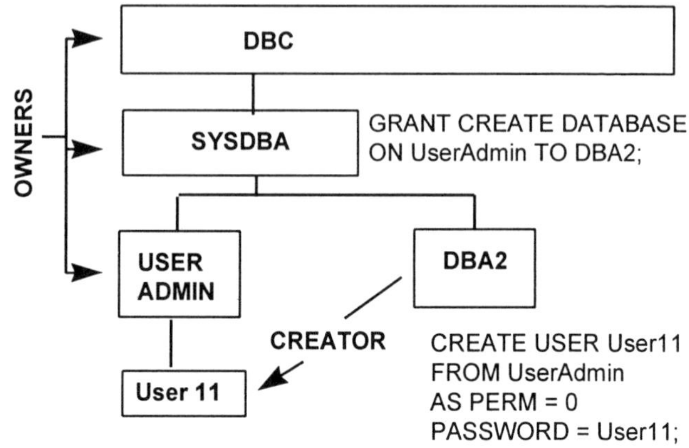

Figure 17-3

For Example, in Fig. 17-3, BA2 is the CREATOR. Rows for all access rights on User11 are automatically inserted into DBC.AccessRights.

These rights can be revoked.

User11 is the CREATED object. Rows for all access rights except CREATE/DROP DATABASE/USER are automatically inserted into DBC.AccessRights.

These rights can be revoked.

DBC, SYSDBA and UserAdmin are all OWNERS. No rows are inserted into DBC.AccessRights on their behalf, but each has the IMPLICIT right to grant any rights over User11 to themselves whenever they wish. Should they choose to grant themselves rights, rows validating those privileges will be inserted into DBC.AccessRights.

An owner's right to grant (or re-grant) himself or herself rights over any owned object CANNOT be revoked.

MONITOR PRIVILEGES

Special privileges are also available for access to the Teradata Performance Monitor - a special protocol which permits the TSA to monitor and control the work flow through the Teradata system even if, for some reason, normal access via SQL is blocked.

The specific privileges are:

MONITOR	All the following privileges:
ABORTSESSION	Aborts any outstanding request or on going transaction of one or more Teradata sessions and, optionally, logs off the sessions.
MONSESSION	Gathers information about logged on sessions and overall system usage on a session-by-session basis.
SETSESSRATE	Sets the frequency at which session-level performance data is updated in the Teradata system.
MONRESOURCE	Gathers information on each processor's availability and performance.
SETRESRATE	Sets the frequency at which processor resource usage data is updated in the Teradata system.

The GRANT Statement

To grant a privilege, the grantor must:

Be an owner of the object.

Hold all the privileges to be conferred with the GRANT option.

The recipient of an explicitly granted privilege may be:

UserName	A specified user or database.
PUBLIC	All users and databases in the Teradata system.
ALL Username	The named user or database and all of its descendents both current and future.

The syntax of the GRANT statement is shown in *Fig. 17-4*.

```
        { ALL [ PRIVILEGES ]                                                  }
        { ALL BUT privilege [, privilege ] . . .                              }
        { privilege [,privilege ] . . .                                       }
GRANT   { MONITOR [ PRIVILEGES ]                                              }
        { MONITOR BUT NOT privilege [,privilege ] . . .                       }
        { UPDATE ( [ALL BUT ] ColumnName [, ColumnName ] . . . )              }
        { REFERENCES ( [ ALL BUT ] ColumnName [, ColumnName ] . . . )         }

  * ON  [ DatabaseName               ]  TO  [ UserName [ . . . , UserName ] ]
        [ DatabaseName.ObjectName    ]      [ PUBLIC                        ]
        [ ObjectName                 ]      [ ALL  UserName                 ]

        [ WITH GRANT OPTION ]

        { ; }

        * NOT REQUIRED IF THE KEYWORD "MONITOR" IS USED
```

Figure 17-4

Notes on Granting Privileges

If the "ALL [PRIVILEGES]" option is used, only the privileges for which the grantee has the GRANT option will be granted.

The INDEX privilege is only available at the table level. The execution of CREATE or DROP INDEX statements is permitted if the user holds either the INDEX or the DROP TABLE privilege.

To UPDATE or DELETE rows using a WHERE clause, the user must also have SELECT privilege on the object.

To GRANT SELECT on a view, the owner of the view must have SELECT WITH GRANT OPTION on the underlying object.

If the Keyword "MONITOR" is used in the GRANT statement, the privilege being granted must be one of the monitor privileges.

If a ColumnName is included with the keywords "UPDATE" or "REFERENCES" and the specified grantee already has the specified right at the table level with the specified grant authority, Teradata accepts the statement, but takes no action.

The REVOKE statement

The form of the REVOKE statement is similar to that of the GRANT. *(See Fig. 17-5)*

To execute the REVOKE statement, the user must have the rights being revoked, together with the GRANT option.

If the "[GRANT OPTION FOR]" is specified, only the grant authority itself is removed.

If the "ALL [PRIVILEGES]" option is used, only the privileges for which the grantee has the GRANT option will be revoked.

```
REVOKE    [GRANT OPTION FOR ]
           ALL [ PRIVILEGES ]
          { ALL BUT privilege [, privilege ] . . .
            privilege [,privilege ] . . .
            MONITOR [ PRIVILEGES ]
            MONITOR BUT NOT privilege [,privilege ] . . .
            UPDATE ( [ALL BUT ] ColumnName [, ColumnName ] . . . )
            REFERENCES ( [ ALL BUT ] ColumnName [, ColumnName ] . . . ) }

* ON [ DatabaseName                ] {FROM} [ UserName [ . . . , UserName ] ]
     [ DatabaseName.ObjectName     ] {TO  } [ PUBLIC                       ]
     [ ObjectName                  ]        [ ALL  UserName                ]

          [ WITH GRANT OPTION ]
          { ; }

          * NOT REQUIRED IF THE KEYWORD "MONITOR" IS USED
```

Figure 17-5

What REVOKE does and does not do

The REVOKE statement is "passive" in that it only removes rows from the DBC.AccessRights table, and never adds them. *For example*, a user has been granted the SELECT privilege at the database level, a single row is inserted into DBC.AccessRights with the Allness Flag set to "Y".

Later, another user with the requisite privileges attempts to revoke the select privilege from the user for table "X". A confirmation message is received which indicates the REVOKE was successful, yet a subsequent test reveals that the user can still execute select statements against table "X".

When the RDBMS received the REVOKE instruction, it accessed the DBC.AccessRights table for a row specifically authorizing the user to SELECT from table "X" and did not find a row representing the exact privilege referenced.

There was a row authorizing the user to SELECT from all tables in the database, but since the privilege it referenced was not specifically for table “X”, it was ignored. Since the REVOKE is ”passive”, ***it does not:***

Remove the database level authorization.

Replace it with a row authorizing the SELECT for every other table in the database.

Teradata assumes that a user with the high level of privilege needed to revoke the privileges of another user is capable of confirming that the privilege being revoked does in fact exist.

To understand why the REVOKE request was confirmed without action, requires an understanding of the rule that:

An unauthorized user attempting to access the system should not derive any useful information as a result of the failed attempt.

A response informing the user that no action was taken would have violated this rule, since the user would have obtained the additional information that the privilege did not exist. *A “Revoke accepted” message therefore merely serves to inform the user that the SQL statement was syntactically correct.*

Transfer of Ownership and Access Rights

While the “GIVE” statement transfers ownership of a user or database from one owner to another, the access rights held by the given object, no matter how they were obtained, are completely unchanged as a result of the “GIVE”. Unrecognized, this can easily lead to unfortunate consequences.

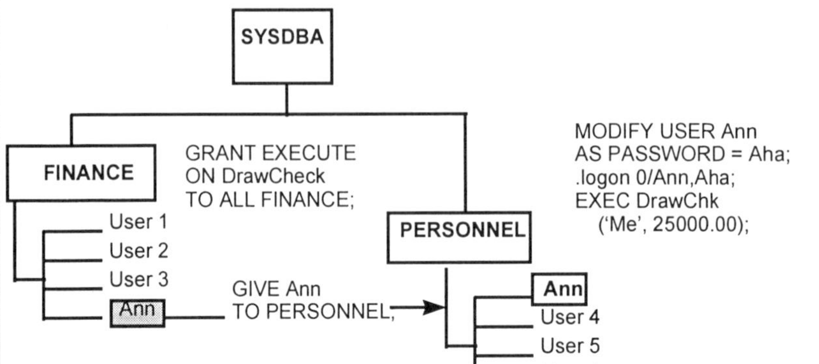

Figure 17-6

For Example, in *Fig. 17-5* The Finance Dept. grants each trusted employee EXECUTE privilege on the DrawCheck macro on an "all username" basis:

Ann joins the organization and inherits the privilege. Ann is eventually promoted to a managerial position with Personnel. The TSA consequently GIVES Ann to Personnel. Since Ann arrived in Personnel as a result of a GIVE transaction, her privilege to draw checks is still intact. She is however still a trustworthy employee.

Her new manager, on the other hand, seizes an opportunity. As Ann's new owner, he changes her password, logs on as Ann and draws himself a large check. The manager is never heard of again. The following morning, Ann has some difficulty logging on to the system, but the problem is fixed by providing her with a new password. It is some time before the loss is discovered.

Conclusions

While we have attempted to address some of the interesting SQL-type issues involved in access and security management as far as the granting and revoking of privileges is concerned, data security is a highly complex issue, and not a matter for casual consideration. The Teradata Database enjoys the highest security rating of any relational database product, but we must continue to recognize that however skillful the Security Administrator might be in putting sophisticated security measures in place, there is always someone who, given enough time, will manage to circumvent them.

Hands On Exercises

From Chapter 16, you should have created the MyName user with zero bytes of permanent space.

1. Logon as Classics and grant update on Book to Myname.

2. Logon as MyName, and increase the Price_Amount of all books by 10 percent. (This should succeed).

3. Reverse the price increase from all the books from publisher 104 only. (This should fail since the SQL has a WHERE clause).

4. Logon as Classics, and grant SELECT on Books to MyName.

5. Logon again as Myname and again attempt to reverse the price increase, first from publisher 104 and then from all the other books. (This should now succeed).

6. Experiment on your own with until you feel you have a good understanding of access rights. *This is the last Hands On exercise, so you may feel free to take any advantage of the Classics database you wish.*

7. ***When the objects are no longer needed***, submit the following SQL to clean up:

```
DELETE Database Classics;
DROP Database Myname;
```

and finally, use the same logon used to create the Classics database to:

```
DROP Database Classics;
```

18 Report Writing

A Vice President of the eighth largest company in the world, walked into the office of the Teradata System Administrator - a long-term friend - who was busily engaged at the keyboard of his PC. Without waiting for the TSA to look up, the VP explained that he really needed a new report in a hurry, but was getting the run-around from MIS. Without looking up, the TSA asked him what exactly he needed. The VP explained, but seemed a little dismayed because while he was talking, the TSA never once interrupted his activity at the keyboard. After what seemed like several minutes of awkward silence the VP, in some frustration asked, “Well, can you help me. How long will it take, and how many thousands of dollars will it cost ?”. Finally the TSA looked up from the keyboard, smiled and said, “You’ve got it, and its free - I wrote the BTEQ script while you were talking.”

This type of story it is not particularly unusual amongst users of the Teradata Database. While there certainly are more sophisticated report writing programs than BTEQ available in the market place, the raw power of Teradata’s SQL and the straight forward no-nonsense nature of BTEQ are often combined for ad hoc reporting - with impressive results.

BTEQ is an ancient utility, conceived early in Teradata’s time of innocence. Until fairly recently it was bundled with the rest of the Teradata software at no additional cost. Sometimes however, the old, the tried and the tested methods are simpler to use, faster to execute and less trouble-prone than many of the flashy newcomers.

BTEQ .EXPORT Command

```
.EXPORT  { DATA               { FILE    = filename    } }
           INDICDATA            DDNAME  = ddname
           REPORT               (IBM only )
           DIF [datalabels]
        [ ,LIMIT = n  ] [ ,CLOSE | OPEN   ]

.EXPORT RESET;
```

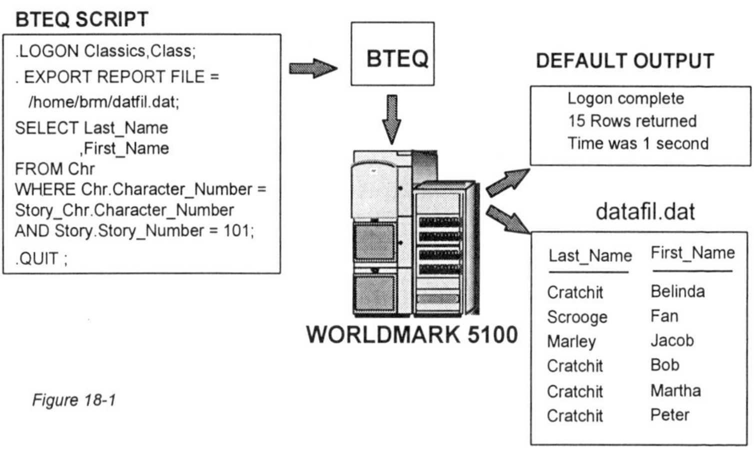

Figure 18-1

The BTEQ .EXPORT command is used to separate the results of an SQL SELECT from the accompanying response messages. *Fig. 18-1* shows how the selected report is redirected to one file (datafil.dat), while the response messages, (logon confirmation, number of rows returned etc.) continue to be directed to the default output file. Also shown in Fig. 18-1 is the syntax for the .EXPORT command.

BTEQ .EXPORTs data in four different formats:

DATA	Binary data or "flat-file" records suitable as input for another application.
INDICDATA	Same as DATA, but preceded with one indicator bit per column returned, rounded up to the next full byte, to signal the presence of NULLs in the data.
REPORT	User-readable output with column headings and underscores. This is the default, and must be]used for generation of reports.
DIF	Data Interchange Format suitable for PC applications.

.EXPORT RESET is used take BTEQ out of EXPORT mode and return all output to the default output file.

BTEQ Format Control Commands

Including the .EXPORT command, the BTEQ command set has 55 commands which are fully explained in the "Teradata DBS BTEQ Manual". While these commands are few in number, they are powerful in function. With some overlap, they can be categorized as:

Session control commands
File control commands
Sequence control commands
Format control commands.

The following is a short list of the main format control commands, which specify the way BTEQ presents information for screen or printer-oriented output. Items shown within square brackets are optional. Items within square brackets separated by a slash "/" are alternatives:

.[SET] DEFAULTS

Resets BTEQ format command options to the values that were set when BTEQ was first invoked.

.[SET] ECHOREQ [ON/OFF]

Specifies whether or not a copy of the Teradata SQL requests and BTEQ commands should be placed in the standard output stream.

.[SET] FOLDLINE [ON/OFF] [, / n / ALL]

Splits each line of a report into two or more lines after the specified columns. This compresses the report into a smaller width.

.[SET] FOOTING [NULL, 'string ']

Specifies the footer text string that appears at the bottom of each page of a report. Supports substitution values &DATE, &TIME, &PAGE, and &n (nth value in a SELECT) anywhere in a footer string.

.[SET] FORMAT [ON/OFF]

Enables or disables all of the page-oriented formatting commands. When FORMAT is OFF, BTEQ ignores the configuration of *FOOTING, FORMCHAR, HEADING, PAGEBREAK, PAGELENGTH and RTITLE.*

.[SET] FORMCHAR [ON/OFF/'HEX sequence 'xb']

Provides format control for printing reports. The 'HEX sequence option translates into a printer escape sequence (for example, "0C"XB or 'oc'xb).

.[SET] HEADING [NULL, 'string']

Specifies a header that appears at the top of each page of a report. Supports substitution values &DATE, &TIME, &PAGE, and &n (nth value in a SELECT) anywhere in the HEADING string. The HEADING and RTITLE options are alternate versions of the same command except that HEADING does not automatically provide the page number and date. If the string is NULL, the HEADING is copied from the SELECT statement that generated the rows.

. [SET] NULL [AS] ['string']

Changes the default for a null field resulting from an SQL SELECT from a question mark "?" to another character or character string.

.[SET] OMIT [ON/OFF] [, / n / ALL]

Excludes specified columns returned from SQL SELECT statements. The OMIT command is useful to underscore a field, or cause a page break at a non-displayed field. OMIT only affects detailed data. If the specified column has subtotaling, the subtotals are not omitted.

. [SET] PAGEBREAK [ON/OFF] [, / n / ALL]

Instructs the printer to eject a page whenever the value for one or more specified columns changes.

. [SET] PAGELENGTH n

Specifies the maximum number of lines on a printed page of output. The default is 55.

. [SET] RTITLE ['string ']

Specifies a title that appears at the top of each page of a report. Titles specified by the RTITLE command automatically include the date and page number. If the string is NULL, the report title is copied from the SELECT statement that generated the rows.

. [SET] SEPARATOR ['string ' / n]

Specifies the width and contents of the string to be placed between the columns in a report. Default is 2 blanks.

. [SET] SESSION CHARSET [code / 'charstring ']

Identifies the name of the character set for the current session. (Code specifies the numeric code for the character set and charstring specifies the name of the character set. The name cannot exceed 30 characters).

. [SET] SIDETITLES [ON / OFF] [0 , withlist, ALL]

Positions titles to the left of the data values returned by a SELECT statement.

("Withlist" specifies a list of numbers, from 1 to 10, separated by commas, that identify the WITH clauses associated with the SIDETITLES command. The number 1 specifies the first WITH clause, 2 specifies the second, and so on. If 0 is specified, instead of "withlist", SIDETITLES are turned off for any part of the response that is not summarized by a WITH clause). The defaults are ON for totals and subtotals, and OFF for all other cases.

. [SET] SKIPDOUBLE [ON/<u>OFF</u>] [, / n / <u>ALL</u>]

Inserts two blank lines in the report whenever the value of a specified column changes.

. [SET] SKIPLINE [ON/<u>OFF</u>] [, / n / <u>ALL</u>]

Inserts one blank line in the report whenever the value of a specified column changes.

. [SET] SUPPRESS [ON/OFF] [, / n / ALL]

Replaces all consecutively repeated values with blank characters.

. [SET] TITLEDASHES [ON / OFF] [0 , withlist, ALL]

Enables or inhibits a line of dash characters immediately before a report summary line generated by a WITH clause.

Withlist specifies a list of numbers, from 1 to 10, separated by commas, that identify the WITH clauses associated with the TITLEDASHES command. The number 1 specifies the first WITH clause, 2 specifies the second, and so on. If you specify 0, instead of a withlist number, then side titles are turned off for any part of the response that is not summarized by a WITH clause).

. [SET] UNDERLINE [ON/OFF] [, / n / ALL]

Inserts a dashed line across the entire width of a report whenever the value of one or more specified columns changes.

[SET] WIDTH n

Specifies the maximum number of characters for each line of the report. The default is 75 characters.

These commands can be learned in a few minutes, but can shorten application development time from weeks to minutes. For Example:

At the beginning of an SQL class, a student expressed deep concern that she had recently been given one month to develop a report from the Teradata Database. The report was purely for internal use and so its general layout and the method used to create it had been largely left up to her. Nevertheless it was a high profile project, and because she had very little experience with the Teradata Database, she was naturally concerned about meeting the deadline.

By the end of the second day, she had developed the following BTEQ formats and SQL needed to generate the a similar report to that required by the project (See *Fig. 18-2) - and she had done it in less than one hour*:

```
.SET FORMAT;
.SET PAGEBREAK ON 1;
.SET RTITLE 'SALES BY PUBLISHER//NUMBER &1//&2';
.SET OMIT ON 1,2;
.SET SUPPRESS ON 3,4;
.SET WIDTH 72;
SELECT Book.Publisher_Number
        ,Publisher_Name
        ,Book.Book_Number
                        (TITLE 'NUMBER', FORMAT 'zzz9')
        ,Book_Name      (TITLE 'TITLE', FORMAT 'x(20)')
        ,Sales_Date     (TITLE 'DATE',
                        FORMAT 'MMMbDDbYYYY')
        ,Sales_Quantity (TITLE 'QTY', FORMAT 'zzz9')
        ,Sales_Quantity * Price_Amount (TITLE 'AMOUNT',
                        FORMAT '$$$,$$9.99',
                        NAMED TSls)
    FROM Book, Publisher, Book_Sales_History
    WHERE Book.Book_Number =
            Book_Sales_History.Book_Number
    AND Book.Publisher_Number =
            Publisher.Publisher_Number
    WITH SUM(TSls)
                        (TITLE 'TOTAL AMOUNT',
                        FORMAT '$$$,$$9.99')
    BY Book.Publisher_Number
    WITH SUM(TSls)
                        (TITLE 'GRAND TOTAL',
                        FORMAT '$$$,$$9.99')
    ORDER BY 3,4,5;
```

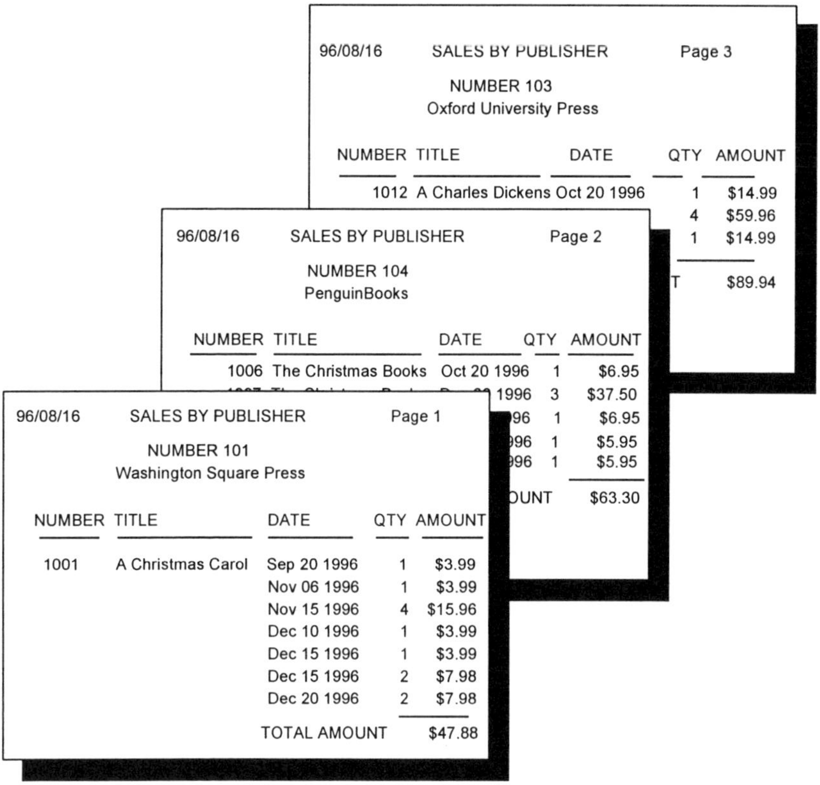

Figure 18-2

Conclusion

Thus, in its revolutionary Version 2 Release 2 implementation of SQL, Teradata successfully defends the high principles of its former proprietary SQL, while peacefully co-existing with the often-conflicting standards of ANSI. In doing so it provides its customers with more power and more flexibility than any other database vendor. Add to that the huge volumes of data that Teradata routinely handles with ease, and you have a system more than capable of meeting the challenge of the 21st century.

Solutions to Hands On Exercises

The output provided in this section may differ from actual results if the data is unordered.

Chapter 4

1. Log on to BTEQ in interactive mode (*See Chapter 3)*.

Logon: **.LOGON 0/Classics;**

Password: **Class;**

2. Select all the columns and all the rows from the STORY table.

```
SELECT *
FROM Story;
```

This response will scroll horizontally off your screen. There are a number of ways of dealing with this problem which are covered in later chapters. Column names have been folded for readability.

```
*** Query completed. 16 rows found. 7 columns
returned.

*** Total elapsed time was 0.31 seconds.
```

Story Number	Story Name	Published Year	Chapter Quantity	Page Quantity	Author Number
105	A Christmas Tree	1859	1	15	101
101	A Christmas Carol	1843	5	63	101
117	The Holly Tree	1849	3	28	101
109	Our Mutual Friend	1865	67	822	101
112	The Cricket on the Hearth	1845	3	104	101
115	Hard Times	1854	37	298	101
106	What Christmas Is As We Get Older	1859	1	4	101
114	Martin Chuzzlewit	1844	54	837	101
116	A Tale of Two Cities	1859	45	404	101
103	Doctor Marigold	1859	2	5	101
108	Great Expectations	1860	59	526	101
110	The Chimes	1844	4	102	101
107	The Haunted Man	1848	3	70	101
113	David Copperfield	1850	64	950	101
104	To Be Taken with a Grain of Salt	1859	1	3	101
102	The Seven Poor Travellers	1861	3	22	101

3. Select the Story_Name and the Published_Year from the STORY table for those stories published in 1859. Order the result by Story_Name:

```
SELECT  Story_Name
        ,Published_Year
    FROM Story
    WHERE Published_Year = 1859
    ORDER BY Story_Name
    ;
```

```
*** Query completed. 5 rows found. 2 columns
      returned.

*** Total elapsed time was 0.27 seconds.

Story_Name                              Published_Year

A Christmas Tree                                  1859
A Tale of Two Cities                              1859
Doctor Marigold                                   1859
To Be Taken with a Grain of Salt                  1859
What Christmas Is As We Get Older                 1859
```

4. Quit BTEQ:

   .quit;

Chapter 5

1. List all the tables, views and macros in the "Classics" database.

HELP DATABASE Classics;

```
*** Help information returned. 17 rows.

*** Total elapsed time was 0.26 seconds.
```

Table/View/Macro name	Kind	Comment
AddTitle	T	Form of Address
Author	T	Author of Story
Book	T	Published Volume
Chr	T	?
Book_Sales_History	T	?
Book_Story	T	?
Chr_Chr	T	?
Chr_Description	T	?
Event	T	?
MainEvents	M	?
Publisher	T	?
Relationship	T	?
Story	T	?
Story_Chr	T	?
Story_Story	T	?
StoryView	V	?

2. Submit the "HELP" and "SHOW" commands for the Story table:

HELP TABLE Story;

```
*** Help information returned. 7 rows.
*** Total elapsed time was 0.27 seconds.
```

Column Name	Type	Comment
Story_Number	I2	?
Story_Name	CV	?
Published_Year	I2	?
Chapter_Quantity	I2	?
Page_Quantity	I2	?
Header_Code	CF	?
Author_Number	I1	?

SHOW TABLE Story;

```
*** Text of DDL statement returned.
*** Total elapsed time was 0.16 seconds.

CREATE SET TABLE CLASSICS.Story ,FALLBACK ,
     NO BEFORE JOURNAL,
     NO AFTER JOURNAL
     (
      Story_Number SMALLINT,
      Story_Name VARCHAR(32) NOT CASESPECIFIC,
      Published_Year SMALLINT,
      Chapter_Quantity SMALLINT,
      Page_Quantity SMALLINT,
      Header_Code CHAR(2) NOT CASESPECIFIC,
      Author_Number BYTEINT)
UNIQUE PRIMARY INDEX ( Story_Number );
```

3. EXPLAIN query number 2 from the exercise following Chapter 4:

How close was the estimated number of rows returned ?

EXPLAIN SELECT Story_Name
,Published_Year
FROM Story
WHERE Published_Year = 1859
ORDER BY Story_Name;

```
*** Help information returned. 13 rows.
*** Total elapsed time was 0.47 seconds.
```

Explanation

1) First, we lock a distinct CLASSICS."pseudo table" for read on a RowHash to prevent global deadlock for CLASSICS.Story.
2) Next, we lock CLASSICS.Story for read.
3) We do an all-AMPs RETRIEVE step from CLASSICS.Story by way of an all-rows scan with a condition of ("CLASSICS.Story.published_year = 1859") into Spool 1, which is built locally on the AMPs. Then we do a SORT to order Spool 1 by the sort key in spool field1. The size of Spool 1 is estimated to be 3 rows.
   The estimated time for this step is 0.15 seconds.
4) Finally, we send out an END TRANSACTION step to all AMPs involved in processing the request.

➔ The contents of Spool 1 are sent back to the user as the result of statement 1.

➔ The total estimated time is 0 hours and 0.15 seconds.

Chapter 6

1. Select the Story_Number and Story_Name for each Story where th Story_Name contains the word "Christmas" (not case specific). Order the report by Story_Name.

```
SELECT Story_Number
        ,Story_Name
        FROM Story
        WHERE Story_Name LIKE '%Christmas%'
        ORDER BY Story_Name;
```

```
*** Query completed. 3 rows found.
    2 columns returned.
*** Total elapsed time was 0.25 seconds.

Story_Number  Story_Name
          101  A Christmas Carol
          105  A Christmas Tree
          106  What Christmas Is As We Get
               Older
```

2. List the major events in the life of Charles Dickens from the Events table which occurred between the years 1824 and 1830 inclusive.

Order the report by Event_Year.

(You might find it helpful to "SHOW" the "Event" table for the column names).

```
SELECT Event_Year
       ,Event
       FROM Event
WHERE Author_Number = 101
AND Event_Year BETWEEN 1824 and 1830
ORDER BY 1;
```

```
*** Query completed. 7 rows found.
    2 columns returned.
*** Total elapsed time was 0.29 seconds.
```

Event_Year	Event
1824	Attends Wellington House Academy
1824	Works in blacking warehouse
1824	Father imprisoned for debt
1827	Leaves Wellington House Academy
1827	Office Boy with attorney's firm
1828	Reporter in Doctor's Commons
1829	Meets Maria Beadnell

Chapter 7

1. SELECT the current DATE, TIME and USER.

SELECT DATE,TIME,USER;

```
 *** Query completed. One row found.
      3 columns returned.
 *** Total elapsed time was 0.04 seconds.

Date         Time         User
96/11/26     12:05:53     CLASSICS
```

2. SELECT the calendar date 6 months from today.

SELECT ADD_MONTHS(DATE,6);

```
 *** Query completed. One row found.
One column returned.
 *** Total elapsed time was 0.03 seconds.

ADD_MONTHS(Date, 6)

1997-05-26
```

3. Select approximately 10 percent of the rows from the "CHR" table. Limit the Last_Name to 10 characters and the First_Name to 7.

```
SELECT Character_Number
        ,Last_Name (CHAR(10))
        ,First_Name (CHAR(7))
FROM Chr
WHERE Character_Number MOD 10 = 1;
```

```
*** Query completed. 5 rows found.
3 columns returned.
 *** Total elapsed time was 0.26 seconds.
```

Character_Number	Last_Name	First_Name
1001	Scrooge	Ebeneze
1021	Taunton	?
1041	Swidger	William
1031	Pickleson	?
1011	Fezziwig	?

Chapter 8

A customer has ordered 50 copies of Book # 1008, at the regular price less 20% discount. State tax must be charged at 8 ½ percent. Prepare a statement with today's date as the order date in the following format. You will need to initialize BTEQ as:

```
.SET FOLDLINE ON;
.SET SIDETITLES;
```

Column	Format
Book Name	Character 20
Order Date	MM/DD/YYYY
Regular Price	Floating Dollar with commas, decimals and zero suppress
Order Quantity	Zero suppress
Discount Rate	Zero suppress and Percent sign
Discount	Floating Dollar with commas, decimals and zero suppress
Tax	Floating Dollar with commas, decimals and zero suppress
Total Due	Floating Dollar with commas, decimals and zero suppress

```
.SET FOLDLINE ON;
.SET SIDETITLES;
SELECT
Book_Name
        (FORMAT 'X(20)', TITLE 'Book Name')
,DATE
        (FORMAT 'MM/DD/YYYY', TITLE 'Order Date')
,Price_Amount
        (FORMAT '$z,zz9.99',   TITLE 'Regular Price')
,50     (FORMAT 'z9', TITLE 'Order Quantity', NAMED OQty)
,20     (FORMAT 'z9%', TITLE ' Discount Rate',
                          NAMED DRate)
```

```
,Price_Amount * OQty * Drate /100 (
        FORMAT '$z,zz9.99', TITLE 'Discount',
                              NAMED Disc)
,(Price_Amount * Oqty - Disc) * .085
        (FORMAT '$z,zz9.99', NAMED Tax)
,((Price_Amount * Oqty) - Disc) + Tax
        (FORMAT '$z,zz9.99',TITLE 'TotalDue')
FROM Book
WHERE Book_Number = 1008;
```

```
*** Query completed. One row found. 8
columns returned.

*** Total elapsed time was 0.26 seconds.

     Book Name         David Copperfield
     Order Date        06/30/1997
     Regular Price     $     6.95
     Order Quantity   50
     Discount Rate    20%
      Discount         $    69.50
      Tax              $    23.63
      TotalDue         $   301.63

.SET DEFAULTS;
```

Chapter 9

1. Build a report which lists the Story_Number and the total number of characters per story from the Story_Chr table. Order the report by Story_Number.

```
SELECT Story_Number
       ,COUNT(Character_Number)
       FROM Story_Chr
       GROUP BY 1
       ORDER BY 1;
```

```
*** Query completed. 5 rows found.
     2 columns returned.

*** Total elapsed time was 0.33 seconds.

Story_Number  COUNT(Character_Number)

         101                       15
         102                        8
         103                        8
         104                        3
         105                       12
```

2. Modify the report above to list each Character_Number by Story_Number and provide a subtotal of the number of characters per story, as well as a final grand total. The report should be ordered by Character_Number within Story_Number, and both subtotals and the grand total should have appropriate titles.

```
SELECT  Story_Number
         ,Character_Number
        FROM Story_Chr
        WITH COUNT(Character_Number)
                      (TITLE 'Sub Total')
        BY Story_Number
        WITH COUNT(Character_Number)
        (TITLE 'Grand Total');
```

```
 *** Query completed. 52 rows found.
     2 columns returned.
 *** Total elapsed time was 0.74 seconds.

Story_Number  Character_Number

         101              1003
         101              1005
         101              1006
         101              1007
         101              1010
         101              1011
         101              1012
         101              1013
         101              1014
         101              1015
         101              1016
         101              1008
         101              1004
         101              1002
         101              1001
Sub Total                   15
```

```
          102          1019
          102          1021
          102          1022
          102          1023
          102          1020
          102          1024
          102          1018
          102          1017
Sub Total                 8
          103          1027
          103          1029
          103          1030
          103          1031
          103          1028
          103          1032
          103          1026
          103          1025
Sub Total                 8
          104          1035
          104          1034
          104          1033
Sub Total                 3
          105          1036
          105          1041
          105          1039
          105          1043
          105          1045
          105          1046
          105          1047
          105          1048
          105          1042
          105          1044
          105          1040
          105          1038
Sub Total                12
Grand Total              46
```

Chapter 10

1. Prepare SQL statements which access the Chr table and calculate a total count of:

   Last names which are missing (NULL).
   First names which are missing (NULL).
   Characters with both First and Last Names.

**SELECT COUNT(*)
FROM Chr
WHERE Last_Name IS NULL;**

```
*** Query completed. One row found.
    One column returned.
*** Total elapsed time was 0.30 seconds.

 Count(*)

        4
```

**SELECT COUNT(*)
FROM Chr
WHERE First_Name IS NULL;**

```
*** Query completed. One row found.
    One column returned.
*** Total elapsed time was 0.30 seconds.

 Count(*)

       13
```

```
SELECT COUNT(*)
       FROM Chr
       WHERE Last_Name IS NOT NULL
       AND First_Name IS NOT NULL;
```

```
 *** Query completed. One row found.
     One column returned.
*** Total elapsed time was 1.04 seconds.

   Count(*)

        31
```

2. Use the "CASE" statement to query the Book_Sales_History table to determine the percent of total sales represented by sales of book 1001.

```
SELECT SUM (
       CASE WHEN Book_Number = 1001
       THEN Sales_Quantity * 100
       ELSE 0
       END) / SUM(Sales_Quantity)
   FROM Book_Sales_History;
```

```
 *** Query completed. One row found.
           One column returned.
 *** Total elapsed time was 0.35 seconds.

(Sum(<CASE  expression>)/Sum(Sales_Quantity))

                                           31
```

Chapter 11

Provide a list of story names from the Story table starting with the second word of the title, and ending with the first word. Title the output field, "Story Names'.

Example:

```
Story Name

Christmas Carol A
Haunted MAN The
Holly Tree The
```

```
SELECT SUBSTR(Story_Name,
              INDEX(story_Name,' ') +1)
              || ' ' ||
              SUBSTR(Story_Name,1,
              INDEX(story_Name,' ') -1)
              (TITLE 'Story Names')
  FROM Story
  ORDER BY 1;
```

```
*** Query completed. 16 rows found.
    One column returned.
*** Total elapsed time was 0.46 seconds.
```

```
Story Names

Be Taken with a Grain of Salt To
Chimes The
Christmas Carol A
Christmas Is As We Get Olde What
Christmas Tree A
Chuzzlewit Martin
Copperfield David
```

```
Cricket on the Hearth The
Expectations Great
Haunted Man The
Holly Tree The
Marigold Doctor
Mutual Friend Our
Seven Poor Travellers The
Tale of Two Cities A
Times Hard
```

Chapter 12

1. Use EXISTS to SELECT the total Sales_Quantity of Book 1001 from the Book_Sales_History for the month of December- *only if we sold any.*

```
SELECT Book_Number,
        SUM(Sales_Quantity)
       FROM Book_Sales_History
       WHERE (Sales_Date MOD 10000)/100 = 12
       AND Book_Number = 1001
       AND EXISTS
              (SELECT *
              FROM Book_Sales_History
              WHERE Book_Number = 1001
              AND (Sales_Date MOD 10000)/100 = 12)
       GROUP BY 1;
```

```
 *** Query completed. One row found.
     2 columns returned.
 *** Total elapsed time was 0.46 seconds.
```

Book_Number	Sum(Sales_Quantity)
1001	4

2. SELECT the Last_Name and First_Name of all Characters from story number 103, first as a subquery, then as a join.

```
SELECT Last_Name
      ,First_Name
      FROM Chr
      WHERE Character_Number in
            (SELECT Character_Number
            FROM Story_Chr
      WHERE Story_Number = 103);
```

```
*** Query completed. 8 rows found.
    2 columns returned.
*** Total elapsed time was 0.66 seconds.
```

Last_Name	First_Name
Marigold	Doctor
Di Velasco	Renaldo
Mim	?
Marigold	?
Pickleson	?
Marigold	Sophy
Marigold	Sophy
Marigold	Willum

```
SELECT Last_Name
      ,First_Name
      FROM Chr, Story_Chr
      WHERE Chr.Character_Number =
            Story_Chr.Character_Number
      AND Story_Number = 103;
```

```
*** Query completed. 8 rows found.
    2 columns returned.
*** Total elapsed time was 0.35 seconds.
```

```
Last_Name      First_Name

Marigold       Willum
Marigold       Doctor
Marigold       Sophy
Mim            ?
Marigold       ?
Marigold       Sophy
Di Velasco     Renaldo
Pickleson      ?
```

3. Use EXPLAIN to evaluate the results of Exercise 2 (above) and determine which is the more efficient.

```
EXPLAIN SELECT Last_Name
              ,First_Name
      FROM Chr
      WHERE Character_Number in
      (SELECT Character_Number FROM Story_Chr
      WHERE Story_Number = 103);
```

```
*** Help information returned. 24 rows.
*** Total elapsed time was 0.79 seconds.
```

```
Explanation
--------------------------------------------------------------
1) First, we lock a distinct CLASSICS."pseudo table"
for read on a RowHash to prevent global deadlock for
CLASSICS.Story_Chr.
2) Next, we lock a distinct CLASSICS."pseudo table"
for read on a RowHash to prevent global deadlock for
CLASSICS.Chr.
3) We lock CLASSICS.Story_Chr for read, and we lock
CLASSICS.Chr for read.
4) We do an all-AMPs RETRIEVE step from CLASSICS.Chr
by way of an all-rows scan with no residual conditions
into Spool 2, which is redistributed by hash code to
all AMPs.  Then we do a SORT to order Spool 2 by row
```

```
hash.The size of Spool 2 is estimated to be 40 rows.
The estimated time for this step is 0.08 seconds.
5) We do an all-AMPs JOIN step from Spool 2 (Last Use)
by way of an all-rows scan, which is joined to
CLASSICS.Story_Chr with a condition of
("CLASSICS.Story_Chr.Story_number = 103").Spool 2
 and CLASSICS.Story_Chr are joined using an inclusion
merge join,with a join condition of
("Spool_2.Character_number =
CLASSICS.Story_Chr.Character_Number").The result goes
into Spool 1, which is built locally on the AMPs.
The size of Spool 1 is estimated to be 2 rows. The
estimated time for this step is 0.20 seconds.
6) Finally, we send out an END TRANSACTION step to all
AMPs involved in processing the request.
-> The contents of Spool 1 are sent back to the user
as the result of statement 1. The total estimated time
is 0 hours and 0.28 seconds.
```

```
EXPLAIN SELECT Last_Name
              ,First_Name
      FROM Chr, Story_Chr
      WHERE Chr.Character_Number =
Story_Chr.Character_Number
      AND Story_Number = 103;
```

```
 *** Help information returned. 20 rows.
     *** Total elapsed time was 0.69 seconds.
```

Explanation

```
1) First, we lock a distinct CLASSICS."pseudo table"
for read on a RowHash to prevent global deadlock for
CLASSICS.Chr.
2) Next, we lock CLASSICS.Chr for read.
3) We do a single-AMP RETRIEVE step from
CLASSICS.Story_Chr by way of the primary index
"CLASSICS.Story_Chr.Story_number = 103" with no
```

```
residual conditions into Spool 2, which is
redistributed by hash code to all AMPs. Then we do a
SORT to order Spool 2 by row hash.
The size of Spool 2 is estimated to be 2 rows.  he
estimated time for this step is 0.13 seconds.
4) We do an all-AMPs JOIN step from Spool 2 (Last Use)
by way of a RowHash match scan, which is joined to
CLASSICS.Chr. Spool 2 and CLASSICS.Chr are joined
using a merge join, with a join condition of
("CLASSICS.Chr.Character_number =
Spool_2.Character_Number").
The result goes into Spool 1, which is built locally
on the AMPs.
The size of Spool 1 is estimated to be 2 rows.
The estimated time for this step is 0.17 seconds.
 ) Finally, we send out an END TRANSACTION step to all
AMPs involved in processing the request.
> The contents of Spool 1 are sent back to the user as
the result of statement 1. The total estimated time is
0 hours and 0.30 seconds.
```

4. Using the EXPLAIN, determine how many rows are returned as a result of the following SELECT:

```
SELECT Story_Name
       , Last_Name
       FROM Chr, Story_Chr, Story
       WHERE Chr.Character_Number =
         Story_Chr.Character_Number
       AND Story.Story_Number =
       Story_Chr.Story_Number;
```

```
*** Help information returned. 28 rows.
 *** Total elapsed time was 1.06 seconds.
```

Explanation

1) First, we lock a distinct CLASSICS."pseudo table" for read on a RowHash to prevent global deadlock for CLASSICS.story_chr.
2) Next, we lock a distinct CLASSICS."pseudo table" for read on a RowHash to prevent global deadlock for CLASSICS.story.
3) We lock a distinct CLASSICS."pseudo table" for read on a RowHash to prevent global deadlock for CLASSICS.chr.
4) We lock CLASSICS.story_chr for read, we lock CLASSICS.story for read, and we lock CLASSICS.chr for read.
) We do an all-AMPs JOIN step from CLASSICS.story by way of a RowHash match scan with no residual conditions, which is joined to CLASSICS.story_chr. CLASSICS.story and CLASSICS.story_chr are joined using a merge join, with a join condition of ("CLASSICS.story.Story_Number = CLASSICS.story_chr.Story_number"). The result goes into Spool 2, which is redistributed by hash code to all AMPs. Then we do a SORT to order Spool 2 by row hash. The size of Spool 2 is estimated to be 8 rows. The estimated time for this step is 0.12 seconds.
6) We do an all-AMPs JOIN step from Spool 2 (Last Use) by way of a RowHash match scan, which is joined to CLASSICS.chr. Spool 2 and CLASSICS.chr are joined using a merge join, with a join condition of ("CLASSICS.chr.Character_number = Spool_2.Character_Number"). The result goes into Spool 1, which is built locally on the AMPs. **The size of Spool 1 is estimated to be 8 rows**. The estimated time for this step is 0.15 seconds.
7) Finally, we send out an END TRANSACTION step to all AMPs involved in processing the request.
-> The contents of Spool 1 are sent back to the user as the result of statement 1. The total estimated time is 0 hours and 0.27 seconds.

Now delete the WHERE clauses. This will result in a full cartesian product join. Determine how many rows will now be returned.

```
EXPLAIN SELECT Story_Name
              , Last_Name
       FROM Chr, Story_Chr, Story;
```

Explanation

```
1) First, we lock a distinct CLASSICS."pseudo table"
for read on a RowHash to prevent global deadlock for
CLASSICS.story_chr.
2) Next, we lock a distinct CLASSICS."pseudo table"
for read on a RowHash to prevent global deadlock for
CLASSICS.story.
3) We lock a distinct CLASSICS."pseudo table" for read
on a RowHash to prevent global deadlock for
CLASSICS.chr.
4) We lock CLASSICS.story_chr for read, we lock
CLASSICS.story for read, and we lock CLASSICS.chr for
read.
5) We do an all-AMPs RETRIEVE step from
CLASSICS.story_chr by way of an all-rows scan with no
residual conditions into Spool 2, which is duplicated
on all AMPs. The size of Spool 2 is estimated to be 64
rows. The estimated time for this step is 0.16
seconds.
6) We do an all-AMPs JOIN step from CLASSICS.story by
way of an all-rows scan with no residual conditions,
which is joined to Spool 2 (Last Use). CLASSICS.story
and Spool 2 are joined using a product join, with a
join condition of ("(1=1)"). The result goes into
Spool 3, which is duplicated on all AMPs.  The size of
Spool 3 is estimated to be 512 rowsThe estimated time
for this step is 0.26 seconds.
7) We do an all-AMPs JOIN step from CLASSICS.chr by
way of an all-rows scan with no residual conditions,
which is joined to Spool 3 (Last Use).CLASSICS.chr and
```

```
Spool 3 are joined using a product join, with a join
condition of ("(1=1)"). The result goes into Spool 1,
which is built locally on the AMPs. The size of Spool
1 is estimated to be 512 rows. The estimated time for
this step is 0.20 seconds.
8) Finally, we send out an END TRANSACTION step to all
AMPs involved in processing the request.
-> The contents of Spool 1 are sent back to the user
as the result of statement 1. The total estimated time
is 0 hours and 0.62 seconds.
```

Chapter 13

1(a). Create a report by first selecting all Book_Numbers, Book_Names and Publisher_Numbers from the Book table, and then use the MINUS operator to eliminate "Penguin Books" from the report.

```
SELECT Book_Number
         ,Book_Name (char(20))
         ,Book.Publisher_Number
        FROM Book
MINUS
SELECT Book_Number
         ,Book_Name (char(20))
         ,Book.Publisher_Number
        FROM Book, Publisher
        WHERE Book.Publisher_Number =
                  Publisher.Publisher_Number
        AND Publisher_Name = 'Penguin Books'
        ORDER BY 1;
```

```
*** Query completed. 6 rows found.
    3 columns returned.
*** Total elapsed time was 0.88 seconds.
```

Book_number	Book_Name	Publisher_Number
1000	A Christmas Carol	?
1001	A Christmas Carol	101
1003	Great Expectations	103
1004	Our Mutual Friend	103
1009	Martin Chuzzlewit	106
1012	A Charles Dickens Ch	103

1(b). Perform the same request as a subquery.

```
SELECT Book_Number
        ,Book_Name (char(20))
        ,Book.Publisher_Number
        FROM Book
        WHERE Publisher_Number NOT IN
        (SELECT Publisher_Number
        FROM Publisher
        WHERE Publisher_Name = 'Penguin Books')
        ORDER BY 1;
```

2. From a subquery SELECT the Book_Number and SUM(Sales_Quantity) from the Book_Sales History table, and store them in a derived table called "TEMP" as "Book_Number" and "SumSales". From the outer query, SELECT the average of SumSales. (In this way you are taking an aggregate of an aggregate)

```
SELECT  AVG(SumSales) (Format 'zz9')
        FROM (SELECT Book_Number
                   ,SUM(Sales_Quantity)
                    FROM Book_Sales_History
        GROUP BY Book_Number) AS TEMP
                    (Book_Number, Sumsales);
```

```
 *** Query completed. One row found.
      One column returned.
 *** Total elapsed time was 0.46 seconds.

Average(Sumsales)
                4
```

Chapter 14

1. Insert a row into the author table for Author_Number 103 and leave all other columns NULL. Use the non-positional form of the INSERT.

```
INSERT INTO AUTHOR (Author_Number)
      VALUES (103);
```

```
*** Insert completed. One row added.
*** Total elapsed time was 0.31 seconds.
```

2. Update the row you have just inserted with the following data:

Last_Name:	Bronte
First_Name:	Charlotte
Birth_Date:	Apr 21 1816
Died_Date:	Mar 31 1855

```
UPDATE Author SET Last_Name ='Bronte'
                  ,First_Name = 'Charlotte'
                  ,Birth_Date = 'Apr 21 1816'
                  ,Died_Date = 'Mar 31 1856'
               WHERE Author_Number = 103;
```

```
*** Update completed. One row changed.
*** Total elapsed time was 0.26 seconds.
```

3. Use the positional form of the INSERT to add another row into the Author table:

Author Number:	104
Last_Name:	Bronte
First_Name:	Emily
Birth_Date:	Jul 30 1818
Died_Date:	Dec 19 1848

```
INSERT Author VALUES
(104, 'Bronte','Emily','Jul 30 1818','Dec 19 1848');
```

```
*** Insert completed. One row added.
*** Total elapsed time was 0.30 seconds
```

4. SELECT both rows to confirm the successful INSERT/UPDATE.

```
SELECT Author_Number
        ,Last_Name
        ,First_Name
        FROM Author
        WHERE Author_Number IN (103,104);
```

```
*** Query completed. 2 rows found.
    3 columns returned.
*** Total elapsed time was 0.26 seconds.
```

Author_Number	Last_Name	First_Name
104	Bronte	Emily
103	Bronte	Charlotte

5. With a single statement, DELETE the rows for Author_Number 103 and 104. (Remember the default for DELETE is ALL).

```
DELETE FROM Author
        WHERE Author_Number IN (103,104);
```

```
*** Delete completed. 2 rows removed.
```

Chapter 15

1. Ensure that all the Bronte sisters have been deleted from the Author table.

```
DELETE FROM Author
        WHERE Author_Number IN (103,104);
```

```
*** Delete completed. 2 rows removed.
```

2. Create a parameterized macro called "NewAuthor" to re-insert the Bronte sisters into the Author table with a reconfirmation message to the user in the format " *Insert of Charlotte Bronte successful.* "

```
REPLACE MACRO NewAuthor
          (ANbr SMALLINT
          ,LName CHAR(20)
          ,FName CHAR(10)
          ,BDate DATE FORMAT 'mmmbddbyyyy'
          ,DDate DATE FORMAT 'mmmbddbyyyy')
   AS ( SELECT 'INSERT OF '||
                 :Lname ||  ' ' ||
                 :Fname ||
                ' SUCCESSFUL' (TITLE '');
   INSERT INTO Author VALUES (
                 :ANbr
                ,:LName
                ,:FName
                ,:BDate
                ,:DDate);
      );
```

```
*** Macro has been replaced.
*** Total elapsed time was 4.30 seconds
```

3.

3. Execute the NewAuthor macro using the positional form to insert a row into the Author Table for:

Author Number	104,
Last_Name	Bronte
First_Name	Emily
Born:	Jul 30 1818
Died:	Dec 19 1848

EXEC NewAuthor
(104, 'Bronte','Emily','Jul 30 1818','Dec 19 1848');

```
*** Query completed. One row found.
      One column returned.
*** Total elapsed time was 0.64 seconds.

INSERT OF Bronte Emily  SUCCESSFUL
*** Insert completed. One row added.
```

4. Execute the NewAuthor macro again, this time using the non positional form to insert the following information into the Author table:

Author Number	103
Last Name	Bronte
First Name	Charlotte

EXEC NewAuthor
(ANbr = 103, Lname = 'Bronte', Fname = 'Charlotte');

```
 *** Query completed. One row found. One column
returned.
 *** Total elapsed time was 0.61 seconds.

INSERT OF Bronte  Charlotte  SUCCESSFUL
*** Insert completed. One row added.
```

Chapter 16

Create a User from the Classics database with your last name (MyName), perm space of one million bytes, and a password of your initials:

```
CREATE USER MyName AS
      PERM=1000000, PASSWORD = MyInitials;
```

```
*** User has been created.
*** Total elapsed time was one minute
     and 9.57 seconds.
```

Create a table in that user called "MyFriends", with the following columns:

FNbr	SMALLINT NOT NULL
Last_Name	CHAR(15)
First_Name	CHAR(10)
AddressLine1	CHAR(30)
AddressLine2	CHAR(30)
City	CHAR(20)
State_Code	CHAR(2)
Zip	INTEGER

The Primary Key is FNbr .
The Non-Unique Primary Index is Last_Name.
Compress AddressLine 1 to zero space if NULL.
Create a Non-unique secondary index on City and State_Code.
Comparisons should be non case-specific except for State_Code which should be upper case.

```
CREATE TABLE MyName.MyFriends
        (FNbr                  SMALLINT  NOT NULL
                               PRIMARY KEY
        ,Last_Name             CHAR(15)
                               NOT CASESPECIFIC
        ,First_Name            CHAR(10)
                               NOT CASESPECIFIC
        ,AddressLine1 CHAR(30)
                               NOT CASESPECIFIC
                               COMPRESS
        ,AddressLine2 CHAR(30)
                               NOT CASESPECIFIC
        ,City                  CHAR(20)
                               NOT CASESPECIFIC
        ,State_Code            CHAR(2) UPPERCASE
        ,Zip                   INTEGER)
        PRIMARY INDEX          (Last_Name)
        INDEX                  (City,State_Code);
```

```
*** Table has been created.
*** Total elapsed time was 7.75 seconds.
```

Populate the table with a few rows.

```
INSERT INTO MyName.MyFriends
        (101,'Marshall','Mary',NULL
        ,'202 Rainbow Avenue'
        ,'Someplace Pretty','CA',91099);
```

```
*** Insert completed. One row added.
*** Total elapsed time was 0.33 seconds.
```

Create a view called FriendsView which accesses all the columns and all the rows of the table with titles and formats.

```
REPLACE VIEW MyName.FriendsView AS
      SELECT FNbr          (TITLE 'Number',
                                 FORMAT 'zzz9')
             ,Last_Name    (TITLE 'Last Name',
                                 FORMAT 'x(20)')
             ,First_Name   (TITLE 'First Name',
                                 FORMAT 'x(10)')
             ,AddressLine1       (TITLE 'Address')
             ,AddressLine2       (TITLE '')
             ,City         (TITLE 'City')
             ,State_Code   (TITLE 'State')
             ,Zip          (FORMAT '9(5)')
            FROM MyName.MyFriends ;
```

```
 *** View has been created.
 *** Total elapsed time was 5.19 seconds.
```

SELECT all columns and all rows from the VIEW.

```
.SET FOLDLINE ON;
.SET SIDETITLES;
SELECT * FROM MyName.FriendsView;
.SET DEFAULTS;
```

```
 *** Query completed. One row found. 8 columns
returned.
*** Total elapsed time was 0.29 seconds.

    Number         101
Last Name          Marshall
First Name         Mary
   Address         ?
                   202 Rainbow Avenue
      City         Someplace Pretty
     State         CA
       Zip         91099
```

Experiment, have fun, and finally, logon as Classics and submit the following SQL:

DELETE DATABASE MyName;

```
*** Database's tables deleted.
*** Total elapsed time was 12.82 seconds.
```

The DELETE statement will drop all tables views and macros in the MyName user, but will leave the user definition,which we will use in the Chapter 17, in the DD/D.

Modify user MyName to set permanent space to zero bytes.

MODIFY USER MyName AS PERM = 0;

```
*** Database/User has been modified.
*** Total elapsed time was 3.95 seconds.
```

Chapter 17

1. Logon as Classics and grant UPDATE on Book to Myname.

GRANT UPDATE on Classics.Book to Myname;

```
*** Grant accepted.
*** Total elapsed time was 0.83 seconds.
```

2. Logon as MyName, and increase the Price_Amount of all books by 10 percent.(*This should succeed.)*

```
UPDATE Classics.Books
      SET Price_Amount = Price_Amount * 1.1;
```

3. Reverse the price increase from all the books from publisher 104 only. (*This should fail* since the SQL has a WHERE clause.)

```
UPDATE Classics.Books
      SET Price_Amount = Price_Amount / 1.1
      WHERE Publisher_Number = 104;
```

```
*** Failure 3523 The user does not have SELECT
access to Classics.Books. Statement# 1, Info =0
*** Total elapsed time was 0.11 seconds.
```

4. Logon as Classics, and grant SELECT on Books to MyName.

GRANT SELECT on Classics.Book to Myname;

```
*** Grant accepted.
*** Total elapsed time was 0.83 seconds.
```

5. Logon again as Myname and again attempt to reverse the price increase, first from publisher 104 and then from all the other books.(*This should now succeed).*

```
UPDATE Classics.Books
    SET Price_Amount = Price_Amount / 1.1
    WHERE Publisher_Number = 104;

UPDATE Classics.Books
    SET Price_Amount = Price_Amount / 1.1
    WHERE Publisher_Number NOT = 104;
```

6. Experiment on your own with until you feel you have a good understanding of access rights. This is the last Hands On exercise, so you may feel free to take any advantage of the Classics database you wish.

7. When the objects are no longer needed, submit the following SQL to clean up:

```
DELETE Database Classics;
DROP Database Myname;
```

```
DELETE DATABASE MyName;
```

```
*** Database's tables deleted.
*** Total elapsed time was 12.82 seconds.
```

and use the same logon used to create the Classics database to

```
DROP Database Classics;
```

"Classics" Database Create Script

```
/* THE FOLLOWING BTEQ  SCRIPT IS PROVIDED IN ELECTRONIC */
/* FORM ON THE DISKETTE WHICH ACCOMPANIES THIS BOOK    */
/* AS CRTCLASS.TXT.  MODIFY THE FIRST .LOGON STATEMENT  */
/* BELOW. IF THERE ARE ANY INACCURACIES IN THIS SCRIPT   */
/* KINDLY EMAIL  brianmar@netcomuk.co.uk                 */

/* ************************************************************************************************ */

.LOGON 0/SYSDBA,

/* ************************************************************************************************ */


CREATE USER Classics AS PERM = 5000000,
        PASSWORD = CLASS;

GRANT ALL ON Classics TO Classics
        WITH GRANT OPTION;

.LOGON Classics,Class;

   CREATE TABLE  Classics.AddTitle ,FALLBACK ,
   NO BEFORE JOURNAL,
   NO AFTER JOURNAL
   (
   Title_Code              CHAR(3),
   Add_Title               CHAR(10) NOT CASESPECIFIC)
   UNIQUE PRIMARY INDEX( Title_Code );

   COMMENT ON Classics.AddTitle IS 'Form of Address';
```

```
CREATE TABLE  Classics.Author ,FALLBACK,
NO BEFORE JOURNAL,
NO AFTER JOURNAL
 (
Author_Number        BYTEINT,
Last_Name            CHAR(20) NOT CASESPECIFIC,
First_Name           VARCHAR(10) NOT CASESPECIFIC,
Birth_Date           DATE FORMAT 'mmmbddbyyyy',
Died_Date            DATE FORMAT 'mmmbddbyyyy')
UNIQUE PRIMARY INDEX( Author_Number );

COMMENT ON Classics.Author IS 'Author of Story';

CREATE TABLE  Classics.Book ,FALLBACK ,
NO BEFORE JOURNAL,
NO AFTER JOURNAL
(
Book_Number          SMALLINT,
Book_Name            VARCHAR(30) NOT CASESPECIFIC,
Publisher_Number     SMALLINT,
Published_Date       DATE,
Price_Amount         DECIMAL(5,2),
Book_Type            CHAR(1)        NOT CASESPECIFIC)
UNIQUE PRIMARY INDEX( Book_Number );

COMMENT ON Classics.Book IS 'Published Volume';

CREATE TABLE Book_Sales_History, FALLBACK,
NO BEFORE JOURNAL,
NO AFTER JOURNAL
 (
Book_Number          SMALLINT
,Sales_Date          DATE
,Sales_Quantity      SMALLINT)
PRIMARY INDEX  (Book_Number);
```

```
CREATE TABLE  Classics.Book_Story, FALLBACK ,
NO BEFORE JOURNAL,
NO AFTER JOURNAL
(
Book_Number                  SMALLINT,
Story_Number                 SMALLINT)
PRIMARY INDEX  ( Book_Number );

CREATE TABLE  Classics.Chr, FALLBACK,
NO BEFORE JOURNAL,
NO AFTER JOURNAL
 (
Character_Number             INTEGER,
Last_Name                    CHAR(12)       NOT CASESPECIFIC,
First_Name                   VARCHAR(10) NOT CASESPECIFIC,
Title_Code                   CHAR(3)        NOT CASESPECIFIC,
Description_Number           SMALLINT)
UNIQUE PRIMARY INDEX( Character_Number );

CREATE TABLE  Classics.Chr_Chr, FALLBACK,
NO BEFORE JOURNAL,
NO AFTER JOURNAL
 (
Character_Number                 INTEGER,
Related_to_Character_Number   INTEGER,
Relationship_Code               CHAR(3)        NOT CASESPECIFIC)
PRIMARY INDEX( Character_Number );

CREATE TABLE  Classics.Chr_Description ,FALLBACK ,
NO BEFORE JOURNAL,
NO AFTER JOURNAL
(
 Description_Number          SMALLINT,
Description                   VARCHAR(50) NOT CASESPECIFIC)
UNIQUE PRIMARY INDEX( Description_Number );
```

```
CREATE TABLE  Classics.Event ,FALLBACK ,
NO BEFORE JOURNAL,
NO AFTER JOURNAL
 (
Event_Number         SMALLINT,
Event                VARCHAR(40) NOT CASESPECIFIC,
Event_Year           SMALLINT,
Author_Number        BYTEINT)
UNIQUE PRIMARY INDEX( Event_Number );


CREATE TABLE  Classics.Publisher ,FALLBACK ,
NO BEFORE JOURNAL,
NO AFTER JOURNAL
(
Publisher_Number     SMALLINT,
Publisher_Name       VARCHAR(20) NOT CASESPECIFIC,
Area_Code            SMALLINT,
Phone_Number         INTEGER)
UNIQUE PRIMARY INDEX( Publisher_Number );

CREATE TABLE  Classics.Relationship ,FALLBACK,
NO BEFORE JOURNAL,
NO AFTER JOURNAL
(
Relationship_Code    CHAR(3)        NOT CASESPECIFIC
,Relationship        VARCHAR(16)  NOT CASESPECIFIC)
UNIQUE PRIMARY INDEX( Relationship_Code );
```

```
CREATE TABLE  Classics.Story ,FALLBACK,
NO BEFORE JOURNAL,
NO AFTER JOURNAL
(
Story_Number          SMALLINT,
Story_Name            VARCHAR(32)  NOT CASESPECIFIC,
Published_Year        SMALLINT,
Chapter_Quantity      SMALLINT,
Page_Quantity         SMALLINT,
Header_Code           CHAR(2),
Author_Number         BYTEINT)
UNIQUE PRIMARY INDEX (Story_Number);

COMMENT ON Classics.Story.Story_Number IS 'Unique Story ID';
COMMENT ON Classics.Story.Story_Name IS 'Story Name';
COMMENT ON Classics.Story.Published_Year IS
'Year originally published';
COMMENT ON Classics.Story.Chapter_Quantity  IS
'Number of chapters';
COMMENT ON Classics.Story.Page_Quantity IS 'Number of pages';
COMMENT ON Classics.Story.Author_Number IS 'Author  ID';

CREATE TABLE  Classics.Story_Chr ,FALLBACK ,
NO BEFORE JOURNAL,
NO AFTER JOURNAL
 (
Story_Number          SMALLINT,
Character_Number      INTEGER)
PRIMARY INDEX( Story_Number );

CREATE TABLE  Classics.Story_Story ,FALLBACK,
NO BEFORE JOURNAL,
NO AFTER JOURNAL
 (
Story_Number          SMALLINT
,In_Story_Number      SMALLINT)
UNIQUE PRIMARY INDEX( Story_Number );
```

```
REPLACE MACRO MainEvents AS (
   SELECT Event
            ,Event_Year
         FROM Event
          ORDER BY Event_Number;);

REPLACE VIEW StoryView
(SNbr, SName, Yr, Chptr, Pge, Auth)
AS
SELECT Story_Number
          ,Story_Name
          ,Published_Year
          ,Chapter_Quantity
          ,Page_Quantity
          ,Author_Number
          FROM Story;

   REPLACE Macro MainEvents AS (
   SELECT Event_Year
            ,Event
          FROM Event
          ORDER BY Event_Year;
   );

  INSERT AddTitle ('MR','Mr');
  INSERT AddTitle ('MRS','Mrs');
  INSERT AddTitle ('MIS','Miss');
  INSERT AddTitle ('MST','Master');
  INSERT AddTitle ('CAP','Captain');
  INSERT AddTitle ('LIL','Little');
  INSERT AddTitle ('THE','The');

  INSERT Author (101,'Dickens','Charles','Feb 07 1812', 'Jun 09 1870');
  INSERT Author (102,'Austen','Jane','Dec 16 1775','Jul 18 1817');

  INSERT Book (1000, 'A Christmas Carol',,,, 'F');
  INSERT Book (1001, 'A Christmas Carol',101, 670331, 3.99, 'P');
  INSERT Book (1002, 'Christmas Tales',104, 950430, 6.99, 'P');
  INSERT Book (1003, 'Great Expectations',103, 940120, 5.95, 'P');
```

```
INSERT Book (1004, 'Our Mutual Friend',103, 951030, 10.95, 'H');
INSERT Book (1005, 'The Christmas Books',104, 710605, 0, 'P');
INSERT Book (1006, 'The Christmas Books',104, 850502, 6.95, 'P');
INSERT Book (1007, 'The Christmas Books',104, 951130, 13.50, 'H');
INSERT Book (1008, 'David Copperfield',104, 950805, 6.95, 'P');
INSERT Book (1009, 'Martin Chuzzlewit',106, 940228, 20.00, 'H');
INSERT Book (1010, 'Hard Times',104, 950410, 6.95, 'P');
INSERT Book (1011, 'A Tale of Two Cities',104, 851110, 5.95, 'P');
INSERT Book
(1012, 'A Charles Dickens Christmas',103, 760615,14.99, 'H');
INSERT Book (1013, 'The Christmas Books',104,570601,,'P');
INSERT Book (1014, 'The Christmas Books',104,460201,,'P');

INSERT Book_Sales_History  (1001,961215,1);
INSERT Book_Sales_History  (1001,961220,2);
INSERT Book_Sales_History  (1001,961210,1);
INSERT Book_Sales_History  (1005,961010,5);
INSERT Book_Sales_History  (1005,961130,1);
INSERT Book_Sales_History  (1007,961220,3);
INSERT Book_Sales_History  (1008,961020,1);
INSERT Book_Sales_History  (1009,961030,2);
INSERT Book_Sales_History  (1012,961205,4);
INSERT Book_Sales_History  (1012,961020,1);
INSERT Book_Sales_History  (1006,961020,1);
INSERT Book_Sales_History  (1005,961215,1);
INSERT Book_Sales_History  (1001,961115,4);
INSERT Book_Sales_History  (1011,961215,1);
INSERT Book_Sales_History  (1011,961105,1);
INSERT Book_Sales_History  (1012,961215,1);
INSERT Book_Sales_History  (1001,961106,1);
INSERT Book_Sales_History  (1001,960920,1);

INSERT Book_Story (1001,101);
INSERT Book_Story (1002,112);
INSERT Book_Story (1002,102);
INSERT Book_Story (1003,108);
INSERT Book_Story (1006,101);
INSERT Book_Story (1006,110);
INSERT Book_Story (1005,101);
```

```
INSERT Book_Story (1007,101);
INSERT Book_Story (1007,102);
INSERT Book_Story (1007,110);
INSERT Book_Story (1008,113);
INSERT Book_Story (1009,114);
INSERT Book_Story (1010,115);
INSERT Book_Story (1011,101);
INSERT Book_Story (1011,110);
INSERT Book_Story (1011,112);

INSERT Chr  (1001, 'Scrooge','Ebenezer','Mr ',101);
INSERT Chr  (1002, 'Marley','Jacob','Mr ',102);
INSERT Chr  (1003, 'Scrooge','Fan','Mis',);
INSERT Chr  (1004, 'Cratchit','Bob','Mr',);
INSERT Chr  (1005, 'Cratchit','Martha','Mis',);
INSERT Chr  (1006, 'Cratchit','Belinda','Mis',);
INSERT Chr  (1007, 'Cratchit','Peter','Mst',);
INSERT Chr  (1008, 'Cratchit','Tim','Mst',);
INSERT Chr  (1018, 'Cratchit',,'Mrs',);
INSERT Chr  (1009, 'Wilkins','Dick','Mr',103);
INSERT Chr  (1010, 'Fezziwig',,'Mr',120);
INSERT Chr  (1011, 'Fezziwig',,'Mrs',121);
INSERT Chr  (1012, ,'Fred',,);
INSERT Chr  (1013, ,'Joe',,104);
INSERT Chr  (1014,'Topper',,'Mr',);
INSERT Chr  (1015, ,'Belle', 'Mis',);
INSERT Chr  (1016,'Dilber',,'Mrs',);
INSERT Chr  (1017,'Crusoe', 'Robin',,105);
INSERT Chr  (1019,'Doubledick','Richard','Mr',106);
INSERT Chr  (1020,'Marshall','Mary','Mis',);
INSERT Chr  (1021,'Taunton',,'Cap',107);
INSERT Chr  (1022,'Taunton',,'Mrs',);
INSERT Chr  (1023,,'Ben',,108);
INSERT Chr  (1024,'Watts ESQ','Richard',,109);
INSERT Chr  (1025,'Marigold','Doctor','Mr',110);
INSERT Chr  (1026,'Marigold',,'Mrs',);
INSERT Chr  (1027,'Marigold','Willum','Mr',);
INSERT Chr  (1028,'Marigold','Sophy','Lil',);
INSERT Chr  (1029,'Marigold','Sophy','Mis',122);
```

```
INSERT Chr  (1030,'Mim',,'Mr ',111);
INSERT Chr  (1031,'Pickleson',,'Mr',);
INSERT Chr  (1032,'Di Velasco','Renaldo','Mr ',);
INSERT Chr  (1033,'Derrick','John','Mr',);
INSERT Chr  (1034,'Harker',,,113);
INSERT Chr  (1035,'Juryman','Haunted','The',);
INSERT Chr  (1036,'Denham','Edmund','Mr ',115);
INSERT Chr  (1037,'Longford',,'Mr',);
INSERT Chr  (1038,'Redlaw',,'Mr ',116);
INSERT Chr  (1039,'Swidger','George','Mr ',117);
INSERT Chr  (1040,'Swidger','Philip','Mr ',);
INSERT Chr  (1041,'Swidger','William','Mr ',);
INSERT Chr  (1042,'Swidger','Millie','Mrs',118);
INSERT Chr  (1043,'Tetterby','Adolphus','Mr',);
INSERT Chr  (1044,'Tetterby','Dolphus','Mst',);
INSERT Chr  (1045,'Tetterby','Johnny','Mst',119);
INSERT Chr  (1046,'Tetterby','Sally','Mis',);
INSERT Chr  (1047,'Tetterby','Sophia','Mrs',);
INSERT Chr  (1048,'Scroggins','Giles',,114);

INSERT Chr_Chr (1001,1002,'PAR');
INSERT Chr_Chr (1002,1001,'PAR');
INSERT Chr_Chr (1001,1003,'BRO');
INSERT Chr_Chr (1003,1001,'SIS');
INSERT Chr_Chr (1004,1001,'EMP');
INSERT Chr_Chr (1001,1004,'EMR');
INSERT Chr_Chr (1004,1005,'DAU');
INSERT Chr_Chr (1004,1006,'DAU');
INSERT Chr_Chr (1004,1007,'SON');
INSERT Chr_Chr (1004,1008,'SON');
INSERT Chr_Chr (1004,1018,'WIF');
INSERT Chr_Chr (1005,1004,'FAT');
INSERT Chr_Chr (1006,1004,'FAT');
INSERT Chr_Chr (1007,1004,'FAT');
INSERT Chr_Chr (1008,1004,'FAT');
INSERT Chr_Chr (1018,1004,'HUS');
INSERT Chr_Chr (1018,1005,'MOT');
INSERT Chr_Chr (1018,1006,'MOT');
INSERT Chr_Chr (1018,1007,'MOT');
```

```
INSERT Chr_Chr (1018,1008,'MOT');
INSERT Chr_Chr (1009,1010,'EMP');
INSERT Chr_Chr (1010,1011,'HUS');
INSERT Chr_Chr (1011,1010,'WIF');
INSERT Chr_Chr (1001,1010,'EMP');
INSERT Chr_Chr (1010,1001,'EMR');
INSERT Chr_Chr (1001,1012,'NEP');
INSERT Chr_Chr (1012,1001,'UNC');
INSERT Chr_Chr (1014,1012,'FRI');
INSERT Chr_Chr (1012,1014,'FRI');
INSERT Chr_Chr (1015,1001,'SWE');
INSERT Chr_Chr (1001,1015,'SWE');
INSERT Chr_Chr (1016,1001,'EMP');
INSERT Chr_Chr (1001,1016,'EMR');
INSERT Chr_Chr (1021,1022,'SON');
INSERT Chr_Chr (1022,1021,'MOT');
INSERT Chr_Chr (1025,1026,'HUS');
INSERT Chr_Chr (1026,1025,'WIF');
INSERT Chr_Chr (1027,1025,'FAT');
INSERT Chr_Chr (1025,1027,'SON');
INSERT Chr_Chr (1026,1027,'DIL');
INSERT Chr_Chr (1027,1026,'FIL');
INSERT Chr_Chr (1028,1025,'DAU');
INSERT Chr_Chr (1028,1026,'DAU');
INSERT Chr_Chr (1028,1027,'GDA');
INSERT Chr_Chr (1027,1028,'GFA');
INSERT Chr_Chr (1029,1025,'ADA');
INSERT Chr_Chr (1030,1031,'EMR');
INSERT Chr_Chr (1031,1030,'EMP');
INSERT Chr_Chr (1031,1032,'AKA');
INSERT Chr_Chr (1032,1031,'AKA');
INSERT Chr_Chr (1033,1035,'EMP');
INSERT Chr_Chr (1035,1033,'EMR');
INSERT Chr_Chr (1036,1037,'AKA');
INSERT Chr_Chr (1037,1036,'AKA');
INSERT Chr_Chr (1037,1038,'NEP');
INSERT Chr_Chr (1038,1037,'UNC');
INSERT Chr_Chr (1039,1037,'FAT');
INSERT Chr_Chr (1039,1040,'SON');
```

```
INSERT Chr_Chr (1040,1039,'FAT');
INSERT Chr_Chr (1041,1040,'SON');
INSERT Chr_Chr (1040,1041,'FAT');
INSERT Chr_Chr (1042,1041,'WIF');
INSERT Chr_Chr (1041,1042,'HUS');
INSERT Chr_Chr (1042,1040,'DIL');
INSERT Chr_Chr (1040,1042,'FIL');
INSERT Chr_Chr (1043,1047,'HUS');
INSERT Chr_Chr (1047,1043,'WIF');
INSERT Chr_Chr (1043,1044,'FAT');
INSERT Chr_Chr (1044,1043,'SON');
INSERT Chr_Chr (1043,1045,'FAT');
INSERT Chr_Chr (1043,1046,'FAT');
INSERT Chr_Chr (1045,1043,'SON');
INSERT Chr_Chr (1046,1043,'DAU');
INSERT Chr_Chr (1047,1044,'MOT');
INSERT Chr_Chr (1047,1045,'MOT');
INSERT Chr_Chr (1047,1046,'MOT');
INSERT Chr_Chr (1045,1047,'SON');
INSERT Chr_Chr (1044,1047,'SON');
INSERT Chr_Chr (1046,1047,'DAU');

INSERT Chr_Description (101,'Grasping covetous old man');
INSERT Chr_Description (102,'Deceased');
INSERT Chr_Description (103,'Apprentice at Fezziwig''s');
INSERT Chr_Description (104,'Receiver of stolen goods');
INSERT Chr_Description (105,'Parrot');
INSERT Chr_Description (106,'Enlists in the army');
INSERT Chr_Description (107,'Company Captain');
INSERT Chr_Description (108,'Waiter');
INSERT Chr_Description (109,'Deceased founder of Charity');
INSERT Chr_Description (110,'Cheap Jack');
INSERT Chr_Description (111,'Showman');
INSERT Chr_Description (112,'Amiable but timid giant');
INSERT Chr_Description (113,'Officer of the jury');
INSERT Chr_Description (114,'Ghost');
INSERT Chr_Description (115,'Student');
INSERT Chr_Description (116,'Learned chemist and lecturer');
INSERT Chr_Description (117,'Bold callous ruffian');
```

```
INSERT Chr_Description
(118,'Embodiment of goodness, gentleness, and domesticity');
INSERT Chr_Description (119,'Patient and much endearing');
INSERT Chr_Description (120,'Jovial old merchant');
INSERT Chr_Description (121,'A worthy match to Mr. Fezziwig');
INSERT Chr_Description (122,'Deaf and dumb');

INSERT Event (101,'Born at Landport, Portsmouth' ,1812,101);
INSERT Event (102,'Family moves to Chatham',1817,101);
INSERT Event
(103,'Family moves to Camden Town, London',1822,101);
INSERT Event (104,'Works in blacking warehouse',1824,101);
INSERT Event (105,'Father imprisoned for debt', 1824,101);
INSERT Event (106,'Attends Wellington House Academy',1824,101);
INSERT Event (107,'Leaves Wellington House Academy',1827,101);
INSERT Event (108,'Office Boy with attorney''s firm',1827,101);
INSERT Event (109,'Reporter in Doctor''s Commons',1828,101);
INSERT Event (110,'Meets Maria Beadnell',1829,101);
INSERT Event (111,'Parliamentary Reporter',1832,101);
INSERT Event (112,'First Published Sketch' ,1832,101);
INSERT Event (113,'Marries Catherine Hogarth',1836,101);
INSERT Event (114,'First Visit to America',1842,101);
INSERT Event (115,'Acquires Gadshill Place, Rochester',1856,101);
INSERT Event (116,'Meets Ellen Ternan',1857,101);
INSERT Event (117,'Separated from his wife',1858,101);
INSERT Event (118,'Begins public readings',1858,101);
INSERT Event (119,'Edits "All the Year Round"',1859,101);
INSERT Event (120,'Second series of readings',1861,101);
INSERT Event (121,'Third series of readings',1866,101);
INSERT Event (122,'Second visit to America',1867,101);
INSERT Event (123,'Fourth series of readings',1866,101);
INSERT Event
(124,'Dies at Gadshill - Edwin Drood unfinished',1870,101);

INSERT Publisher (101,'Washington Square Press',212,2232000);
INSERT Publisher (102,'MacMillan Publishing',212,3355100);
INSERT Publisher (103,'Oxford University Press',213,5247000);
INSERT Publisher (104,'Penguin Books',213,6250040);
INSERT Publisher (105,'The Modern Library',312,6612244);
```

```
INSERT Publisher (106,'Every Man''s Library',415,6651000);

INSERT Relationship ('PAR','Partner');
INSERT Relationship ('BRO','Brother');
INSERT Relationship ('SIS','Sister');
INSERT Relationship ('EMP','Employee');
INSERT Relationship ('EMR','Employer');
INSERT Relationship ('DAU','Daughter');
INSERT Relationship ('SON','Son');
INSERT Relationship ('WIF','Wife');
INSERT Relationship ('FAT','Father');
INSERT Relationship ('MOT','Mother');
INSERT Relationship ('NEP','Nephew');
INSERT Relationship ('UNC','Uncle');
INSERT Relationship ('FRI','Friend');
INSERT Relationship ('SWE','Sweetheart');
INSERT Relationship ('BET','Betrothed');
INSERT Relationship ('FIL','Father-in-law');
INSERT Relationship ('DIL','Daughter-in-law');
INSERT Relationship ('ADA','Adopted daughter');
INSERT Relationship ('GDA','Granddaughter');
INSERT Relationship ('GFA','Grandfather');
INSERT Relationship ('AKA','Alias');

INSERT Story(101,'A Christmas Carol',1843,5,63,101);
INSERT Story(102,'The Seven Poor Travellers',1861,3,22,101);
INSERT Story(103,'Doctor Marigold',1859,2,5,101);
INSERT Story(104,'To Be Taken with a Grain of Salt',1859,1,3,101);
INSERT Story(105,'A Christmas Tree',1859,1,15,101);
INSERT Story(106,'What Christmas Is As We Get Older',1859,0,4,101);
INSERT Story(107,'The Haunted Man',1848,3,70,101);
INSERT Story(108,'Great Expectations',1860,59,526,101);
INSERT Story(109,'Our Mutual Friend',1865,67,822,101);
INSERT Story(110,'The Chimes',1844,4,102,101);
INSERT Story(112,'The Cricket on the Hearth',1845,3,104,101);
INSERT Story(113,'David Copperfield',1850,64,950,101);
INSERT Story(114,'Martin Chuzzlewit',1844,54,837,101);
INSERT Story(115,'Hard Times',1854,37,298,101);
INSERT Story(116,'A Tale of Two Cities',1859,45,404,101);
```

```
INSERT Story(117,'The Holly Tree',1849,3,28,101);

INSERT Story_Chr (101,1001);
INSERT Story_Chr (101,1002);
INSERT Story_Chr (101,1003);
INSERT Story_Chr (101,1004);
INSERT Story_Chr (101,1005);
INSERT Story_Chr (101,1006);
INSERT Story_Chr (101,1007);
INSERT Story_Chr (101,1008);
INSERT Story_Chr (101,1010);
INSERT Story_Chr (101,1011);
INSERT Story_Chr (101,1012);
INSERT Story_Chr (101,1013);
INSERT Story_Chr (101,1014);
INSERT Story_Chr (101,1015);
INSERT Story_Chr (101,1016);
INSERT Story_Chr (102,1017);
INSERT Story_Chr (102,1018);
INSERT Story_Chr (102,1019);
INSERT Story_Chr (102,1020);
INSERT Story_Chr (102,1021);
INSERT Story_Chr (102,1022);
INSERT Story_Chr (102,1023);
INSERT Story_Chr (102,1024);
INSERT Story_Chr (103,1025);
INSERT Story_Chr (103,1026);
INSERT Story_Chr (103,1027);
INSERT Story_Chr (103,1028);
INSERT Story_Chr (103,1029);
INSERT Story_Chr (103,1030);
INSERT Story_Chr (103,1031);
INSERT Story_Chr (103,1032);
INSERT Story_Chr (104,1033);
INSERT Story_Chr (104,1034);
INSERT Story_Chr (104,1035);
INSERT Story_Chr (105,1036);
INSERT Story_Chr (105,1038);
INSERT Story_Chr (105,1039);
```

```
  INSERT Story_Chr (105,1040);
  INSERT Story_Chr (105,1041);
  INSERT Story_Chr (105,1042);
  INSERT Story_Chr (105,1043);
  INSERT Story_Chr (105,1044);
  INSERT Story_Chr (105,1045);
  INSERT Story_Chr (105,1046);
  INSERT Story_Chr (105,1047);
  INSERT Story_Chr (105,1048);

  INSERT Story_Story (104,103);

.QUIT;
```

Index

2-Phase Commit, 97
3 Rules of Normalization, 14
3RD Normal form, 14,16,20

A

Access Rights/Privileges, 20,66,120,368-370
    GRANT, 371,373-375
    Mechanisms, 370-372
    REVOKE, 375-377
    Transfer of Ownership, 377-378
Access Module Processor (AMP), 41,44,58,61,67, 89-91,104,128
Account Strings, 125
Activity Transaction Modeling (ATM), 2,83
Aggregates, 31,255
    Aggregate Function, 193
    GROUP BY, 258
    Mixed, 259
    Non-Aggregates, 259
ALIAS, 298,307
ALL, 227,231
Allness Flag, 370,376
ALTER TABLE, 356
American National Standard Institute (ANSI), 23,35, 161-163,235
ANSI Flagger Program, 204
ANY, 230
Application Processor (AP), 50-51
Application Utilities, 96,99-101
    BTEQ, 101-104
    Bulkload, 105-107,116
    FastExport, 113-116
    FastLoad, 108-110
    Multiload, 110-113,116
Archive and Recovery, 136-137
Arithmetic Functions, 233
    Data Conversions, 237
    Operations, 235-236
ASCII Form, 23
Associative Tables, 78,171
AT&T, 4,6,37,38,161
AT&T G.I.S, 6,52
Attributes, 14,17
Automotive Industry, 156

B

Banking and Financial Industry, 153-154
Britton-Lee, 162
BTEQ, 25,96,101-104,273
    Accessing, 181-184
    Batch Mode, 185
    Defaults, 247
    Error Reporting, 188

BTEQ (Continued)
  Export Command, 382
  Format Control Commands, 383-389
  Initialization and Logon, 184
  Output, 186
  Report Writing, 381
Buckets (See Hash Buckets)
BulkLoad (See Application Utilities)
Bynet, 56

C

Call Level Interface (See Programming Interfaces)
Cargo Transportation Industry, 148-149
CASE, 274-276
CASESPECIFIC, 224-225
CAST, 243-244
C.D.C. (Computer Data Corporation), 5
Central Processing Unit (CPU), 36,39,46,125
CHARACTERS (See String Functions)
Citibank, 3,37
Classics Database, 166, 189
Cliques, 135
Clusters, 131-132
COALESCE, 278-279
COLLATION, 346
Column Names, 349-350
COMMENT, 355
Communications Layer, 58,62,89,115
Computed Values, 236
Concatenation (See String Function)
CONSTRAINT, 354-355
Consumer Goods/Retail Supply Industry, 147-148
Continued Hash Flag, 70
Communications Processor (COP), 47-48
Correlated Subquery (See Subqueries)
Crash Dumps, 365
CREATE MACRO (See Macro)
CURRENCY, 249-252
Cylinder Index, 70-72,89,92

D

Data Base Computer (DBC), 343
Data Control Language (DCL), 25,34,192
Data Definition Language (DDL) , 25-29,192
Data Dictionary/Directory (DD/D),17,20,66,196, 204,332,343,345,357, 365
Data Integrity, 331,340
Data Manipulation Language (DML), 5, 30, 104, 192, 323
Data Warehouse, 4,145,159
Data Types, 23-24,233-235
  Comparisons, 244
  Conversions, 242
DATE, 237,239-240
  Formats, 252-254

DATE (Continued)
Handling, 239-242
DBC/1012, 4-6,38-50,161
Deadlock (See Locks)
DELETE Statement, 34,323,328
Derived Tables, 321,322
Disk Array, 51,133-134
RAID 1, 134
RAID 5, 51.134-135
Disk Space, 27,74,
Disk Storage Unit (DSU), 44-45
Distribution of Rows, 74-77
DISTINCT, 199
Domain, 14-16,175-177, 178,301
DROP MACRO (See Macro)

E

ER Diagram, 167
Entity, 9-11,77,167
Major Entity, 77-78,170
Minor Entity, 77,137,171
Sub-Entities, 77-78
EXECUTE Macroname (See Macro)
EXISTS, 300
EXPLAIN, 35,204,213-215,311
EXTRACT Statement, 241

F

FALLBACK, 52,130-133, 346,349
FastExport (See Application Utilities)
FastLoad (See Application Utilities)
FOLDLINE, 207-209
FORMAT, 249
Free Block List, 72
FROM Clause, 298
Foreign Key (FK), (See Keys)
Full Table Scan, 57-58,91-92
Fujitsu, 5

G

Graphical User Interface (GUI), 98
GIVE Statement, 367
GRANT Statement (See Access Rights)
GROUP BY Clause, 257, 258-262
Multiple Columns, 261
Having, 261-262

H

Hanzi, 24
Hardware Failure, 130
Hash
Bucket, 58,62,
Collisions and Duplicates, 64-66
Maps, 58,89
Hashing Algorithm, 58-59, 62-63
HAVING Clause, See GROUP BY
Health Care Insurance Industry, 152-153
HELP, 35,204,205-207
Hierarchical Database, 7,73
Hierarchical Terms, 366-368
Hitachi, 5
Homonyms, 178

I

IBM, 4,38,159,160,162
Input Modification Routine (INMOD),106,108
INNER JOIN (See Joins)
Interface Processor (IFP),39, 41-42,
INTERSECT, 317,320
Indexes, 17,93,172,351
- Non-Unique Index, 18
- Non-Unique Primary Index (NUPI), 64
- Non-Unique Secondary Index (NUSI), 18,86, 89-91,174
- Primary Index, 18, 61-63,67,73-81, 93, 123, 172, 173, 352
- Search by Index, 59-60
- Secondary Indexes, 18, 85-88,172,174,356
  - Subtables, 60,86
  - Selection (Strong/Weak), 91
  - Unique Index, 18
  - Unique Secondary Index (USI), 18,86, 88-89,174

INFORMIX, 162
INSERT Statement, 34,323
- Positional Form, 324, 337-338
- Non Positional Form, 325,338

INSERT SELECT, 325
INTEL, 5,43
I.R.S., 2

J

Join Function, 31,193
Joins, 295,301
- Cartesian Product, 306-307
- Inner, 314
- Outer, 313,314
- Self Joins, 298, 305-306

Journals, 346,349
- AFTER IMAGE, 138,346
- BEFORE IMAGE, 129-130,138,346
- Permanent, 138-140
- Transient, 129

K

K-Mart, 4,37
Kanji, 24,163
Keys, 17,163,167,170,354
- Foreign Key, 11-13,171
- Primary Key, 11-13, 73-74,82,170,352,

L

LIKE Command, 226
- WITH ANY, ALL or SOME, 227
- ESCAPE feature, 228

Linear Performance, 48-49
Local Area Network (LAN), 46,160,181,183
Locks, 121-129
- Automatic, 123-125
- ACCESS, 121
- Deadlock, 128-129
- READ, 121
- WRITE, 121

Locks (Continued)
EXCLUSIVE, 122
Logical Data Model, 16,20
Logical Operators, 217-218
AND, 219
OR, 219
Multiple AND/OR, 220-221
NOT, 222-223
LOGON
(See Teradata LOGON)

M

MACRO, 19,29-30,35,332
CREATE, 333
DROP, 334
EXECUTE, 334
Parameterized, 335
REPLACE, 333
Syntax Options, 337
Main Frame, 39,181
Manufacturing Industry, 157
Massively Parallel, 6,145,161
Master Index, 69-70,89
MicroTDP, 46,48,183
Microsoft Visual Basic, 99
MINUS, 317,319
MODIFY USER/DATABASE, 35
MODULO Operator, 238
MONITOR Privileges, 373
MultiLoad
(See Application Utilities)
Multiple Cursors, 97
Multiple Sessions, 41,104-105
MULTISET, 349

N

NCR3600, 5,50-52,133,181
NCR3550, 53-54,133
NCR, 5-6,38,49-50,54
NAMED Function, 248
Non-Positional Form
(See INSERT)
NULL, 12-13,173,268,271,313,324
Arithmetic &Comparisons, 272
NULLIF, 277,280,283

O

ODBC
(see Programming Interfaces)
Operators
Logical, 217
Range Test, 223-225
Set, 317
ORDER BY Clause, 198,260
Optimizer, 91,94,174,213,230
ORACLE, 162
Oracle Parallel Server, 52
Out of Space Condition, 74
OUTER JOIN (See Joins)

P

Passenger Transportation Industry, 149-150
Parameterized Macros (See Macros)
Parallel Database Extensions (PDE), 54
Parallelism, 35

Parsing Engine (PE), 51,67,89,128
Password, 26,346
Partial String Operator, (See String Functions)
Performance Monitor, 373
Permanent Space (PERM), 26-27,74,345,346
Pharmaceutical Industry, 157
Physical Database, 16,20
PL/1 Program Language, 97
Positional Form (See INSERT)
PowerBuilder, 99
Preprocessor (See Programming Interfaces)
Primary Index (See Indexes)
Primary Key (PK),(See Keys)
Priorities, 121,125-126
Privileges, (See Access Rights)
Project, 31,193
Programming Interfaces, 95
- Call Level Interface (CLI) 40,97,98,105,182
- ODBC Driver, 98-99
- Teradata Preprocessor, 97-98

Public Sector, 155
Publishing Industry, 156

R

RAID (RAID 1 and RAID 5) (see Disk Array)
Range Test Operators, 217
- BETWEEN…AND, 223-225
- UPPER, 225

Relational Database, 7-9, 162,165
RDMS, 120,162,215,305,343, 349,350,376
Relational Query Function, 193
Referential Integrity, 13,74,163,172,331, 338-341,352
Relational Data Model, 8-9,16
Reorganization (REORG), 72
REPLACE MACRO (See Macro)
Resource Usage, 66
Restart Log, 105,110
Retail Industry, 146-147
REVOKE Statement (See Access Rights)
Row Hash, 69,123
Rows, 67
- Locating, 67
- Distribution, 74-76
- Row ID, 65-66,85
- Row Layout, 66
- Rows in Blocks, 108

S

Secondary Index (See Indexes)
Security
- Administrator, 120
- Rating 'C2', 119
- Rules, 66

SELECT Function, 193-196
SELECT Statement, 31,259, 261, 295,336
Sequential Processing, 35
SET, 349

Set Mathematics, 7,22
SET Command, 230,349
Set Operators, 217,317-318,
IN/NOT IN, 229-230
Shared Nothing Architecture,
39-41
SHOW, 204,209-212,351
SIDETITLES, 207-209
Single Node (see Symmetric
Multi-Processing Node)
SOME, 231
SPOOL, 26,70,345,346
STARTUP, 346
String Functions, 285
CHARACTERS, 288-289
Concatenation, 285-286
Index, 292-293
Partial String Operator, 217,
226
SUBSTR/SUBSTRING,
289-292
on Numerics, 290
TRIM, 286-288
Structured Query Language
(SQL), 16,
21-25,95,159-160
Functions, 192
Naming Convention, 170
Multiple Statements, 127
Parser, 66,332
Teradata Enhancements,
34-35
SQL Access Group (SAG), 98
Subqueries, 295-298,
307-310,327
Subqueries (Continued)
Correlated, 163-299
Subtotals, 264-267
Support Environment, 110
Symmetric Multi-Processing
Node (SMP), 54-56
Synonyms, 177
System Administration
(See Teradata)
System FE, 365
T
Tables, 9-11,18,123,347
Derived Tables, 313,
321-322
TeleCommunications Industry,
150-151
Terabyte, 3
Teradata Corporation, 3,159
Teradata Database, 17,48-49,
53,57,121
Teradata Director Program
(TDP), 41,47,182-183
Teradata Enhancements (SQL),
34
Teradata LOGON, 120
Teradata Manager, 98
Teradata ODBC Driver
(See Program.Interfaces)
Teradata Operating System
(TOS), 44,54
Teradata Performance Monitor,
373
Teradata PreProcessor
(See Program Interfaces)
Teradata SQL, 23,204

Teradata Version 2, 54,58,62,163,235
Teradata System Administration, 141,204,365
TEQUEL, 23,161
TITLE, 247
Totals (See WITH and WITH BY)
Transfer of Ownership (See Access Rights)
Transaction Technology Inc., 3
Transaction
  Boundaries, 126-127
  Failure, 129
  Integrity, 336
TRIM (See String Function)

U

Unauthorized User, 119
Uniqueness Value, 65
UNISYS, 160
UNIX Operating System, 50-52
UNION, 31,193,317,318
UPDATE, 34,323,327-328
UPPER, (See Range Test Operators)

V

Version 2 Release 2, (See Teradata Version 2)
VIEW 18-19,357
  CREATE/REPLACE, 358-362
Virtual Net (Vnet), 54
Virtual Table, 19
VISUAL C++, 99
Vproc, 54

W

WHERE Clause, 197,260,313,326
Wild Card Characters, 195,228
WinCLI, 98
Windows NT, 98
Winter Corporation, 143
WITH…BY, 35,262-268
WITH, 266-268
WORLDMARK 5100, 6, 54-55,56,133,181

X

XOR Calculation, 134

Y

Ynet, 5,37,41-45,52,56

Z

ZEROIFNULL, 35,280

Glossary

2 Phase Commit - Coordination of multiple synchronous database updates.

3550 - NCR UNIX-based mid-range, single node, computer system. Supports Teradata Database Version 2.

3600 - NCR UNIX-based massively parallel computer system. Runs Teradata Database (Version 1) on proprietary architecture.

3rd Normal Form - A state where all columns in tables obey the first three rules of normalization . See Normalization.

Access Module Processor - The physical processor or Vproc in the Teradata Database responsible for data maintenance and retrieval.

Account String - A subset of Teradata logon ID.

Application Processor - A UNIX server (or host) to the Teradata Database for Version 1 machines which permits direct user access, network or channel connections to the Teradata Database.

Application Utilities - A number of data maintenance utilities which includes BTEQ, BulkLoad, FastLoad, MultiLoad and FastExport used for large-scale data loading and maintenance.

Attribute - Technically any column in a table, but generally limited to non-key columns.

BTEQ - Basic Teradata Query facility. A program that allows end-users to access the Teradata Database in interactive, background and report-writing mode from all supported platforms.

BulkLoad - AKA **Bulk Data Load** or **BDL**. An application utility available only from an MVS or VM environment for large-scale data maintenance.

Bynet - High speed scaleable interconnect between multiple SMP Units for the Teradata Database Version 2 running in the WorldMark 5100M environment.

Call-Level Interface - A library of routines that reside in the User's address space, and provides the interface between the application program and the TDP or Gateway.

Clique - A collection of SMP Nodes with shared access to disk arrays using SCSI interfaces.

Cluster -A group of AMPs, usually four in number, which cooperate to protect each other's data in the event of hardware failure. The level of protection afforded by clusters is known as FALLBACK.

Communications Layer - Collective term for Ynet, Vnet and/or Bynet.

COP - Communications Processor - One kind of interface processor (IFP) on the database computer Version 1. A COP contains a gateway process for communicating with workstations via a LAN.

DD/D - Data Dictionary/Directory - The automatically maintained information about all of the databases, tables, views, macros, and users known to the Teradata Database, including information about ownership, space allocation, accounting, and access right relationships among those objects.

Data Type - Variations of alpha, numeric and byte data recognized by the Teradata Database.

Data Warehouse - Major data storage facility for current and future decision support applications.

DBC/1012 - The hardware of the data base computer. The DBC/1012 stores data and responds to queries about the data.

Data Control Language - A collection of SQL statements that deal with the transfer of ownership and granting and revoking of access rights.

Data Definition Language - A collection of SQL statements that deal with the creation, drop and modification of database objects.

Deadlock - A condition in which two or more transactions are unable to continue because each is waiting for computer resources held by the other. Deadlock resolution calls for the youngest transaction to be rolled back.

Disk Array - An arrangement of 20 disks arranged as 4 ranks of 5 disks each. See RAID

Data Manipulation Language - A collection of SQL statements comprising Select, Insert, Update and Delete.

Domain - A logical data modeling concept for grouping together all columns in the data base which refer to the same real-world person, place, thing or idea.

Disk Storage Unit - A physical disk.

Entity - A real-world person, place, thing or idea of interest in the data model. Each entity becomes a separate and distinct table.

FastLoad - AKA **Fast Data Load**. - An application utility for loading data from a file on the host to a new table on the Teradata Database at high speed. Available from all Teradata supported platforms.

Foreign Key (FK) - A column or columns in a table that directly reference the primary key column or columns of the same or another table.

Graphical User Interface - A windows-based application language or interface oriented towards graphical screen presentation.

HANZI - Chinese 2-byte characters.

Hash or Hashing - A method of transforming an index value from a table into an address of a physical storage area. The purpose is to store and retrieve data efficiently, minimizing average search time. In the Teradata DBS, one result of hashing calculates a hash bucket value which is used to identify the AMP responsible for that particular item of data.

Hash Bucket - See Hash.

Hashing Algorithm - The arithmetical calculation to which data values are input which results in a hash bucket value plus a remainder. See Hash.

Hierarchical Database - Non-relational database which requires the user to navigate top to bottom through the tables in hierarchical fashion until the required data is located.

Interface Processor - A physical processor on the DBC/1012 or the NCR 3600 responsible for interface between the host and the Teradata hardware. The IFP parses the SQL, generates AMP instructions and interfaces with the AMPs across the Ynet.

Index - A means of ordering and locating rows on disk for efficient access and processing. See Primary Index and Secondary Index.

Input Modification Routine - A user-written routine, generally in COBOL or C which pre-processes input data before passing it to BulkLoad, FastLoad, MultiLoad or FastExport, resulting in a single seamless utility operation.

Journals - Tables maintained by the RDBMS to protect against various kinds of failure. The journals of most interest to the user include system journals, such as the Transient Journal, which protects against transaction failure, the Recovery Journal for fallback-protected tables, and user defined Permanent Journals as an archive option.

KANJI - A dialect of Japanese characters. Supported by Teradata in Version 2 Release 2.

Logical Data Model A collection of tables in 3rd normal form which model a business enterprise. The logical data model is constructed according to the rules of set mathematics and is independent of the RDBMS on which it might eventually be implemented.

Macro - One or more SQL statements that are stored in the Teradata DBS and can be executed by a single EXECUTE statement. A macro can have multiple statements and substitutable parameters. Each macro execution is treated as an implicit transaction.

Massively Parallel - A term used to describe Teradata's implementation of dividing the workload amongst large numbers of loosely coupled processors (or CPUs) in such a way that each processor can perform its portion of a task in parallel with all the others.

MultiLoad - Teradata's most sophisticated application utility which permits up to 20 DML statements to be applied to up to 5 target tables under various conditions, at speeds generally exceeding those of BulkLoad and BTEQ.

Node - See Symmetric MultiProcessing Node.

Normalization - A number of rules (generally 3) which determine the correct table for an attribute or column based on the relationship between that attribute and the primary key.

NULL - An SQL keyword. The state of missing or unknown data as distinct from zeros or spaces.

Open Database Connectivity - A standardized protocol and set of calls for portability of SQL database applications between participating vendors.

Parser - A collective name for a number of Teradata programs which are resident on the IFP, COP or PE and are responsible for the syntax check, object resolution, optimization, and generation of AMP instructions for SQL statements.

PE - Parsing Engine - A physical processor in Teradata Version 1 machines, or a Vproc in Teradata Version 2. Responsible for parsing the SQL, generation of AMP instructions and interface with the other processors across the Communications Layer.

PERM - AKA **Permanent Space** or **MaxPerm**. The amount of space, expressed in bytes, allocated to a database or user for permanent storage of data in tables.

Physical Data Model - The collection of tables with primary and secondary indexes assigned, which is actually implemented on the RDBMS. The logical model usually differs from the logical model for performance reasons.

Primary Index - The column or group of columns in a table most often used for access. The Teradata Database uses the primary index as a distribution index.

Primary Key - A column or group of columns which uniquely identifies each row of a table. A Primary Key must be unique, not null and never changed.

RAID - Redundant Array of Inexpensive Disks . A method of sharing and duplicating the data between the elements of a Disk Array for protection against hardware failure. Teradata presently supports two varieties of RAID, RAID 1 which uses mirroring of data, and RAID 5 which uses parity.

Referential Integrity - The strict observance of PK/FK relationships amongst relational tables. If values (other than null) in all columns identified as FK have identical counterparts in PK columns of the same or another table, the database is said to have referential integrity.

Relational Database - A collection of tables with PK and FK relationships which model a business enterprise, and are constructed according to the rules of set mathematics.

Secondary Index - A subtable which references a column or group of columns in a table as an alternate access path to the primary index. Secondary indexes may be unique or non-unique.

SET - A collection of related fields that may take the form in SQL of a list of values or an imbedded SELECT.

Symmetric MultiProcessing Node - A group of CPUs which are tightly-coupled to mutually cooperate and function as a single super-powerful CPU. The Teradata Database Version 2 PEs and AMPs run as virtual processes (Vprocs) in UNIX, on one or more SMP Nodes on the NCR 3550, 4100 or WordMark 5100 hardware.

Spool - A file on the Teradata DBS that holds the result of SQL statement processing until it can be examined by the user or application program.

Subset - A smaller set within a larger set. (see SET).

Terabyte - A trillion bytes of data.

Teradata Manager - A powerful windows-based PC application which permits a Teradata administrator to monitor and control multiple Teradata implementations from a single station.

TEQUEL - Teradata SQL (Obsolete). The dialect of SQL implemented by Teradata prior to the introduction of ANSI standards.

TDP - Teradata Director Program AKA **Traffic Director Program**. Host-based software responsible for the registration and transmission of SQL between a user and the Teradata Database. In a channel-connected environment, TDP becomes responsible for ensuring the correct delivery of requests and responses between all the users on the host system and the Teradata Database. In a network environment, a smaller version of TDP known as Micro TDP or MTDP provides a similar service to a single user.

TOS - Teradata Operating System. Developed for the DBC/1012 and the NCR 3600 (Version 1) machines. Teradata Version 2 runs on UNIX and does not require TOS. It does however require a small number of minor modifications to the standard UNIX, knows as PDE - Parallel Database Extensions.

Version 1 - The original implementation of Teradata on the DBC/1012 and NCR 3600 which required proprietary hardware and TOS.

Version 2 - The Teradata Database as a purely software product running in the UNIX environment with virtual instead of physical processors. Teradata Version 2 is presently supported on the NCR 3550, 4100 and the Worldmark 5100.

View - An alternate way of organizing and presenting information in the Teradata DBS. A view, like a table, has rows and columns. However, the rows and columns of a view are not stored but are selected from the base table whenever the view is referenced. Views may be used to simplify SQL or to enforce security at the row or column level.

Virtual Table See View.

Vproc - Virtual Processor. Distinct from the physical processors needed by Teradata Version 1. In Teradata Version 2, PEs and AMPs run as separate programs on top of the UNIX operating system in SMP units. Vprocs communicate with each other within an SMP using a memory-sharing protocol known as the Vnet (virtual net), and between SMPs by the scaleable high speed interconnect known as the Bynet.

WinCLI - A powerful windows-based Call-Level Interface to the Teradata Database used primarily for the Teradata Manager.

WorldMark 5100 - The massively parallel computer system which was introduced by NCR in late 1995 and he most powerful engine yet for the Teradata Database (Version 2).

Ynet - The original proprietary, high-speed intelligent interconnect at the heart of Teradata's Version 1 implementation of massively parallel architecture. The Ynet was substantially redesigned for Teradata Version 2, and it was replaced by the Vnet within an SMP unit, and the Bynet between SMP units.

List of Acronyms

2GL	2nd Generation Language
3GL	3rd Generation Language
AMP	Access Module Processor
ANSI	American National Standards Institute
AP	Application Processor
ATM	Application Transaction Modeling
BTEQ	Basic Teradata SQL
Bynet	"Banyan" Net
CLI	Call Level Interface
COP	Communications Processor
CPU	Central Processing Unit
DBC/1012	Data Base Computer
DCL	Data Control Language
DD/D	Data Dictionary/Directory
DDL	Data Definition Language
DML	Data Manipulation Language
DSU	Disk Storage Unit
FK	Foreign Key
FTS	Full Table Scan
GUI	Graphical User Interface
IFP	Interface Processor
INMOD	Input Modification Routine
MIPS	Millions of Instructions per Second
NUPI	Non Unique Primary Index
NUSI	Non Unique Secondary Index
ODBC	Open Database Connectivity
PDE	Parallel Database Extensions
PE	Parsing Engine
PK	Primary Key

RAID	Redundant Array of Inexpensive Disks
RDBMS	Relational Database Management System
SAG	SQL Access Group
SCSI	Small Computer Standard Interface
SMP	Symmetric Multi-Processing Node
SQL	Structured Query Language
TDP	Teradata Director Program
TOS	Teradata Operating System
UPI	Unique Primary Index
USI	Unique Secondary Index
Vnet	Virtual Net
Vproc	Virtual Processor
WinCLI	Windows Based Call Level Interface
XOR	Exclusive Or calculation
YNET	Ynet

Another book by the same author:

The Teradata Database
Application and Archive/Recovery Utilities

Following on from the first volume in the series, "The Teradata Database - Introduction and SQL", this book continues the fascinating journey into the world of large-scale data maintenance and disaster recovery. In doing so, it becomes an irreplaceable guide for those who can afford the luxury of a classroom education in the Teradata Database, and essential reading for those who cannot.

With hundreds of easy-to-follow examples and practical exercises, the reader is gently but firmly led to the discovery of how to create efficient and powerful data maintenance applications quickly and effortlessly.

As an added bonus, the book includes a detailed examination of the Teradata Archive and Recovery options needed to protect the data against catastrophic hardware or software failure.

Published by
Education in Parallel

You are invited to E-Mail the author at:
brianmary@yahoo.com